The Journalist as Reformer

Henry Demarest Lloyd in Boston, 1902.
Courtesy of the State Historical Society of Wisconsin, no. WHi (X3) 13467.

THE JOURNALIST AS REFORMER

Henry Demarest Lloyd and
Wealth Against Commonwealth

RICHARD DIGBY-JUNGER

Contributions in American History, Number 168
Jon L. Wakelyn, Series Editor

GREENWOOD PRESS
Westport, Connecticut • London

Library of Congress Cataloging-in-Publication Data

Digby-Junger, Richard.
  The journalist as reformer : Henry Demarest Lloyd and Wealth
against commonwealth / Richard Digby-Junger.
    p.   cm.—(Contributions in American history, ISSN 0084–9219
; no. 168)
  Includes bibliographical references (p.   ) and index.
  ISBN 0-313-29957-9 (alk. paper)
  1. Lloyd, Henry Demarest, 1847–1903. 2. Journalists—United
States—19th century—Biography. 3. Social reformers—United
States. I. Title. II. Series.
PN4874.L56D54   1996
070′.92—dc20   95–50453
  [B]

British Library Cataloguing in Publication Data is available.

Library of Congress Catalog Card Number: 95–50453
ISBN: 0-313-29957-9
ISSN: 0084–9219

First published in 1996

Greenwood Press, 88 Post Road West, Westport, CT 06881
An imprint of Greenwood Publishing Group, Inc.

Printed in the United States of America

The paper used in this book complies with the
Permanent Paper Standard issued by the National
Information Standards Organization (Z39.48–1984).

10 9 8 7 6 5 4 3 2 1

Copyright Acknowledgments

The author and publisher gratefully acknowledge permission to use the following sources:

From *WLT: A Radio Romance* by Garrison Keillor, Copyright © 1991 by Garrison Keillor. Used by permission of Viking Penguin, a division of Penguin Books USA Inc.

From *WLT: A Radio Romance* by Garrison Keillor, Copyright © 1991 by Garrison Keillor. Used by permission of Faber and Faber Ltd., United Kingdom.

folder 1, box 1, series I; folder 5, box 2, series I; folder 6, box 2, series I; folder 8, box 2, series I—Inglis Interview, RG 1—John D. Rockefeller Papers, Rockefeller Family Archives, Rockefeller Archive Center, North Tarrytown, New York.

The reminiscences of Nicholas Kelley, in the Collection of the Columbia Oral History Research Office.

Every reasonable effort has been made to trace the owners of copyright materials in this book, but in some instances this has proven impossible. The author and publisher will be glad to receive information leading to more complete acknowledgments in subsequent printings of the book and in the meantime extend their apologies for any omissions.

To Linda

Contents

Acknowledgments

The retelling of a life, even a narrowly focused effort such as this, requires the contributions of many, and I owe more than a few debts of gratitude for assistance in the preparation of this book. No study of Henry Demarest Lloyd can be undertaken without consulting his collected papers, ably supervised at the State Historical Society of Wisconsin by Harry Miller. Although the majority of Lloyd's materials were microfilmed two decades ago, Harry and his staff have continued to collect Lloyd-related materials, which they made available to me. Meanwhile, the Lloyd family donated additional documents to the Chicago Historical Society, and Archie Motley was especially helpful in accessing them.

Professor James L. Baughman, of the University of Wisconsin-Madison, read and criticized early versions of this manuscript, and I am deeply grateful to him for his many suggestions and support over the years. Professors Stephen Vaughn, Allan G. Bogue, and Paul Boyer also made a number of useful criticisms, for which I am appreciative. The late Mary Ann Yodelis-Smith provided both criticisms and encouragement, and I will miss her. Professor Jay M. Jernigan, of Eastern Michigan University, was helpful to me in more ways than he will ever know, and I thank him.

A number of libraries and collections allowed me to make extensive use of their holdings, and their librarians were of great assistance. The Library of Congress provided newspapers and other materials from its vast holdings, as did the libraries of the State Historical Society of Wisconsin, the University of Wisconsin-Madison, Northwestern University, Chicago Historical Society, New York Public Library, and New York Historical Society. Elsa Meyers helped me locate many early Lloyd family materials at the New Jersey Historical Society. Gary J. Arnold of the Ohio Historical Society helped with the Washington Gladden Collection, as did Darwin H. Stapleton of the Rockefeller Archive Center. Richard A. Shrader of the University of North Carolina Southern Historical Collection assisted me with the Ethelbert Stewart papers and John McCutcheon searched the archives of the *Chicago Tribune* for me. Carley R. Robison made the William Salter papers available to me at Knox College. Ronald J. Grele of the Oral History Research Office of Columbia University was helpful, as was Donald A. Ritchie, associate historian of the United States Senate.

Lloyd's granddaughter, Georgia Lloyd, provided me with copies of some of Lloyd's scarcer books and the Lloyd biography written by her great aunt, Caro Lloyd Stroebell. She also provided me with encouragement but no interference, for which I will always be grateful. Professor I. M. Destler, of the University of Maryland at College Park, the son of the late Chester M. Destler, donated his father's research notes and interviews on Lloyd to the State Historical Society of Wisconsin at my suggestion. Although severely disorganized, the materials revealed information that Destler could not put in his biography and I thank Donna Sereda, of the State Historical Society, for her help in accessing them. Pennsylvania oil country historian Ernest C. Miller found documents for me that I would not have otherwise been able to access at the Drake Well Museum and I deeply appreciate his assistance. The Graduate School and the College of Liberal Arts and Sciences of Northern Illinois University provided funding for the research and writing of this book.

Professor John Wakelyn of Catholic University of America was extremely supportive of my work and I am appreciative to him. John Dan Eades, Margaret Maybury, and Jodie McCune of Greenwood Press made this book possible.

Introduction: The Voice of the People Shall Be Heard

The crowd was thinning a few minutes after 10:00 P.M. on the evening of May 3, 1886, as radical newspaperman Samuel Fielden finished an impromptu speech. A cold rainshower had chased much of his audience away from his delivery wagon podium parked at the end of a drab, warehouse lined Chicago block known as Haymarket Square. Desperate to keep his remaining listeners, Fielden openly defied them to rise up against their employers. What did it matter whether one killed oneself by overwork or by fighting the capitalistic enemy, he demanded. "What is the difference?" he asked.

His question went unanswered for at that moment, two hundred Chicago policemen surrounded Fielden's impromptu podium. Their leader, Captain John Bonfield, accused Fielden of breaching the peace and ordered him and his crowd to disperse. Fielden and another speaker, Albert R. Parsons, were angry at the interruption and reminded Bonfield that their gathering was peaceful and that they had a legitimate right of free speech. As they argued, a powerful dynamite bomb flew through the air, sparks showering from its lighted fuse, and exploded near the front of the police ranks, killing Patrolman Mathias J. Degan instantly. The remaining policemen charged the frightened crowd, indiscriminately shooting and beating anyone in an attempt to catch the person who had thrown the bomb. As the smoke cleared, the bodies of seven dead or dying and sixty wounded police officers were left on the bloody street, along with an unrecorded number of dead and injured audience members.

In the wake of the bombing, panic reigned in Chicago as long harbored fears of a bloody, French style revolution involving the city's many immigrant residents were finally released. The police retaliated against anyone considered an anarchist.   More than two hundred men and women were arrested and hundreds more assaulted or illegally deprived of their rights for transgressions as minor as bragging in a saloon.   When the actual bomb thrower could not be found (he or she never was), a grand jury indicted thirty-one men, a number reduced to eight for convenience.   None of the eight could be linked to the actual bombing.   Some were not even present at Haymarket, but they were charged with a total of sixty-nine felony counts of accessory before the fact and general conspiracy, the latter punishable under Illinois law by death.[1]

At the moment of the explosion, one of the best known of the generation of social reformers to emerge from Haymarket was resting an ocean away. Thirty-nine-year-old Henry Demarest Lloyd had been plagued for more than a year by a case of nervous prostration that he could not overcome, the result of his work as a reporter and editor for the *Chicago Tribune*.   Finally at ease in England, he could not sympathize with Haymarket, even when his labor newspaper friend John Swinton wrote him with the sensational details. Disbelieving the magnitude of the hysteria that gripped Chicago, Lloyd predicted that the city's legal system would sort out and punish those responsible for the incident and the police overreaction.   Swinton, who was in New York, was decidedly less certain.   In a return letter dated the day before the grand jury issued its indictments, he pleaded, "Can't you do something to help secure those accused men a fair trial?"—a reference to Lloyd's influence as a newspaperman. Lloyd's still disbelieving response was that the "dynamitards" had secured an able lawyer "who will employ all the resources of the law in their behalf."[2]

It was not until Lloyd's return to Chicago a month later that he discovered how wrong he had been.   Not even the most capable Philadelphia lawyer could have obtained a fair trial for the Haymarket anarchists in 1886 Chicago. Distressed by the evolving miscarriage of justice, he met with each of the men in their jail cells to hear their stories.   He found them vastly different from the cold blooded cop-killing image fostered in the Chicago press.   Seven of the men were not unlike the young radical that Lloyd had been two decades previously, working for a national organization opposed to tariffs.   "Philosophically, Free Traders and Anarchists occupy similar ground," he wrote in a notebook following his meetings.   "Both look to the time when men will be good enough and intelligent enough to do without government and regulation."   Although Lloyd repudiated violence, he considered the Chicago police at least partially responsible for the Haymarket incident, noting, "Are there not in the whole chain of events circumstances which make it consistent with justice to lessen the punishment legally decreed?"   He also asked,

Shall we be safe in setting—by the State—the precedent of arrest without warrant, search without warrant, and condemnation to death for being 'leaders'? . . . State's Attorney Grinnell claims that socialists are not to be believed!   As if the fact that a man believed in extending to machines, etc., the principles of the post-office incapacitated him from telling the truth. The worst foreigners are the men who are introducing European continental methods of government by police.[3]

Lloyd's judgment was not shared by the general public. The *Chicago Tribune* denounced the anarchists as "loathsome murderers," "infamous scoundrels," and "godless foreigners." The *Chicago Inter-Ocean* noted that they had "violated every law of God and man." William Bross, Lloyd's father-in-law and a *Tribune* owner, wrote in his diary, "A hard looking lot. . . . Cut Throats—nothing less." More than one letter writer begged Illinois Governor Richard J. Oglesby to "Hang the dirty sons of bitches."[4]

Ultimately, four of the eight—August Spies, Adolph Fischer, George Engel, and Albert Parsons—were hanged together on November 11, 1887. William Bross wrote in his diary, "The anarchists—four of them—were hanged at 11:54 A.M. The Law, thank the Lord, is vendicated [*sic*]." Carl Sandburg, then the nine-year-old son of a Swedish railroad worker living in nearby Galesburg, Illinois, later recalled the jubilation of townspeople when they heard of the executions. It was only with time, he later wrote, that "the feeling grew on me that I had been a little crazy, 'off my nut.'" To Lloyd, the executions were like a death in the family. He gathered with friends at his suburban Chicago mansion that evening, sang a song to the condemned men, "Voice of the Gallows," that he had written to the tune "Annie Laurie," and cried. One of the condemned men, Albert Parsons, declared from the gallows before his death, "Let the voice of the people be heard." That night, Lloyd responded in his notebook, "The voice of the people shall be heard."[5]

The Haymarket Square bombing has few equals as a defining moment in American history. It has been likened to a Third Great Awakening: a revival of the American conscience and spirit. Others have compared it to the 1837 murder of abolitionist editor Elijah Lovejoy, which reinvigorated abolitionism, or New York's 1911 Triangle Shirtwaist fire, which ignited twentieth-century urban reform efforts. It had a similar effect on Henry Demarest Lloyd, forever changing the way he viewed mankind and society. Lloyd's pre- and post-Haymarket reform activities have been amply chronicled, but his journalistic and literary efforts have been ignored, especially by historians of American radicalism and reform. For all of his empires of reform, Lloyd was a man of words, a journalist and nonfiction writer, who used a variety of media to lobby the public and government for the improvement of social conditions. He crusaded for the rights of the late nineteenth-century poor—consumer, worker, labor unionist, farmer, and aged. In doing so, he produced an enviable body of writings, including the 1881 "Story of a Great Monopoly," the first article length exposé of the Standard Oil Company, his seminal 1894 book *Wealth Against Commonwealth*, and a body of speeches. These and the other major works that he wrote (in contrast to his posthumous writings, which were reassembled and edited from sketchy notes) need to be looked at anew, as they stand on their own and not on their latter day reputation. History has many interpretations, but it is best to understand Lloyd as he really wrote, not the socialist radical image fostered by his sister after his untimely death and popularized by radical and reform historians.[6]

Lloyd borrowed from a number of traditions for his writings and speeches. Although not unknown, advocacy journalism was far from common before Lloyd, especially when used to support improvements in social conditions. Printer and newspaperman Benjamin Franklin argued in 1731 that "Printers are educated in the Belief that when Men differ in Opinion, both Sides ought equally to have the Advantage of being heard by the Publick [sic]." The Revolutionary War made such impartiality impractical and even dangerous. Benjamin Edes and John Gill's *Boston Gazette*, described by the governor of Massachusetts as "an infamous weekly paper which has swarmed with Libells of the most atrocious kind," was the most quoted of the Patriot press, but others were almost as vociferous. The best known advocate journalist was Thomas Paine, who turned from writing poems and articles about marriage for the *Pennsylvania Magazine* to his pamphlet *Common Sense* in early 1776. The First Amendment, which took effect in 1791, provided protection for political discussions in the press, and many nineteenth-century journalists became advocates for political parties, especially in cities with competing newspapers. *Frank Leslie's Illustrated Monthly* published a report in 1858 that forced New York and Brooklyn city officials to monitor the healthfulness of milk, and other urban journals published reports on social problems during the 1860s and 1870s. Still, impartiality remained a goal of many American journalists until and even after the Civil War. Cincinnati's first newspaper, the *Centinel of the North-Western Territory*, promised that it was "Open to all Parties, but Influenced by None" in 1793. The *Racine* (Wisconsin) *Argus* noted fifty years later, "We shall endeavor to weigh, with candor, and judge with impartiality every measure, let it emanate from whatsoever source." Historian Thomas C. Leonard has explained, "Journalism was a business with a common sense rule: boosting paid, knocking did not." Only when he became independently wealthy was Lloyd able to make a career out of writing and speaking about social change.[7]

Lloyd's nonfiction was steeped in the nineteenth-century literature of social protest. English writers such as William Makepeace Thackeray, Charles Dickens, and Anthony Trollope set the standard for this type of literature with journalistic style novels and serialized magazine short stories that chronicled the human misery of the Industrial Revolution through the use of fictional characters and settings. Thomas Carlyle decried "The Gospel of Mammonism" in 1844, writing, "We have profoundly forgotten everywhere that *Cash-Payment* is not the sole relation of human beings." Elizabeth Barrett's 1844 "The Cry of The Children" was a poetic protest against child labor. Charles Kingsley described "The Men Who Are Eaten" in *Alton Locke*, a 1850 exposé of sweat shops. In the United States, the Fugitive Slave Act of 1850 was the stimulus for Harriet

Beecher Stowe's 1857 *Uncle Tom's Cabin*, the well-researched story of a fictitious Southern slave family. Rebecca Harding Davis spent months observing working conditions in American iron and textile mills but fictionalized her short stories, "Life in the Iron Mills" and "A Story of Today," which appeared in the *Atlantic Monthly* in 1861 and 1862. Edward Eggleston, Mark Twain, Charles Dudley Warner, and David Ross Locke used novels to expose the social implications of fake land booming during the 1870s, something Lloyd would do with facts in a newspaper article in 1884. Helen Hunt Jackson novelized the treachery perpetrated against California's Native Americans in her 1884 *Ramona*. Novelist-journalists such as Stephen Crane, Frank Norris, Jack London, and Theodore Dreiser continued the tradition in their late nineteenth and early twentieth-century social protest novels and short stories. For years after *Wealth Against Commonwealth* was published, readers badgered Lloyd for a fictionalized account of his factual study, and Lloyd finally admitted in 1898, "It is a curious fact of history that political liberty progresses only by the help of legal fictions; and I suppose our economic growth can only be accomplished by the same use of illusion." However, Lloyd considered himself a "photographer of facts." He used literary effects in *Wealth*, his other books, and many of his speeches, but he refused to fictionalize. It was the ghost of Oliver Twist who asked for "more" in *Millionaires Against Miners*, not a reincarnation.[8]

Lloyd had a number of earlier books and magazine articles on monopolies and trusts to aid him. Congressional and state legislative investigators conducted periodic probes of industrial combinations beginning in 1873. Lloyd made extensive use of information collected by one such body, New York State's Hepburn Commission. Beginning in the 1860s, a variety of writers also protested what they viewed as abuses perpetrated by the captains of industry. Charles Francis Adams, Jr., called for government regulation of the railroads in several *North American Review* articles in 1869 and 1870, arguing, "It is useless for men to stand in the way of steam engines." Henry George popularized antimonopoly sentiment in an 1871 booklet, *Our Land and Land Policy*, and revived the subject in his 1880 *Progress and Poverty*. D. C. Cloud capitalized on agrarian dissent against trusts to sell five editions of his *Monopolies and the People*, published in 1872 and 1873, warning as would Lloyd: "While we have no titled aristocracy in this country, under the fostering care of the government an aristocracy of wealth has sprung up among us more despotic in its nature than exists in the old world." Thomas A. Bland pressed for the restoration of the "American system of free competition" in his 1881 *The Reign of Monopoly*. Congregationalist minister Josiah Strong denounced slums, mass immigration, and despotic capitalists in his 1885 *Our Country*. In an 1887 *North American Review* article, a Lloyd acquaintance, James F. Hudson, held that "no monopolies are consistent with the spirit of popular institutions." Thomas S. Denison fictionalized the industrial monopoly question and evoked what historian James Truslow Adams called the American dream in his 1885 *An Iron Crown, or the Modern Mammon*. Edward Bellamy's *Looking Backward, 2000-1887* was science fiction against laissez-faire capitalism and Social Darwinism, and there was a wide variety of antimonopoly writings in magazines and newspapers between 1887 and 1892. As popular as many of these earlier writings were, they did not have the national political impact of Lloyd. Antitrust historian John B. Clark has observed,

Lloyd['s "Story of a Great Monopoly] is fairly entitled to much of the credit for crystallizing the growing sentiment for federal regulation of [the] railroads. . . . [Before] no serious demand for federal legislation was made and no important legislative effort was made by Congress. . . . Now the public interest was exhibited in the large numbers of petitions which flowed into Congress, and numerous bills for the regulation of the railroads were introduced in each house.[9]

Lloyd also made use of alternative nineteenth century media forms. An alternative press—newspapers and magazines advocating particular minority views—had developed during the first half of the nineteenth century, but was not widely known or used. Black, abolitionist, American Indian, women's, utopian, and labor publications appeared as early as the 1820s, offering perspectives that were too sensitive, specialized, or controversial for the mainstream press. Ex-slave Frederick Douglass, the editor of the best known antebellum black newspaper, *North Star*, wrote in his autobiography, "In my judgment a tolerably well conducted press in the hands of persons of the despised race, would . . . prove a most powerful means of removing prejudice and awakening an interest in them." Nineteenth-century feminist suffrage editors openly rejected the conventions of the mainstream press, often with a sense of pride, to support women's issues.William Lloyd Garrison's *The Liberator*, produced between 1831 and 1865, was only one of a host of abolitionist newspapers. Almost all of the alternative press published letters to the editor, providing access to anyone who could write. Abolitionist newspapers even published the speeches of freed slaves who could not write. The alternative press waxed and waned as their various causes did, but continued throughout the nineteenth century. Persons who felt disenfranchised or could not write had the public podium open to them.[10]

In turn, Lloyd's writings were influential on the muckrakers. Those men and women who wrote about monopolies, trusts, and the social problems of the industrial revolution shortly before and after Lloyd's death in 1903 found a powerful precursor in Lloyd. His writings have also served as models for advocate journalists and other reform writers.

Lloyd is no stranger to biographers. His sister wrote a two volume history of his life in 1912, nine years after he died at the age of fifty-six in 1903. Caro Lloyd Strobell honored the memory of her brother in her book, but she was a socialist and tried to link her brother to the Socialist Party, which he never joined. At the height of McCarthyism in 1951, Daniel Aaron called Lloyd a Progressive in his book, even though Lloyd had died before Progressivism became socially acceptable. In 1957, Lloyd's grandson-in-law cast him as one of America's greatest radicals, a role Lloyd probably would have enjoyed but did not live up to. The most comprehensive study of Lloyd's life was published in 1963—Chester M. Destler's *Henry Demarest Lloyd and the Empire of Reform*. Destler spent more than thirty years researching and writing his book, but his scholarly detachment was compromised by an obsession for too many details in Lloyd's life. The resulting manuscript was so long that it had to be cut in half for publication, and it still lacks cohesiveness and organization, especially when discussing Lloyd's writings. Destler did not have available to him the personal journals of Lloyd's wife or his sister or selected correspondence related to Lloyd's finances that were kept from him by family members. Nor was he able to include quotations from a John D. Rockefeller interview conducted during the 1910s that revealed the extent of Rockefeller's knowledge about Lloyd and *Wealth Against Commonwealth* and how Lloyd had angered him. More recently, Jay Jernigan has written a useful, if short, study of Lloyd, and John L. Thomas attempted, with partial success, to relate Lloyd to fellow reformers Henry George and Edward Bellamy. To date, no one has adequately examined Lloyd's writings within the broader context of his life.[11]

In this biography, Lloyd's life is organized into three sections. The first two chapters look at how his education as a lawyer, with its inherent predilection for the advocacy of a client, merged with his infatuation with the newspaper business to steer him toward journalism and a career with the *Chicago Tribune*. The second portion examines Lloyd's most influential advocacy works, beginning with his 1881 "Story of a Great Monopoly" *Atlantic Monthly* article—the first article-length attack of John D. Rockefeller and the Standard Oil Company—and culminating in the 1894 *Wealth Against Commonwealth*, Lloyd's nonfictional opus against monopolies and industrialization that pre-dated by more than a decade Ida Tarbell's better known *History of the Standard Oil Company*. The final chapters consider Lloyd's lesser recognized writings following *Wealth*, especially the many speeches he delivered—works complicated and enervated by money, personal, and family problems, and by Lloyd's eclectic personality, philosophies, and interests.

The book begins by examining Lloyd's early life, the contrast between years spent living in rural America and his adolescence on the streets of Civil War era New York City. Even at an early age, Lloyd showed a predilection toward writing. It was those experiences that influenced him to write "The voice of the people shall be heard" in the wake of the Haymarket Square bombing and executions.

NOTES

1. The Haymarket bombing is described in Bruce Nelson, *Beyond the Martyrs* (New Brunswick, NJ: Rutgers University Press, 1988); Ann Masa, "Chicago's Martyrs: A Parable for the People," *Chicago History*, 25(Summer 1986): 59; Paul Avrich, *The*

Haymarket Tragedy (Princeton, NJ: Princeton University Press, 1984); Carl Guarneri, "Haymarket Though the Anarchist's Eyes," *Reviews in American History*, 13(March 1985): 76–79; Phillip S. Foner, ed., *The Autobiographies of the Haymarket Martyrs* (New York: Monad Press, 1983); Voltarine deCleyre, *The First Mayday: The Haymarket Speeches, 1895-1910* (Minneapolis: Cienfuegos Press, 1980); Foster Rhea Dulles, *Labor in America: A History* (New York: Thomas Y. Crowell, 1966), 122–125; Henry David, *History of the Haymarket Affair* (New York: Farrar and Rinehart, 1936); Lucy Parsons, ed., *Famous Speeches of the Eight Chicago Anarchists* (New York: Arno Press, 1969); Michael J. Schaack, *Anarchy and Anarchists* (Chicago: F.J. Schulte, 1889); and M. M. Trumbull, *The Trial of the Judgement* (Chicago: Health and Home Publishing, 1888).

2. Bross MS Diary, 25 February, 11 March, and 26 August 1886, William Bross papers, Chicago Historical Society (hereafter Bross, CHS); John Swinton to HDL, 26 May 1886, and HDL to Swinton, 8 June 1886, both in Henry Demarest Lloyd Papers, State Historical Society of Wisconsin (hereafter HDL, Wisc.).

3. "Free Speech," n.d., circa 1886; HDL, small notebook G, circa 1886; HDL notebook, November 1887; and "Notes on Haymarket Anarchist Trial, November 1887," all in Henry Demarest Lloyd papers, microfilmed edition, State Historical Society of Wisconsin, Madison, 1971 (hereafter HDL, mf.); Adolph Fischer to HDL, 4 November 1887; Charles H. Hamm to HDL, 13 December 1887; HDL to Aaron Lloyd, 10 November 1887; all in HDL, Wisc.; "Their Reasons for Signing," 5 November 1887; "What Shall Be Done with the Anarchists," 6 November 1887, and "Mr. Lloyd's Demand for Justice," 10 November 1887, all in *Chicago Tribune*; Caro Lloyd Strobell, *Henry Demarest Lloyd, 1847-1903: A Biography*, vol. 1 (New York: G. P. Putnam's Sons, 1912), 92–93; and John L. Thomas, *Alternative America: Henry George, Edward Bellamy, Henry Demarest Lloyd and the Adversary Tradition* (Cambridge, MA: Belknap Press, 1983), 208.

4. *Chicago Inter-Ocean*, 6 May 1886, as quoted in Henry David, *The History of the Haymarket Affair* (New York: Farrar & Rinehart, Inc., 1936), 209; HDL, "Petition for the Pardoning of the Anarchists," 8 November 1887, HDL, Wisc.; Bross MS diary, 11 November 1887, CHS; and undated petition to "Governor Richard J. Oglesby," *Chicago Tribune*, 10 November 1887, in CLS, *Lloyd*, II, 333–339.

5. HDL, "Hymn to the Gallows," 11 November 1887; "Execution of the anarchists," 11 November 1887; "Anarchists-Bar Association Speech," December 1887; Adolph Fischer to HDL and William W. Salter, 4 November 1887; HDL to Aaron Lloyd, 10 November 1887; Robert W. Patterson to HDL, 31 December 1887; Samuel J. Fielden to CLS, 25 August 1905; and Jessie Dale Pearce to CLS, n.d., before 24 October 1907, all in HDL, Wisc.; HDL 1887 and 1893 notebooks and typed MS, "Execution of the Anarchists," n.d., after 11 November 1887, all in HDL, mf.; Bross MS diary, 10, 11 November 1887, CHS; HDL to William M. Salter, 20 October 1887; Francis F. Browne to HDL, n.d., before 6 November 1887; JBL to Salter, 6 November 1887; and HDL to Salter, 21 December 1887; all in William M. Salter papers, Knox College Archives; Nathaniel Hong, "They Hang Editors, Don't They? Free Speech and Free Press Issues in the Haymarket Case, 1886," unpublished paper delivered to the Association for Education in Journalism and Mass Communication Convention, Minneapolis, MN, August 1990; CLS, *Lloyd*, I, 86; and Avrich, *Haymarket*, 301–308.

6. William Strauss and Neil Howe, *Generations: The History of America's Future, 1584 to 2069* (New York: Morrow, 1991), 92–96; Sidney Lens, *Radicalism in America*

(Cambridge, MA: Schenkman Publishing Co., 1982), 170; and J. Joseph Huthmacher, *Senator Robert F. Wagner and the Rise of Urban Liberalism* (New York: Atheneum Press, 1968).

7. *Centinel of the North-Western Territory* as cited in John Nerone, *The Culture of the Press in the Early Republic: Cincinnati, 1793-1848* (New York: Garland Publishing, 1989), 1-22; Jeff Smith, *Printers and Press Freedom: The Ideology of Early American Journalism* (New York: Oxford University Press, 1988), 115-119; Stephen Botein, "Printers in the American Revolution," in *The Press and the American Revolution*, ed. Bernard Bailyn and John B. Hench (Boston: Northeastern University Press, 1980), 11-58; *Racine Argus*, 2 March 1837, as cited in Jacqueline Fix, "The Establishment of Wisconsin's Territorial Newspapers, 1833-1848," (Masters thesis, University of Wisconsin, 1961); Arthur M. Schlesinger, *Prelude to Independence: The Newspaper War on Britain, 1764-1776* (Westport, Ct: Greenwood Press, 1957); Philip Davidson, *Propaganda and the American Revolution, 1763-1783* (Chapel Hill, NC: University of North Carolina Press, 1941); Curtis D. MacDougall, *Interpretative Reporting*, 8th ed. (New York: Macmillan Publishing, 1982), 79-81; and Thomas C. Leonard, *The Power of the Press: The Birth of American Political Reporting* (New York: Oxford University Press, 1986), 109.

8. HDL, *A Strike of Millionaires Against Miners or the Story of Spring Valley* (Chicago: Belford-Clarke Co., 1890), 109; HDL to Lee Meriwether, 26 November 1898, in HDL, Wisc.; Robert Miraldi, *Muckraking and Objectivity: Journalism's Colliding Traditions* (New York: Greenwood Press, 1990), 41-46; Richard D. Altick, *Victorian People and Ideas* (New York: W. W. Norton & Co., 1973), 33-141; William E. Buckler, *Prose of the Victorian Period* (Boston: Houghton Mifflin Co., 1958); *The Portable Victorian Reader*, ed. Gordon S. Haight (New York: Viking Press, 1972); Walter E. Houghton, *The Victorian Frame of Mind, 1830-1870* (New Haven: Yale University Press, 1957), 196-217; Edward L. Cassidy, "Muckraking in the Gilded Age," *American Literature*, 13(May 1941): 134-141; Vernon Louis Parrington, *Main Currents in American Thought*, III (New York: Harcourt, Brace and Co., 1930), 316-319; Robert E. Spiller, et al., *Literary History of the United States*, 3d ed. (New York: Macmillan, 1963), 1107-1134; and Henry Walcott Boynton, *Journalism and Literature* (Boston: Houghton Mifflin and Co., 1904).

9. D. C. Cloud, *Monopolies and the People*, 5th ed. (Davenport, IA: Day, Egbert, & Fidlar, 1873), 13; John B. Clark, *The Federal Trust Policy* (Baltimore: Johns Hopkins University Press, 1931), 17-32; Hans B. Thorelli, *The Federal Anti-Trust Policy: Organization of an American Tradition* (London: George Allen and Unwin, 1954), 132-142; Edward Chase Kirkland, *Dream and Thought in the Business Community, 1860-1900* (Ithaca, NY: Cornell University Press, 1956); Ralph L. Nelson, *Merger Movements in American Industry, 1895-1956* (Princeton, NJ: Princeton University Press, 1959); Saul Engelbourg, *Power and Morality: American Business Ethics, 1840-1914* (Westport, CT: Greenwood Press, 1980); Thomas K. McCraw, *Prophets of Regulation* (Cambridge, MA: Belknap Press, 1984), 1-56; Naomi R. Lamoreaux, *The Great Merger Movement in American Business, 1895-1904* (New York: Cambridge University Press, 1985); Steven L. Piott, *The Anti-Monopoly Persuasion: Popular Resistance to the Rise of Big Business in the Midwest* (Westport, CT: Greenwood Press, 1985); and W. Elliot Brownlee, *Dynamics of Ascent: A History of the American Economy* (Chicago: Dorsey Press, 1988).

10. Armistead S. Pride, "*Rights of All*: Second Step in Development of Black Journalism," *Journalism History*, 4(Winter 1977): 129–131; Jannette L. Dates and William Barlow, "Introduction: A War of Images," in *Split Image: African Americans in the Mass Media*, ed. Dates and Barlow (Washington D.C.: Howard University Press, 1990), 6–11; Roland E. Wolseley, *The Black Press, U.S.A.* (Ames: Iowa State University Press, 1990), 28–37; Bernell Tripp, *Origins of the Black Press, 1827–1847* (Northport, AL: Vision Press, 1992), 44–81; Clarence E. Walker, *Deromanticizing Black History: Critical Essays and Reappraisals* (Knoxville: The University of Tennessee Press, 1991), 87–98; Sally Taylor, "Marx and Greeley on Slavery and Labor," *Journalism History*, 6(Winter 1979–80): 103–106, 122; Sean Wilentz, *Chants Democratic: New York City and the Rise of the American Working Class, 1788–1850* (New York: Oxford University Press, 1984); Dan Schiller, *Objectivity and the News: The Public and the Rise of Commercial Journalism* (Philadelphia: University of Pennsylvania Press, 1981), 25–46; Lauren Kessler, *The Dissident Press: Alternative Journalism in American History* (Beverly Hills, CA: Sage Publications, 1984), 48–73; Robert H. Walker, *The Reform Spirit in America: A Documentation of the Pattern of Reform in the American Republic* (New York: Putnam, 1976), 76–77; John L. Thomas, *The Liberator: William Lloyd Garrison, A Biography* (Boston: Little, Brown and Co., 1963); and Merton L. Dillon, *The Abolitionists: The Growth of a Dissenting Minority* (New York: W.W. Norton, 1979), 36–40.

11. John L. Thomas, *Alternative America: Henry George, Edward Bellamy, Henry Demarest Lloyd and the Adversary Tradition* (Cambridge, MA: Belknap Press, 1983); E. Jay Jernigan, *Henry Demarest Lloyd* (Boston: Twayne Publishers, 1976); Chester M. Destler, *Henry Demarest Lloyd and the Empire of Reform* (Philadelphia: University of Pennsylvania Press, 1963); Harvey O'Connnor, "Henry Demarest Lloyd: The Prophetic Tradition," in ed. Harvey Goldberg, *American Radicals: Some Problems and Personalities* (New York: Monthly Review Press, 1957), 79–90; Daniel Aaron, *Men of Good Hope: A Story of American Progressives* (New York: Oxford University Press, 1951), 133–171; and Strobell, *Lloyd*.

1

Lloyde

Henry Demarest Lloyd was born in New York City on May Day 1847, the first child of Aaron and Maria Lloyd. His birthplace was a redbrick, gambrel-roofed house owned by David James Demarest, his maternal grandfather, located near the present-day Washington Square section of lower Manhattan. The first written reference to Henry was by his father Aaron, an apology to his father for ignoring a family tradition of naming first born sons after their paternal grandfather. "My desire was to name Henry after you," Aaron explained, "but Maria's heart seemed so set before marriage to name him after her brother that I could insist upon my wishes in the matter no longer."[1]

Henry was shaped by a variety of influences during his earliest years. He lived in a number of small, rural towns, including one on the edge of the frontier, and they burned a preference for a simpler, more pastoral America into his subconscious. His father's oppressive religiosity was a more direct influence, helping to shape his later thoughts, actions, and writings. The burgeoning urbanism of mid-nineteenth-century New York City, especially the human by-products discharged by the industrial revolution, became a focus for Henry. A Columbia University education convinced him that the future of America depended upon the contributions of upper-class men of good character, and he set out to become one. In the study of law, Henry learned advocacy, the espousal of another's cause, and carried that philosophy into his first job as a publicist. But it was a penchant for writing, nurtured in part by his proximity to New York's newspaper center, Printing House Square, that eventually led young Henry Demarest Lloyd to journalism, and it was the eventual combination of writing and advocacy that made *Wealth Against Commonwealth* and his other articles, speeches, and books special.

The young Henry came from distinguished stock. His mother was a New York blue blood, a direct lineal descendant of David De Marest, one of the first Dutchmen to tame the Manhattan wilderness in the mid-seventeenth century. De Marest's progeny Americanized their last name, but the next ten generations were all buried on or in the immediate vicinity of Manhattan Island. Henry's maternal grandfather David James Demarest built a house in suburban Greenwich Village in 1835. He was proud of his Dutch Huguenot ancestry, speaking and teaching the language to his children and serving as an elder in the nearby Reformed Dutch Church, but he could not fail to recognize the growing ethnic homogeneity of early nineteenth-century New York City and he married outside his nationality. Henry's mother, Maria Christie, was educated at an expensive finishing school that specialized in the eighteenth-century English romantic tradition. Maria was not an especially talented student, but she was polished into a socially correct, highly marriageable patrician woman who would have been in her element in any upper-class Knickerbocker home.[2]

Henry's father Aaron came from a more radical background. He traced his American lineage to Mehitable Goffe, a daughter of one of the English regicides who executed King Charles I in 1649. Following the restoration of Charles II in 1660, Goffe escaped across the Atlantic to the more politically tolerant Commonwealth of Pennsylvania, and her descendants eventually owned land above some of the same oil deposits that Henry would write about in *Wealth Against Commonwealth*. One of her progeny, Rebecca Ball, was a cousin to Mary Ball, George Washington's mother, and another wintered with Washington at Valley Forge.[3]

Of all his ancestors, Henry was the most like his paternal grandfather. As a teenager, John Crilly Lloyd served in the War of 1812 and was briefly imprisoned by the British in Canada. In compensation for his military service, he was given 160 acres of Eastern New Jersey woodland within view of New York City. However, farming was not his calling, and John Lloyd worked variously as a tailor, landlord, land speculator, commissioner of deeds, postmaster, and justice of the peace. In 1828, he became a Jackson Democrat, one of the first to support Old Hickory in his predominantly Federalist settlement, and his support won him a patronage position as postmaster. With the Whig victory of William Henry Harrison in 1840, John Lloyd remained a Democrat, and he defiantly cast his final ballot for the party of Jefferson and Jackson the day before his death in 1881. Like his grandson, John Lloyd was an enemy of elitism. He joined with his hero Andrew Jackson in opposing the Second National Bank in 1836 and wrote a broadside challenging a local bank in 1840. Another 1840s John Lloyd broadside called on voters to "behold the fiend exclusive privilege and monopoly standeth on the pinnacle of the temple power, grinding the face of the workingman." Although Henry disdained his beloved Democratic politics, his radicalism and dislike of elitism were reminiscent of his grandfather.[4]

Henry's father Aaron was markedly different from his grandfather. John Lloyd separated from his wife soon after the birth of their only child and Aaron spent his formative years living on the Pennsylvania farm of his paternal grandparents. At the age of ten, Aaron joined his father in New Jersey and began attending the nearby Reformed Dutch Church. Two of his uncles were ministers in the Reformed Dutch Church, a nationalistic subdenomination of Presbyterianism that stubbornly clung to the centuries-old Puritanical precepts of Protestant reformers John Calvin and John Knox. John Lloyd wanted Aaron to become a mechanic, but Aaron heard another calling. He found in the strict discipline of Calvinism compensation for the love and guidance denied to him by the lack of a mother, and it was this same discipline that he tried to instill in Henry and that led to a lasting break between the two. In spite of John Lloyd's wishes, Aaron graduated from Rutgers College in 1842 and the New Brunswick Theological Seminary in 1845 as a fully ordained Dutch Reformed minister.[5]

Aaron's first assignment was as an assistant pastor at a New York City parish in 1845, and it was there that he met and courted comely Maria Demarest. Their marriage in February 1846 was more advantageous to him than her. To Maria, Aaron was a socially acceptable, well educated, if not altogether prosperous husband. To Aaron, Maria represented an ancestral connection to the Dutch Reformed faith that he did not have and a path into the Knickerbocker aristocracy of antebellum New York City. In one ceremony, he advanced his career and compensated for his own less than prosperous childhood. Fifteen months after their marriage, Henry was born, just as Aaron was preparing for the first pastorate of his own.[6]

Aaron's religion was the first important influence in young Henry's life. The industrial revolution, the changing role of women in society, ecumenism, and the growth of less strident denominations had induced many early nineteenth century Presbyterians to stray from the strict precepts of the sovereignty of God and predestination as outlined by John Calvin and John Knox. Orthodox traditionalists such as Aaron viewed these developments with alarm and endeavored to protect their faith by reaffirming its founding tenets. One of Maria's cousins was a Dutch Reformed minister and church official who summarized the faith's opposition to modernism in an 1856 book, *History and Characteristics of the Reformed Protestant Dutch Church*. "The Reformed Dutch Church must do her part in the war against [God's] enemies," David D. Demarest wrote. "She must maintain her distinctive character and vigorously carry on the work of extension, or be absorbed by the surrounding large denominations."[7]

The home was the first line of defense in the war against doctrinal impurity, and children were the pawns. In his book, David D. Demarest argued that the primary function of Dutch Reformed parents was to "earnestly and carefully admonish [their children] to the cultivation of true piety; to engage their punctual attendance on family worship, and take them with them to the hearing of the Word of God." Parents who failed in this holy mission faced the prospects of public condemnation, reprimand, and eternal damnation. As an ordained minister of the faith, Aaron was more than mindful of this duty, he was obsessed by it, and as a result Henry came to regard religion as the most arduous regiment of his life as a result.   Initially Henry enjoyed what his younger sister Caro later characterized as "vivid impressions of Jesus" learned at his mother's knee, but Aaron's schedule of three church services per week, twice daily devotional sessions, and two prayers at each meal wore thin over time. In between times, Henry was subjected to "a great deal of well meant exhortation . . . and an occasional funeral and anniversary meeting." Aaron demanded attendance at his religious observances, and Henry was so dutiful that he missed only three sessions during his entire childhood.[8]

Henry felt first apprehension, then guilt, and finally disgust at his father's demands. As he grew, he was also experiencing the normal psychological need of a boy to gain his father's love and approval, which was denied to him because Aaron thought his son lacked piety. The resulting emotions left a mark on Henry's mental complexion for the rest of his life and even damaged his own efforts at fathering. Henry never reconciled his relationship with his father, even after he broke with the Dutch Reformed Church. Aaron's obsession left his oldest son with another, annoying tendency as well. As Henry later explained, "During my 'apprenticeship' I contracted the habit of not listening to what was said, though trying to look as intelligent as possible. This habit of not listening, but wandering in my mind in wayward paths of my own, is now a great annoyance to me when I want to listen to lectures, speeches, etc."[9]

Aaron Lloyd's religious fervor was beneficial to Henry in at least one respect. Aaron was involved in a controversy in 1855 when the General Synod of the Dutch Reformed Church expelled its North Carolina chapter for supporting slavery. The slavery dispute hurt the Dutch church both in terms of membership and money, as it did other churches, and it took years for the Dutch to mend their differences. Still, Aaron was so proud of his opposition to slavery that he donated a book on the Dutch Reformed dispute to the New York Historical Society fifty years later. Though there are no other significant early records on the subject, Henry was almost certainly exposed to abolitionism through his father. He became acquainted with Wendell Philips as part of his first full-time job and made a variety of references to abolitionism in his writings.   He was probably also exposed to *The Liberator*, the leading abolitionist newspaper and one of the best known alternative newspapers of the nineteenth century. Such a publication could have influenced the interest in alternative journalism Henry displayed later in life.[10]

Shortly after Henry's birth, Aaron moved his young family to Phelps, an upstate New York community located about twenty-five miles southeast of

Rochester. Henry survived the usual rites of childhood there, including a case of the chicken pox contracted from an older cousin. When he was six, bullies stole grocery money from him, an event Maria Lloyd later recalled as causing him "great mortification." An unusually thick shock of opulent black hair lent Henry an aristocratic look, and a woman once "gave him a gold dollar and said he looked like a young prince," according to his sister Caro. Henry's childhood appearance was marred by amblyopia, a congenital eye condition also known as lazy eye, but the problem was corrected by a New York City physician in 1857.[11]

Moves to churches in New Jersey and New York State followed between 1848 and 1857, but it was Aaron's last pastorate that provided Henry with a distaste for agriculture. In the immediate years before the Civil War, the Reformed Dutch faith experienced a dramatic growth in its Western membership, and to meet the demand, the church was forced to provide ministers. Aaron's call came in 1857 to Pekin, a central Illinois settlement located about fifty miles north of the state capital of Springfield. Although the exact cutting edge of the frontier had moved beyond Pekin by the late 1850s, the town retained most of its primitive heritage. Above-ground wooden pipes carried the sometimes fetid drinking waters of the Illinois River to the poorly constructed homes of residents; immigrant farmers stood around street corners discussing agricultural conditions in a variety of languages.[12]

For all of its unpleasantries, Pekin advanced Henry's exposure to the American reform tradition first gleaned from his grandfather John Lloyd. The reform-minded Republican party had been born in the West only a few years before, and it was sweeping Illinois during the time Henry lived there. The newly organized Pekin Republican Party faced formidable opposition from leftover Whigs and Know-Nothings, not to mention a hard-core constituency of Democrats, but it made up for its lack of support with mighty aspirations. One observer predicted that "strong local prejudices and feelings in various sections of the county" would determine the election of 1858. That was the year that a lanky Springfield lawyer named Abraham Lincoln faced the "Little Giant," Democratic U. S. Senator Stephen Douglas, in a series of seven public debates held around the state of Illinois. Although their comments on slavery have been most remembered, the leading local issue of the debates was the Illinois Central Railroad, which had been forced into receivership earlier in the year. To get back on its feet, the railroad was seeking an exemption from the Illinois corporate earnings tax. Douglas and other Democrats supported keeping the tax as a means of insuring control over the ambitious railroad. Lincoln, who had previously practiced law for the Illinois Central, endorsed an exemption as an aid to farmers and businessmen. Although there was no debate in Pekin, Henry and his father could have traveled to several other nearby sites to hear the issues debated. In the November election, Lincoln lost Pekin and surrounding Tazewell County by only 156 votes, and the settlement stood directly on the line between Lincoln's Republican support to the North and Douglas's solidly Democratic South. Pekin and the Lincoln-Douglas debates provided Henry with an unparalleled lesson in reform and politics.[13]

Henry displayed a proclivity for writing and speechmaking in Pekin. In his first preserved "book," a penciled composition written on sermon paper and titled "Notebook by Henry Demarest Lloyd . . . containing an account of Natural Philosophy, of birds, beasts . . . and other miscellaneous matter," Henry discussed his school studies and the prairie sights around him. He revealed an early sensitivity toward criticism, warning his "readers": "The critical world will please remember that [these compositions] are the productions of a young person and not of an old and experienced [person] who is well acquainted with all the different customs of the world. . . . [This notebook] was not written for the ordeal of criticism but to distribute among men thereby to promote the knowledge and happiness of mankind." He must have pleased his teacher in one essay, "A Speech in the Defense of Composition Writing," by noting, "Some of you sit down to write [compositions] in a fit of passion because Mr. Blenkirous makes you . . . [but] he only does it for your own benefit." Other essays documented the "Domestic Entertainments of the Ancients" and "The Humble Bee."[14]

In spite of such distractions, Henry's Pekin adventure began to wear thin almost from the start. Aaron was probably allergic to the flora and fauna of the Illinois River Valley and was sick so often that he was unable to preach or work. The New York bred Maria never adjusted to her rural surroundings or neighbors. The financial panic of 1857 created economic problems for Pekin as well, bringing an abrupt end to the Illinois land boom and reducing the attendance and collections at Aaron Lloyd's struggling church. The panic hurt Aaron in another way, for he and his father had been speculating in Illinois land since 1844. Aaron had even considered buying Illinois land along a never-built Lake Huron Mississippi River canal. The failure of his land investments left Aaron cash poor with little hope of recouping his losses through his church work.[15]

It was in Pekin that Henry came to know the drudgery of nineteenth century agriculture. He and his three younger brothers were forced to hand plant and tend eleven acres of corn to feed their family and provide a small cash crop. They worked long and hard on the hot Illinois prairie, but their efforts could not make up for Aaron's land losses and inadequate salary. Pushed toward bankruptcy, Aaron asked for another ministry, but the Dutch Reformed Church could find nothing else for him in 1860, probably because he was a non-Dutch minister. With no other option, Aaron quit the ministry, sold his Pekin house, and moved his family back to New York City. They settled in the same house in whicht Henry had been born some fourteen years earlier. Although he never hated farmers, Henry had little nice to say about agriculture or its practitioners for the rest of his life, even during his years as a Populist.[16]

The New York City of 1860 was vastly different from what it had been during Maria's childhood or even at the time of Henry's birth in 1847. The walking city of New York disappeared forever between 1830 and 1860 as the city's population quadrupled and its narrow boundaries leapfrogged. William Cullen Bryant complained in his *New York Evening Post* that commerce was "devouring inch by inch" the wilderness shoreline of Manhattan. Lawyer and diarist George Templeton Strong noted that he attended a party in 1856 "in thirty-seventh!!!—it seems but the other day that thirty-seventh Street was an imaginary line running through a rural district and grazed over by cows." New York was becoming the first real city in America, and its residents had a ringside seat for one of the most important developments in nineteenth-century American history.[17]

Henry's home near Washington Square was at the heart of the reinvented New York, and the best and worst of urban life were on daily view for him. Novelist Henry James wrote of his childhood on the "Square" at about the same time as Henry that "it was here, as you might have been informed on good authority, that you had come into a world which appeared to offer a variety of sources of interest." Yet a few blocks away was the notorious Five Points, the worst slum in pre-Civil War America. Prostitutes walked the streets or called from windows, criminals openly plied their trade, and pigs rooted for garbage. Nowhere else in America were the extremities of wealth and poverty so conveniently displayed, and they provided a lesson that was not lost on the adolescent Henry.[18]

A short walk beyond Washington Square lay America's first information center. Beginning in the early 1830s, a new type of newspaper, the penny press, had started in New York City. Where older newspapers had chronicled partisan politics or commerce for a small readership of upper-class businessmen, the penny press told the story of New York's birth as a world metropolis to the city's rapidly expanding middle class. As the city grew, the penny newspapers became the only source of information for residents, and their publishers amassed both power and fortunes on the pennies of their readers. The *New York Sun*, *New York Herald*, *New York Tribune*, and *The New York Times* celebrated their influence and affluence with massive new office buildings constructed near Washington Square in an area known as Printing House Square. Here one could tread in the footsteps of celebrity editors such as Moses Yale Beach, Horace Greeley, James Gordon Bennett, and Henry J. Raymond. Coming from a family that stressed newspaper reading, Henry feasted on the New York press and came under its influence and mystique. Not surprisingly, both he and his younger brother Demarest worked as newspapermen as adults. Lloyd was rejected as a writer for the *New York Tribune* but was hired by the *Chicago Tribune*. Demarest worked a decade for the *New York Tribune* before he became a Broadway dramatist.[19]

Tempering such distractions was the reality of everyday existence in Civil

War era New York City. Deprived of his ministry, Aaron opened a small bookstore a short distance from his father-in-law's house, specializing in theological titles, prayer books, bibles, history, and juvenile literature, but money was hard to come by. War-induced double-digit inflation made even a minister's salary seem opulent compared to the slim profits of a bookstore. To make ends meet, Maria and her two daughters did their own housework while Henry and his two brothers worked after school at the nearby Mercantile Library. Still, the sale of some of Aaron's precious religious tracts was necessary to finance a trip to Grandfather Lloyd's house in New Jersey, and Henry got a new pair of boots one winter with the proceeds from a sale of some of the family's silverware.[20]

Such an abrupt change in economic and social status was not lost on the adolescent Henry. In the smaller towns that he had grown up in, he had enjoyed the distinction of moving about upper-class juvenile society as the son of a minister. With its upper class of new wealth, New York turned up its nose at tradesmen, especially less than successful ones such as Aaron, and Henry was now ridiculed by his peers for his family's circumstances, and his father's apparent lack of ambition, where he had once been held in esteem. Aaron did little to help Henry adjust to the new situation. He viewed his new circumstances not as shameful but as a lesson in humility, and he redoubled his daily religious regimen to make the most of it for his children's spiritual growth. Henry was incensed at his father's callousness toward his juvenile suffering and did everything he could to shut Aaron out of his life, working or studying late. Their estrangement became complete during the early 1860s when Henry and his two brothers quit the Reformed Dutch Church of their father and joined Henry Ward Beecher's interdenominational Plymouth Church. Beecher was the most popular American minister of his day, drawing thousands to his Sunday sermons, but theological conservatives such as Aaron considered his ecumenism heretical. Henry's decision was a serious, personal rebuke to Aaron. Maria intervened by coaxing her children to attend the more traditional Church of the Strangers, which claimed among its members Cornelius Vanderbilt and other prominent Knickerbockers, but Henry eventually stopped attending church altogether and remained an agnostic for the rest of his life. Regardless, his father's Calvinist theology stayed with him as an integral, albeit repressed, part of Henry's moral perspective and influenced his future reform inclinations.[21]

Politics was the other major point of contention between Henry and his father. Henry was too young to fight in the Civil War, turning eighteen three weeks after Appomattox, but his father's faith in the secessionist Democratic Party irked him, especially its connection with lower-class elements in society. Aaron and his father John Lloyd were New York Locofoco-Democrats, strongly opposed to Abraham Lincoln's vision of a centralized federal government. John Lloyd so disliked Lincoln that he quit his postmaster's job the day after the Republican was elected to office in 1860 and stopped attending his Reformed

Dutch Church when a member waved an American flag during a Sunday service in celebration of a Northern victory. As such, Locofoco-Democrats were not held in the highest esteem by New York's old line upper class and many considered them traitors to the Union cause. In particular, Henry's maternal grandfather, David James Demarest, was a staunch Unionist Republican, favoring Lincoln's efforts to return stability and decorum to the country. Regardless of his position as a visitor in his father-in-law's house, Aaron persevered in his views and the dinner debates between the Lloyds and the Demarests were intense during the war years. One of Henry's neighbors later recalled, "It used to make my loyal blood boil to see your father reading the [Democratic New York] *Daily News*." In response, Henry and his brothers read the pro Lincoln *New York Tribune*.[22]

Henry tolerated his father's disloyal views until New York City's antidraft riots of 1863. For four July days, mob law reigned in lower Manhattan as lower-class whites protested Lincoln's latest draft order and the growing competition of freed slaves for jobs. Aaron Lloyd supported their opposition to the draft because it was the first time in American history that the federal government, not an individual state, had raised an army. Republicans, including Henry's maternal grandfather, sided with New York Mayor George Opdyke in calling the riots an outrage against public order. When local authorities could no longer control the situation, Secretary of War Edwin Stanton diverted ten Union Army regiments to New York to restore the peace. As a result of the riots and his ongoing antagonism toward his father, Henry eschewed the Democratic party for the rest of his life, even when it became aligned with reform elements late in the nineteenth century. At the same time, he developed a deep-seated fear of mob rule, a concern that manifested itself in his adult writings as a prediction of a French-style revolution in the United States. Father and son discussed politics occasionally after the riots, but Aaron could never convince Henry to vote Democratic, not even in the presidential election of 1896.[23]

Lloyd completed his grammar school education in 1863 and, with the encouragement of his parents, set his sights on Columbia College, now Columbia University. The differences between New York's public schools and the privately-owned Columbia was so dramatic that Maria tried to arrange a year of preparatory study for Henry but the tuition was beyond their means. Aaron asked several wealthy men if they would support Henry through college, a common nineteenth-century practice for ministers, and a prominent New York banker agreed, promising Henry a four-year scholarship in exchange for good grades.[24]

Mid-nineteenth century Columbia College stressed its Episcopalian heritage and classical liberal arts curriculum to its patrician, Knickerbocker clientele, but in an effort to promote social harmony, it occasionally accepted talented students of lesser parentage. Henry was of the latter group, a fact made abundantly clear to him from his first day of classes. The course work epitomized the classical emphasis that had earmarked Columbia's founding in 1754, and newer, more suspect disciplines such as science, history, and contemporary literature were eschewed for the most part in favor of traditional Greek and Roman studies. Change came slowly. One particularly detested textbook of Henry's day was said to have been in use for at least thirty years. Ironically, what the school lacked in academics it made up for in athletics. Unlike modern-day Columbia, the baseball "nine" of Lloyd's era was undefeated and its other teams were nearly as good.[25]

The faculty was little better than the curriculum. The one exception was Francis Lieber, a professor of political economy and public law. Fritz, as his students called him, was German born and educated, and lectured with an intellectual intensity that frightened the college's new president, Frederick A. P. Barnard.   So as not to offend the school's conservative trustees, Barnard restricted Lieber to teaching less impressionable graduate students beyond his undergraduate political economy class. Regardless, his radical politics and ideas radiated through the halls of Columbia like a forbidden fruit, and Henry took all of his undergraduate classes and spent hours with him after school. Lieber was fascinated by the publicity process, and he taught Lloyd how news was made and how to get a newspaper to print a story without identifying the true source, the art of a mid-nineteenth century press agent. Although Henry eventually fell out of step with Lieber's politics, his publicity techniques formed part of the basis for Henry's advocacy writings.[26]

The Columbia faculty influenced Henry in one other respect.   Their emphasis on noblesse oblige, the moral obligation of the highborn toward society, left an indelible mark on Henry, especially when he became wealthy later in life. Columbia taught its patrician students that public service was a duty and obligation of the upper class in exchange for the privileges it enjoyed, and failure to repay such a debt was a mark of poor character. In a sense, Henry Demarest Lloyd's entire reform career was inspired by his adolescent desire to be wealthy enough to feel guilty about the lower classes. That he would be so influenced by the spirit of noblesse oblige was not surprising considering that the split between Henry and his father occurred at the same time and Henry was eager to distance himself from the vow of poverty his father had seemingly imposed on himself.[27]

There was at least one drawback to Henry's higher education. In an attempt to keep up with his better educated classmates, he developed a habit of working and studying too long and too hard. Henry was a sensitive, emotional individual who always believed that he was operating from a disadvantage, and what began in college as a laudable quest for academic excellence ended up in a lifelong habit.   The unintended result was nervous prostration, a health condition related to chronic overwork that left Henry incapable of caring for himself for months at a time. He was also prone to insomnia and literally had to be read to sleep as an older man. He was far from unusual in these regards, for many in his post-Civil War generation suffered from a variety of stress-related disorders including insomnia, nervous prostration, and depression. Ironically, these conditions were considered marks of good breeding and success, and Henry embraced the stereotype, for better or worse, in his own life.[28]

Henry sharpened his writing and speaking skills at Columbia. His preserved essays, poems, and speeches reveal a growing talent at self-expression. In "Stray Cuttings from the Trail of a Goosequill," Henry wrote, "I was taken from the pinions of one goose to spread the opinions of another." A professor noted on another essay, "In the main, very good indeed, but sometimes inaccurate, at other times odd in expression." Henry contributed editorials to the Columbia student newspaper, one on the college's then lower Manhattan location and another criticizing the school's classical curriculum. He published at least one anonymous poem in the college's yearbook, delivered graduation speeches in both 1866 and 1867, and was characterized as a poet who "tickles your feet with an intellectual straw, trips you up with some humorous rope . . . and throws out so many ready scintillations." in his official class history. To celebrate his growing aestheticism, Henry changed the spelling of his last name to "Lloyde" during his sophomore year in college, a practice he did not drop until after graduation.[29]

Beyond his writings, Henry earned distinction during his junior year at Columbia for being "the man who threw Prex," a reference to Columbia President Frederick A. P. Barnard. Locked doors were a common grievance of mid-nineteenth-century Columbia students, especially when they sought to enter warm classrooms from cold unheated hallways. Lloyd's class briefly considered "no door shall stand between me and my duty" as its official class motto before saner minds prevailed. When spring fever struck in April 1866, an unknown number of Lloyd's classmates excised their demons by breaking open and damaging a locked door. When no one in the junior class would identify the guilty parties, Barnard decided to use the incident to teach the platitudes of propriety and discipline to his pupils. He explained, "I should be wholly wanting in my duty if I failed to do all in my power to protect the property which has been committed to my charge."[30]

To decide if Henry's class would be held collectively liable for the three dollars in damages, Barnard called a military-style court martial before a jury of seniors. Barnard selected two of the school's best known patricians to represent the junior class, Nicholas Fish and George A. DeWitt, scions of two prominent New York families. The class resented his interference and added several non-elites to the defense team, including Henry. On the day of the trial, Fish, DeWitt, and the others set about "to make the affair a great legal frolic" but Lloyd prepared, using a military law textbook to develop a five-part rebuttal to Barnard's charges. Four of his arguments dealt with legal technicalities but his fifth was based on a fundamental tenet of American law, the due process clause of the Fifth Amendment. In front of the senior jury, Henry argued that Barnard had violated the rights of the entire junior class by penalizing all for the misbehavior of a few. Following ten minutes of closed-door deliberation, the seniors allowed Henry's contention. Barnard, recognizing that he had been outmaneuvered by Henry, entered a plea of *nolle prosequi* and agreed to pay for the damages. The junior class "went on its way rejoicing" and Henry became a Columbia College legend.[31]

Henry's newfound popularity was tempered by the reality that his major, political economy, portended few career opportunities upon his graduation in 1867. College diplomas themselves meant little in New York, then a city of self made men. There were two exceptions to this rule. Since Henry had no interest in religion, the law was his only other option. In particular, nineteenth-century attorneys were more literary than their twentieth-century counterparts, a trait Henry found especially appealing. Most of New York City's first generation of literary luminaries, giants such as Washington Irving and William Cullen Bryant, had been lawyers. "The legal profession," historian Thomas Bender wrote, "sustained a commitment to literary breadth and elegance, to classical forms, and to civic republicanism. With the culture of the law and that of literature thus nearly fused, literature inherited the law's commitment to neoclassical order and responsibility in letters and life." As such, a legal career offered Henry a dignified, upper-class occupation and a desired opportunity to write and publish.[32]

Unfortunately, Henry's economic status affected his decision. He was considering two law programs, Harvard and Columbia, when Nicholas Fish, his Columbia door-incident classmate, wrote him in early 1868. Fish recommended Harvard but observed that tuition, room, and board was $700 a year, well beyond Henry's meager means. Determined that a homegrown legal education was better than none at all, Henry enrolled in Columbia's graduate school in January 1868 with the intention of earning a master's degree that would help him pass the New York State bar exam.[33]

Going back to Columbia meant that Henry would study with his former mentor Fritz Lieber. Lieber lectured on constitutional law and legal history, but it was his excursions into legal ethics that most intrigued Henry. Lieber argued that it was the moral duty of lawyers to perform nonpartisan civic public service, an obligation he called national citizenship or civic humanism. Social chaos was the only alternative if upper-class men failed to take their proper place in a democracy, and Lieber believed that unprincipled, opportunistic, low-class entrepreneurs had seized control of the American government in the wake of the Civil War because good, upper-class men had failed to act. According to Lieber, only men of character, educated at a proper institution like Columbia, could save Gilded Age American democracy from disintegrating into anarchy.[34]

Henry also learned about the advocacy nature of the legal profession at

Columbia. At their essence, lawyers are defined as advocates, persons who speak for others. Beginning in the Middle Ages in England, law evolved as a profession of trained advocates advising their clients and arguing their cases in courts. The one-sided nature of the legal profession allows lawyers to represent anyone, since it is not incumbent on a lawyer to determine the guilt or innocence of a particular client. Once representation has been agreed to, a lawyer must argue as persuasively as he or she can for a client or risk losing his or her law license. Henry applied the spirit of the advocacy principle to his journalism, speaking for individuals and groups that he felt were overlooked or underrepresented in American society.[35]

In spite of the allure of Printing House Square, Henry did not immediately embark upon a newspaper career after he completed the requirements for his master's degree and passed the bar exam in spring 1869. Instead, he found work in an allied field. Publicity was still a new pursuit in post-Civil War New York. It had sprung up as an axillary industry to the penny press during the 1830s, feeding on the newspapers' success by "planting" stories or editorials for paying clients. Most of the time the price of a planted story was a bribe to an editor or reporter, usually in tickets, cash, or other property. A press agent was "the only man in the world proud of being called a liar," as one explained. Secrecy was essential, for if the source of a planted story became known, the impact was lessened. Respectable organizations interested in promoting themselves employed agents under unrelated job titles so that few would know their true purpose. Under such circumstances, being a good publicity agent required allegiance to his client, a talent for talking, an ability to write, and an idea of how far the law would stretch—all skills common to a lawyer.[36]

The American Free-Trade League was one of many special interest groups that tried to emulate the success of the abolitionists after the Civil War. Founded in 1864, it began as an organization of merchants and shippers opposed to war tariffs, but by the conclusion of the war, it had attracted a sizable group of ex-abolitionists into its ranks, including William Lloyd Garrison and Wendell Philips, as well as liberal laissez-faire capitalists such as William Cullen Bryant, Ralph Waldo Emerson, E. L. Godkin, David A. White, Henry Ward Beecher, Edward Atkinson, Carl Schurz, Henry George, and Lloyd's Columbia mentor, Francis Lieber. All shared a common belief in liberalism and the benefits of free trade. The League was headquartered in New York City, where the country's leading shippers were located, but it dispatched field workers across the country. There was an unabashed comparison to abolitionism in League literature, one pamphlet noting, "Chattel slavery consists in the power conferred by government upon a few favored individuals to control the labor of their fellow men. . . . [Trade] protection is the same in spirit."[37]

With Lieber's help, the League hired Henry as a colporteur, or field worker, and sent him on the road during the summer of 1869. In preparation for his first job, Henry immersed himself anew in the political economists that he had studied as an undergraduate, men such as Adam Smith, Edmund Burke, Alexis de Tocqueville, Frederic Bastiat, and Richard Cobden. Over the summer of 1869, he traveled to three dozen cities in Ohio and upper New York State, speaking to more than a thousand newspaper editors and community leaders. His skill at generating publicity, learned from Lieber, his knowledge of small-town life, and his enthusiasm for the free trade cause attracted the attention of the national headquarters, and Henry was ushered back to New York City in the fall and promoted to assistant secretary. In reality, his primary function was to generate publicity for the organization both within and without the New York press.[38]

In publicizing free trade, Henry came in contact with the leading journalists of the day. In an 1871 letter to Yale University President Theodore Dwight Woolsey, *Nation* publisher E. L. Godkin, a Free-Trade League member, called Henry "a gentleman in whom you may repose the fullest confidence." William Cullen Bryant published a number of Henry's letters in his free-trade *New York Evening Post* under the pseudonym "No Monopoly," their chief target being *New York Tribune* publisher Horace Greeley. Greeley maintained that the Free-Trade League was a special interest group of "British importers," financed by "British gold," a charge that turned out to be true. In his "No Monopoly" letters, Henry accused Greeley and America's industrialists of seeking high tariffs to create monopolies for certain goods. In one "No Monopoly" letter, Henry demanded that high salt tariffs be reduced to benefit Western meat packers. Greeley responded by calling Henry a "demagogue," to which Lloyd retorted, "If advocating cheap salt, cheap iron, cheap clothing, and cheap necessaries for the people entitles one to the name demagogue, I shall be proud to be called one not only by the monopolists' hired man who edits the *Tribune*, but by every living soul in the world."[39]

The debate raged on the speaker's platform as well. *The New York Times* quoted Henry at a public rally in 1871:

It was folly to say [internal production] could not be maintained without protection. American labor needed nothing but a stout arm. Mr. Greeley and his followers presented us with a theory, which must be eradicated from the minds of all Americans.

Greeley tried to rebut his young adversary, but he was on the losing side of the issue in a city dependent upon foreign trade. In frustration, he complained to Henry, "You have at least a score of free-trade idiots in this city, not counting your society. The *Tribune* stands alone for protectionism."[40]

The "No Monopoly" letters furthered Henry's growing reputation as a skilled writer and young man to watch. In late 1869, the Free-Trade League decided to publish its own newsletter, and it naturally looked to Henry as editor. By design, the *Free-Trader* bore a striking resemblance to Godkin's *Nation*, in both appearance and style, to confuse readers into thinking it was a legitimate magazine and not free-trade propaganda. Distributed free of charge to libraries, schools, churches, and given to a variety of influential people, it featured editorials, book reviews, and articles all in fierce opposition to tariffs and protectionism. Henry acted as the publicist and advocate that he was, observing in one of the first issues, "These 'facts' are conclusive proof that high tariffs do make high prices, and that the [New York] *Tribune* theory that Protection lowers prices is only a *Tribune* theory." In an editorial titled "The Issue of the Future," he argued:

The affirmative position assumed by the Republican Party in reference to slavery has resulted . . . in the complete overthrow and extinction of that infamous institution. The next thing must be something else. What is that something else which must take the place of the slavery agitation . . . . The people may be slow to learn where their money goes, but they are sure to learn in time; and when that time comes, there will be serious reckoning.[41]

The publicity business worked both ways, as Henry discovered to his dismay in October 1870. Greeley's *Tribune* scooped the *Free Trader* by publishing a supposedly confidential list of the Free Trade League's major financial contributors. To no one's surprise, the list included the names of nearly every major importer and overseas banker in New York City, businessmen who stood to gain the most profit from free trade as Greeley had maintained. Henry wrote a letter demanding that the *Tribune* reveal its source for the list but Whitelaw Reid, Greeley's assistant, refused the request, responding, "This is a thing of such constant occurrence in a newspaper office that it attracts no attention." The disclosure created consternation among League officials but apparently had little long-term impact. According to other *Tribune* reports, the Free-Trade League collected over $57,000 in contributions and spent nearly $27,000 in 1870, qualifying it as a major special interest organization. In November, Greeley credited the Free-Trade League with derailing the congressional campaigns of a dozen pro-tariff Republicans, including himself. Still, the morally-minded Henry never forgot the ethical considerations of publishing a stolen document, and refused to do so in his *Wealth Against Commonwealth* in contrast to Ida M. Tarbell in her *History of the Standard Oil Company*.[42]

Henry's free-trade efforts earned him the reputation of an impassioned, intelligent, and compulsive overworker. Years later, a sister of one his college friends told him, "In my first recollection of you, a young law student, arguing with my father upon free-trade, you spoke already with the experience and aplomb of a veteran." His younger brother David added a line about Henry to a Broadway play he wrote in 1882. To distract his ingenue from a discussion of marriage, David had his male romantic lead say, "Let's talk about something soothing. Let's talk about the tariff." As consumed as he was by his free trade work, Henry still had the time to teach night classes at a New York City public high school in 1872 and 1873. He promised his pupils to explore "the origin, development, and proper functions of the state." He made tariffs a case study, inviting both Horace Greeley and Francis Lieber to present their sides on the issue. His intensity made him memorable if distant. One student recalled that Henry was "more than ordinary: there was something grandly stoic about him" but also observed of his shy, emotional nature, "He didn't understand you when you wanted to thank him."[43]

Henry's various discourses on free trade and political economy led him to his first nationally-published writing effort, a letter to the editor of the *Phrenological Journal* in January 1872. The St. Louis-based publication featured an eclectic assortment of literature and philosophy modeled after the *Journal of Speculative Philosophy*, the first American periodical devoted exclusively to philosophy. In words he would eventually come to recant, Henry wrote a response to a critic of political economy, noting that this social science was "a valiant ally of the social reformer" because it denounced "violations of economic law which cause social disorders." To Henry, a true free market system would eliminate "monopolists, subsidies, special legislation, [and] land grants." Although the *Phrenological Journal* did not have a large circulation, it was the start of Henry's professional career, and seeing his words in print renewed a passion for journalism that had been growing in Henry since his days near Printing House Square.[44]

NOTES

1. CLS, "Biographical Sketch of H. D. Lloyd," n.d., circa 1936 and Aaron Lloyd, "Genealogical," n.d., circa 1900, both in HDL, mf; Aaron Lloyd to John C. Lloyd, 9 July 1849, in Lloyd Family Papers, New Jersey History Society (hereafter Lloyd Family Papers); and Mary A. and William H. S. Demarest, *The Demarest Family* (New Brunswick, NJ: Thatcher-Anderson Co., 1938), 214–215, 288–291.

2. CLS, "Biographical Sketch" and Aaron Lloyd, "Genealogy," both in HDL, mf; Maria Lloyd to HDL, November 1889 and 22 November 1889, both in HDL Papers, State Historical Society of Wisconsin (hereafter HDL, Wisc.); CLS, *Lloyd* I, 1–17; Mary and William Demarest, *Demarest Family*, 13–14, 145, 214; Demarest Family Genealogy in James Riker Collection, New York Public Library; CLS, *Lloyd* I, 1–17.

3. CLS, "Biographical Sketch" and Aaron Lloyd, "Genealogy," both in HDL, mf.; CLS, *Lloyd* I, 1–17; and Destler, *Empire of Reform*, 15–16.

4. John C. Lloyd documents, various dates, Lloyd Family Papers; H. A. Holmes, *A Brief History of Belleville*, pamphlet in New Jersey Historical Society; Elizabeth Forte, *Belleville: A Bicentennial Salute* (Belleville, NJ: Privately Printed, 1975); Stuart Galishoff, *Newark, the Nation's Unhealthiest City: 1832-1895* (New Brunswick, NJ: Rutgers University Press, 1988); John C. Lloyd, "The Second Epistle of the Workingmen to their Brethren in All the Land," 1841, HDL, Wisc.; John C. Lloyd, "First Chapter of the Book of Chronicles of the Times," 1840, and unsigned explanation, both in Jessie Bross Lloyd Papers, Chicago Historical Society (hereafter JBL, CHS).

5. Aaron Lloyd to John Crilly Lloyd, March 30, 1823, in Lloyd Family Papers;

"Biographical Sketch", ibid.; CLS, *Lloyd* I, 1–17; various Aaron Lloyd obituaries following his death on 17 December 1905, Lloyd Family Papers and JBL, CHS; and Aaron Lloyd, "Contributions to the Early History of the Reformed Dutch Church of Second River," *New Jersey Historical Society Proceedings, Second Series*, 9(1886): 195–232.

6. Chester M. Destler, "Henry Demarest Lloyd and the Empire of Reform," unpublished draft MS, circa 1950, State Historical Society of Wisconsin, 1–3 (hereafter, HDL, MS); Winthrop S. Hudson, *Religion in America* (New York: Charles Scribner's and Sons, 1974); and Joseph Belcher, *The Religious Denominations in the United States* (Philadelphia: J. E. Potter, 1854), 712–719.

7. CLS Journal, HDL Papers, State Historical of Wisconsin (hereafter CLS Journal); David D. Demarest, *History and Characteristics of the Reformed Protestant Dutch Church* (New York: Board of Publications of the Reformed Protestant Dutch Church, 1856), 205; and Hudson, *Religion*, 165–166.

8. Demarest, *Reformed Protestant Dutch Church*, 165–166 and CLS, *Lloyd* I, 1–17.

9. HDL to the Reverend Quincy Dowd, 6 April 1890, HDL, Wisc.; Aaron Lloyd to John Crilly Lloyd, 12 April 1848, Lloyd Family Papers; CLS, *Lloyd* I, 1–17; Colleen McDannell, *The Christian Home in Victorian America, 1840–1900* (Bloomington: Indiana University Press, 1986), 77–85; Lewis Yablonsky, *Fathers and Sons* (New York: Simon and Schuster, 1982), 46–61, 78–81; Samuel Osherson, *Finding Our Fathers: The Unfinished Business of Manhood* (New York: The Free Press, 1986), 1–43; Edward A. Rotundo, "Manhood in America: The Northern Middle Class, 1770–1920 (Ph.D. diss, Brandeis University, 1982), 197–210; and Robert Kegan, *The Evolving Self* (Cambridge, MA: Harvard University Press, 1982), 73–110.

10. Samuel B. How, *Slaveholding Not Sinful: Slavery, the Punishment of Man's Sin, Its Remedy, The Gospel of Christ* (New Brunswick, NJ: John Terhune, 1856), copy identified as donated by Aaron Lloyd, in New York State Historical Society.

Also see Herbert Aptheker, *Abolitionism: A Revolutionary Movement* (Boston: Twayne Publishers, 1989); David Paul Nord, "Tocqueville, Garrison and the Perfection of Journalism," *Journalism History*, 13(Summer 1986): 56–63; Irving Howe, *The American Newness: Culture and Politics in the Age of Emerson* (Cambridge, MA: Harvard University Press, 1986); Merton L. Dillon, *The Abolitionists: The Growth of a Dissenting Minority* (New York: W. W. Norton, 1979), 36–40; Leonard L. Richards, *"Gentlemen of Property and Standing"* (New York: Oxford, 1970), 22–23; Aileen S. Kraditor, *Means and Ends in American Abolitionism: Garrison and His Critics on Strategy and Tactics, 1834–1850* (New York: Pantheon Books, 1969), 177–255; Charles A. Madison, *Critics and Crusaders: A Century of American Protest* (New York: Frederick Ungar, 1959), 14–38; and Hazel C. Wolf, *On Freedom's Altar: The Martyr Complex in the Abolition Movement* (Madison: University of Wisconsin Press, 1952).

11. Aaron Lloyd to "My Dear Parents," 29 May 1848; Maria to Mrs. John C. Lloyd, 15 June 1848; Aaron to John Crilly Lloyd, 11 July 1848, 9 July 1849, all in Lloyd Family Papers; HDL photograph at age ten; CLS to HDL, 23 December 1898; and Aaron Lloyd to CLS, 11 March 1904, all in HDL, Wisc.; CLS Journal; and Sylvia D. Hoffert, *Private Matters: American Attitudes toward Childbearing and Infant Nurture in the Urban North, 1800–1860* (Urbana: University of Illinois Press, 1989), 142–168.

12. Various obituaries, Aaron Lloyd, circa 17 December 1905 and Thomas N. Gill to Steamer Arndt Letty, 3 August 1857, all in Lloyd Family Papers; Mary and William

Demarest, *Demarest Family*, 214; Arthur Charles Cole, *Centennial History of Illinois: The Era of the Civil War, 1848–1870* (Springfield: Illinois Centennial Commission, 1919), 1–29, 54; Belcher, *Religious Denominations*, 713; Hudson, *Religion in America*, 166; and Demarest, *Reformed Protestant Dutch Church*, 112–115, 183–186, 205.

13. S. S. Marshall to C. Lanphier, 9, 14 October 1858, C. Lanphier papers, Illinois State Historical Society, as cited in Bruce Collins, "The Lincoln-Douglas Contest of 1858 and Illinois' Electorate," *Journal of American Studies*, 20(Fall 1986): 391–420; F. Gerald Ham, *The Papers of Henry Demarest Lloyd: A Guide to the Microfilm Edition* (Madison: State Historical Society of Wisconsin, 1971); Chester M. Destler, "A 'Plebeian' at Columbia: 1863–1869," *New York History*, 27(July 1946): 306–323; and Norman Pollack, *The Populist Mind* (Indianapolis: The Bobbs-Merrill Company, Inc., 1967), 66–68.

Also see Robert H. Walker, *Reform in America: The Continuing Frontier* (Lexington: University Press of Kentucky, 1985); Lawrence Veysey, *The Perfectionists: Radical Social Thought in the North, 1815–1860* (New York: John Wiley and Sons, Inc., 1973), 1–13; Ronald G. Walters, *American Reformers, 1815–1860* (New York: Hill and Wang, 1978); Ross E. Paulson, *Radicalism and Reform: The Vrooman Family and American Social Thought, 1837–1937* (Frankfort: University of Kentucky Press, 1968); David Brion Davis, ed., *Ante-Bellum Reform* (New York: Harper and Row, 1967); John L. Thomas, "Romantic Reform in America, 1815–1865," *American Quarterly*, 17(Winter 1965): 656–681; Roberta Garner, *Social Movements in America* (Chicago: Rand McNally, 1977); Donald F. Tingley, *Essays in Illinois History* (Carbondale: Southern Illinois University Press, 1965); Bessie Louise Pierce and Joe L. Norris, *As Others See Chicago: Impressions of Visitors, 1673–1933* (Chicago: University of Chicago Press, 1933); Kathleen McCarthy, *Noblesse Oblige: Charity and Cultural Philanthropy in Chicago, 1849–1929* (Chicago: University of Chicago Press, 1982); Cole, *Civil War*; Warren Susman, "The Persistence of Reform," in *Culture As History* (New York: Pantheon Books, 1984), 86–97; John Higham and Irving H. Bartlett, *The American Mind in the Mid-nineteenth Century* (New York: Thomas Y. Crowell Co., 1967); and Henry Steele Commager, ed., *The Era of Reform, 1830–1860* (Princeton, NJ: Van Nostrand, 1960).

14. Aaron Lloyd to John Crilly Lloyd, 5 June, 18 September 1857, 31 August, 23 September 1859; all in Lloyd Family Papers and "A Notebook by Henry Demarest Lloyd, Pekin, Tazewell [County], Illinois . . ." in HDL, mf.

15. Elizabeth Middleton Lloyd to John Crilly Lloyd, 17 October 1844; David Lloyd to John Crilly, 5 July 1849; David Lloyd to John Crilly, 16 February 1855; Aaron Lloyd to John Crilly, 27 March, 5 June 1857, 26 September 1857, 31 August, 23 September 1859; all in Lloyd Family papers; "Proposed Canal Between Lakes Erie and Michigan," *Chicago Tribune* (hereafter *C.T.*), 18 November 1894; Cole, *Illinois*, 245–250; and CLS, *Lloyd* I, 10–17.

16. Aaron Lloyd to John Crilly Lloyd, 31 August, 23 September 1859, both in Lloyd Family papers; Cole, *Illinois*, 245–250; and CLS, *Lloyd* I, 10–17.

17. William E. Dodge, *Old New York: A Lecture* (New York: Dodd, Mead and Co., 1880), 22; Charles N. Glaab and A. Theodore Brown, *A History of Urban America* (New York: Macmillan, 1983), 83–106; John C. Teaford, *The Municipal Revolution in America: Origins of Modern Urban Government, 1650–1825* (Chicago: University of Chicago Press, 1975); Eric F. Goldman, "Middle States Regionalism and American

Historiography: A Suggestion," in Goldman, ed., *History and Urbanization: Essays in American History in Honor of W. Stull Holt* (Baltimore: The Johns Hopkins University Press, 1941); Thomas Bender, *New York Intellect: A History of Intellectual Life in New York City from 1750 to the Beginnings of Our Own Time* (Baltimore: Johns Hopkins University Press, 1987), 156–157; Edward K. Spann, *The New Metropolis: New York City, 1840–1857* (New York: Columbia University Press, 1981), 1–23; Paul Boyer, *Urban Masses and Moral Order in America, 1820–1920* (Cambridge: Harvard University Press, 1978), 3–21; Maury Klein and Harvey A. Kantor, *Prisoners of Progress: American Industrial Cities, 1850 to 1920* (New York: Macmillan, 1976), x–xiii; Raymond A. Mohl, *The New City: Urban America in the Industrial Age, 1860–1920* (Arlington Heights, IL: Harlan Davidson, Inc., 1985), 7–52; Cyril E. Black, *The Dynamics of Modernization: A Study in Comparative History* (New York: Harper and Row, 1975); John Higham, *From Boundlessness to Consolidation: The Transformation of American Culture, 1848–1860* (Ann Arbor, MI: William L. Clements Library, 1969); and Richard B. Stott, *Workers in the Metropolis: Class, Ethnicity, and Youth in Antebellum New York City* (Ithaca: Cornell University Press, 1990).

18. Charles Lockwood, *Manhattan Moves Uptown: An Illustrated History* (Boston: Houghton Mifflin Company, 1976), 49–105; Spann, *New Metropolis*, 111–112, 153; Bender, *New York Intellect*; Susan Edmiston and Linda D. Cirino, *Literary New York* (Boston: Houghton Mifflin Co., 1976), 23–31; and Browne, *Metropolis*, 295–303.

19. Michael Schudson, *Discovering the News: A Social History of American Newspapers* (New York: Basic Books, 1978); Dan Schiller, *Objectivity and the News: The Public and the Rise of Commercial Journalism* (Philadelphia: The University of Pennsylvania Press, 1976); Edwin and Michael Emery, *The Press and America*, 6th ed. (Englewood Cliffs, NJ: Prentice-Hall, 1988); 217–220; John W. Tebbel, *The Compact History of the American Newspaper* (New York: Hawthorn Books, 1963); Frank Luther Mott, *American Journalism, A History: 1690–1960* (New York: The Macmillan Co., 1962); Sidney Kobre, *Development of American Journalism* (Dubuque, IA: William C. Brown Co., 1969); Arthur J. Kaul and Joseph P. McKerns, "The Dialectic Ecology of the Newspaper," *Critical Studies in Mass Communication*, 2(1985): 217–233; and Gunther Barth, *City People: The Rise of Modern City Culture in Nineteenth-Century America* (New York: Oxford University Press, 1980), 58–109.

20. Advertisement for "A. Lloyd, dealer in Theological and Misc. Books," n.d., circa 1862, Lloyd Family papers and CLS, *Lloyd* I, 1–17.

21. Wolf, *On Freedom's Altar*, 7–10; Leonard, *Nativism*, 40–43; Altina L. Walker, *Reverend Beecher and Mrs. Tilton: Sex and Class in Victorian America* (Amherst: The University of Massachusetts Press, 1982); Henry Jacob Silverman, "American Social Reformers in the Late Nineteenth and Early Twentieth Century," (Ph.D. diss., University of Pennsylvania, 1963); and Robert M. Crunden, *Ministers of Reform: The Progressives' Achievement in American Civilization, 1889–1920* (New York: Basic Books, Inc., 1982).

22. CLS, *Lloyd,* 1–17; Destler, HDL, MS, 1–3; J. B. Wallace to HDL, 21 June 1894, HDL, Wisc.; and CLS Journal.

23. CLS, ibid.; Aaron Lloyd to HDL, 30 October 1900, in HDL, Wisc.; James McCague, *The Second Rebellion: The Story of the New York City Draft Riots of 1863* (New York: The Dial Press, 1968); and Iver Bernstein, *The New York City Draft Riots: Their Significance for American Society and Politics in the Age of the Civil War* (New York: Oxford University Press, 1990).

24. CLS, ibid., and Destler, HDL, MS, 1–3.

25. Samuel A. Blatchford, *A True History of the Class of 1867 of Columbia College* (New York: C.A. Alvord, 1867), 26–27, in Columbiana Collection, Columbia University; J. H. van Amringe, *An Historical Sketch of Columbia College in the City of New York, 1754–1876* (New York: Macgowan and Slipper, 1876), 73–81; *A History of Columbia University* (New York: Columbia University Press, 1904); Destler, "Plebeian"; and John Disturnell, *New York As It Was and As It Is* (New York: D. Van Nostrand, 1876), 89–92.

26. Blatchford, *Class of '67*, 22–23; Destler, ibid.; and Frank Freidel, *Francis Lieber: Nineteenth-Century Liberal* (Baton Rouge: Louisiana State University Press, 1947).

27. HDL to Samuel Bowles, 9 February 1887 in HDL, Wisc.; John L. Thomas, *Alternative America*, 50; John G. Sproat, *"The Best Men:" Liberal Reformers in the Gilded Age* (New York: Oxford University Press, 1968), 142–168; and Peter J. Frederick, *Knights of the Golden Rule: The Intellectual as Christian Social Reformer in the 1890s* (Lexington: University Press of Kentucky, 1976), 31–77.

28. Joseph F. Kett, *Rites of Passage: Adolescence in America 1790 to the Present* (New York: Basic Books, 1977), 102–168 and Strauss and Howe, *Generations*, 217–227.

29. "Notebook by Henry Demarest Lloyd, Pekin, Illinois, Tazewell, containing an account of Natural Philosophy of birds, beasts," n.d., circa 1859; "Stray Cuttings from the Trail of a Goosequill," n.d., circa 1865; "Thoughts on the Battleground of the Forge," 5 January 1864; undated, untitled editorials, circa 1865; "Valedictory Speech," 30 May 1866; Booklet for the 113th Commencement of Columbia College, 25 June 1867; all HDL, Wisc. and Blatchford, *Class of '67*, 59–60, 87–90.

30. *The Columbiad*, 3(April 1866): 2, in Columbia Collection, Columbia University; entries for 9, 22 December 1864, 10 March 1865, "Minute-Book of the Class of 1867 of Columbia College," MS, Columbian Collection, Columbia University (hereafter Minute-Book); Destler, *Empire of Reform*, 313–314; Blatchford, *Class of '67*, 19–20; and F.A.P. Barnard to HDL, 10 April 1866, in HDL, Wisc.

31. Entries for 3 November 1865, 23 February, 6, 9, 10, 20, 26 April 1866, 30 June 1870, 8 June 1898 "Minute-Book"; Blatchford, *Class of '67*, 34–38; CLS, "Biographical Sketch of H. D. Lloyd," n.d., in HDL, Wisc.; Destler, "Plebeian," 318–320; "Report of Court Martial, May 2, 1866," in HDL, Wisc.; and *Annual Report of the President of Columbia College Made to the Board of Trustees, June 4, 1866* (New York: D. Van Nostrand, 1866) in Columbiana Collection, Columbia University.

32. Bender, *Intellectual New York*, 130–131.

33. Nicholas Fisk to HDL, 1, 5, 15 January 1868, HDL to Fish, 3, 10 January 1868, all in HDL, Wisc. and van Amringe, *Columbia College*, 81–95.

34. Freidel, *Francis Lieber*, 368. On civic republicanism, see Bernard Bailyn, *The Ideological Origins of the American Revolution* (Cambridge: Harvard University Press, 1967); Gordon S. Wood, *The Creation of the American Republic, 1776–1787* (Chapel Hill: University of North Carolina Press, 1969); Garry Wills, *Inventing America: Jefferson's Declaration of Independence* (Garden City, NY: Doubleday, 1978); and Isaac Kramnick, "Republican Revisionism Revisited," *American Historical Review*, 87(July 1982): 629–664.

35. Alexander H. Robbins, *A Treatise on American Advocacy*, 2d ed. (St. Louis: Central Law Journal Co., 1913), 1–26; Lawrence J. Smith, *Art of Advocacy* (New York:

Times Mirror Books, 1992); and James A. Gardner, *Legal Argument: The Structure and Language of Effective Advocacy* (Charlottesville, VA: The Michie Co., 1993).

36. Christopher Lasch, "Journalism, Publicity and the Lost Art of Argument," *Gannett Center Journal*, 4(Spring 1990): 1–12; J. Michael Sproule, "Propaganda Studies in American Social Science: The Rise and Fall of the Critical Paradigm," *Quarterly Journal of Speech*, 73(February 1987): 60–78; Doug Newsom, Alan Scott, and Judy Vanslyke Turk, *This is PR: The Realities of Public Relations* (Belmont, CA: Wadsworth Publishing Co., 1993), 38–44; Richard S. Tedlow, *Keeping the Corporate Image* (Greenwich, CT: JAI Press, 1979); Eric F. Goldman, "Public Relations and the Progressive Surge: 1898–1917," *Public Relations Review*, 4(Fall 1978): 52–61; Neil Harris, *Humbug! The Art of P.T. Barnum* (Boston: Little Brown and Co., 1973); Edward L. Bernays, *Crystallizing Public Opinion* (New York: Boni and Liveright, 1923), 70–83; Emory Holloway, "Whitman as His Own Press-Agent," *American Mercury*, 18(December 1929): 482–488; Will Irwin, "The Press Agent: His Rise and Decline," *Colliers* 48(2 December 1911): 24–25; and H. C. Adams, "What is Publicity?," *North American Review*, 175(December 1902): 896–904.

37. F. A. P. Barnard to David Dudley Field, 1 May 1869, in HDL, Wisc.; undated, unidentified newspaper clipping describing a meeting organized by Aaron Lloyd in New Jersey under the auspices of the New York Free-Trade Association, HDL, mf.; Executive Committee, American Free-Trade League to Richard Rogers Bowker, 21 April 1869, Bowker papers, New York Public Library; Sproat, *Best Men*, 78; Destler, HDL MS, 36; Charles H. Marshall to *New York Evening Post*, 2 October 1903, in Lloyd Family papers; Frederick, *Knights of the Golden Rule*, 36; Howard K. Beale, "The Tariff and Reconstruction," *American Historical Review*, 35(January 1930): 286–291; Thomas, *Alternative*, 23–25; and Browne, *New York*, 399–404.

38. Roeliff Brinkerhoff to CLS, 4 January 1904, HDL, Wisc.; "HDL Private Notebook", n.d., in HDL, mf.; Aaron Lloyd obituary, *New York Herald*, circa 17 December 1903, clipping in Lloyd Family Papers; and Thomas, *Alternative*, 23–35.

39. *New York Evening Post*, 29 May, 1, 18, 25 June, 9, 23, 27 July, 19 October 1869, all clippings in HDL, mf.; Destler, HDL MS, 40–41; and E. L. Godkin to Theodore Dwight Woolsey, 6 December 1869 in *The Gilded Age Letters of E. L. Godkin*, ed. William M. Armstrong (Albany: State University of New York Press, 1974), 142–143.

40. Horace Greeley to HDL, 2 April 1871 and *New York Times*, 25 March 1871, both in HDL, Wisc.

41. *The Free-Trader*, 1(July 1870): 19 and 2(January 1871): 139, Library of Congress.

42. HDL to Whitelaw Reid, 20 October 1870 and "Confidential Free-trade League Treasurer's Report," 1 October 1870, both in Ford Autograph Collection, New York Public Library; and Sproat, *Best Men*, 78–79.

43. William Cullen Bryant to Mr. and Mrs. Fairbank, 14 November 1872; L. D. DeWitt to HDL, circa 27 February 1900; Francis Lieber to HDL, 2, 11 March, 12 April, 18, 27 November 1871; Horace Greeley to HDL, 15, 17, 22, 23, 28 February 1871; Benjamin J. Smith to CLS, 11 October 1906; 1871 notice of HDL's night school class; and CLS Journal; all in HDL, Wisc.; HDL to Richard R. Bowker, 13 June 1870, Bowker papers, New York Public Library; *New York Evening Post* clippings, 18 February, 14 April, 7 October 1871, in HDL, mf.; Browne, *New York*, 682–683; and

CLS, *Lloyd* I, 25.

44. HDL, "Political Economy Not a Failure," *Phrenological Journal*, 54(January 1872): 53–55 and J. Thomas Scharf, *History of Saint Louis City and County* (Philadelphia: Louis H. Everts and Co., 1883), 1587, 1599.

2

Security

One of Henry Demarest Lloyd's Columbia College classmates took a poll of their class shortly before graduation in 1867. Of the twenty-eight respondents, eleven said they planned to become lawyers, three merchants, three ministers, two bankers, one a druggist, and one an engineer. Five had no firm career goals in mind, and the last two claimed they planned to "teach the young . . . how to shoot." It was not unusual for the majority of the class of '67 to have firm career plans, for the calling to an occupation was considered an important rite of passage for among upper-class nineteenth-century young men. One antebellum male guidebook writer warned, not altogether helpfully, that "many individuals mistake their appropriate callings, and engage in employment for which they have neither mental nor physical adaptation." Perhaps the lesson was made a bit clearer in the first Horatio Alger, Jr., book for boys, *Ragged Dick: or Street Life in New York City*, which appeared in 1867. Young men had to plan properly for the future, or hope they too could rescue a grateful rich man from drowning.[1]

For Henry Demarest Lloyd, the choice was a bit less complicated. His infatuation with newspapers and publicity and his inclination toward noblesse oblige and reform drew him to the law and eventually journalism. But underneath his desire to find a comfortable, socially desirable occupation, there was a more pressing concern, a need to achieve a sense of security, both financial and personal, in his life. Even though Lloyd had never truly known the stigma of poverty, he always felt as though he was operating from a point of disadvantage. Therefore, he wanted to establish himself in an occupational and social position of advantage. Only then would he be able to apply his talents and abilities to other causes. It was urgent that he find a secure, well-paying job, make a good marriage, and establish himself and his family in a safe location. In the process, he became involved in two local reforms, joined a failed political party, and made and lost a chance to control one of the most influential newspapers outside of New York City. Still he managed by 1880 to achieve the sense of personal security he desired.

The first of the reform efforts ironically involved his collegiate employer. In a city as yet without a public library, New York's Mercantile Library was a unique institution, sharing its books, magazines, and newspapers with readers in a comfortable setting. To use the facility, patrons had to pay a steep annual fee of ten dollars, making the library inaccessible to all but the wealthy. As a result, by the early 1870s the Mercantile achieved a rather dubious reputation as a place for its young, unmarried, upper-class male members to socialize. One newspaper complained, "Young gentlemen who spend as many leisure hours in these reading-rooms as circumstances indicate are in a fair way to acquire a reputation which will compare very favorably with that gained at the bowling allies, billiard tables, and sipping houses."[2]

The library's reading room was open from nine to nine every day except Sunday. That it was closed on Sunday was not unusual, for as one writer reported in 1869, the difference between weekdays and Sundays was nowhere more apparent than in New York City. "The mighty machine with all its wheels and cranks and levers and cylinders, stops on Saturday night like a clock that has run down," the writer observed, "and does not move again until Monday morning." The Sunday-closing practice was more custom than religious requirement, another observer noting that the city ceased "from labor rather than sin" on Sundays. For whatever reason, hotels emptied, theaters, operas, races, and libraries were closed, and the few newspapers brazen enough to publish Sunday editions were known as "sensation journals."[3]

Lloyd, his brother John, and about twenty-five fellow patrons decided in 1871 that it was time to modernize the Mercantile's Sunday policy. Their plan was to stage a protest at the library's annual board meeting, but the directors, tipped to their scheme in advance, limited attendance to ticket holders and made sure that none of the protesters got a ticket. When Lloyd's group appeared, the New York City police were called to clear the room. As one participant later recalled, the entire group, including Lloyd, was "thrown out bodily." The incident both pleased and alarmed Lloyd's mother. She wrote Lloyd's other brother David, "Wasn't Henry plucky at that first meeting?" but continued, "I am almost sorry that [Lloyd and brother John] have got into the muss, but it may be necessary for them to fight much with evil and wickedness in their way through this crooked world, and they can here acquire some practice. It will cost Henry as much or more than $100, Johnny says."[4]

The protesters regrouped and Lloyd proposed a new tactic, a publicity campaign to embarrass the recalcitrant board. Shortly before the 1872 meeting, the protesters staged an outdoor gathering, complete with a brass band, and invited Henry Ward Beecher, New York's leading theologian, as their main speaker. Beecher, an American Free-Trade League member and Lloyd acquaintance, softened his stance on the preservation of the Sabbath for his young friends and called for the Sunday opening of museums, libraries, and art galleries to relieve ennui and "provide wholesome, moral enlightenment." To the enjoyment of his youthful audience, he confided that "there is too much preaching on Sunday" and maintained that opening the Mercantile Library on Sunday would help "the friendless, the homeless, and the hungry for knowledge." Beecher's comments and the resulting publicity left the board little choice but to retreat from its no-Sunday policy, and as a further gesture of peace, it named Lloyd as its new recording secretary. Lloyd and his band of protesters celebrated their victory with a dinner of lobster salad and champagne. Although their campaign began and ended with the Mercantile, Sunday hours became commonplace throughout New York City during the 1870s.[5]

Lloyd's second reform was directed at a loftier and more entrenched goal, New York's machine-dominated, corruption-riddled municipal government. During their prime, William M. "Boss" Tweed and the Tammany Hall political organization netted an estimated $200 million in graft. Tweed was successful because he centralized his authority, holding several political offices at one time. Once in control, he made an art of bribery, giving away as much as $600,000 in payoffs in one year alone. Tammany Hall kept its power by handing out patronage jobs, controlling as many as twelve thousand government positions. Although Tweed and Tammany Hall maintained separate political organizations, they cooperated when it was necessary to retain control of the entire New York City government.[6]

Lloyd entered the fray against them in early 1871. He wrote a letter to the *New York Tribune* in January, offering a five-dollar contribution to the campaign of H. W. Twombly, a little known New York State assemblyman who had shunned a Tweed bribe. Sounding more like an aged patrician than the landless young man that he was, he wrote, "Thousands in this city are, with myself, consciously disfranchised. Our political liberty is gone and how rapidly our personal liberty and our property shall follow rests with our voters." In June, he asked the New York Political Science Society to "unite and seek through education and the dissemination of correct principles to do away with the ignorance and dishonesty which now characterize American politics." Although he never considered himself a mugwump, he supported governmental reform, telling a friend, "If honest, intelligent and unpartisan, [a new legislature] may put our present plundering officials to the knife and give us a new charter that shall be a ban to official corruption and not a cloak for it."[7]

He joined an anti-Tweed organization, the Young Men's Municipal Reform Association, during the summer of 1871. At the group's request, he wrote a pamphlet explaining the city's complicated election laws. The booklet provided a practical description of the voting procedure, from the proper opening and closing hours of polls to an explanation of the one person, one vote principle and was written in an advocacy style. The association distributed hundreds of copies throughout the city and *The New York Times* reprinted it in a special pre-election article headlined, "Every Man His Own Voter." The paper thanked the Young Men's Association, noting "[the group] deserved public gratitude for bringing [Lloyd's] abilities into the sphere of active politics." On election day, Lloyd volunteered as a poll watcher, pledging to eliminate "fraud in the registration and at the polls in this district and to secure a fair and honest election."[8]

To his joy, the New York City electorate voted Tweed and Tammany Hall out of office. Although the Tammany organization regained power in 1873 and maintained a presence in New York City politics into the twentieth century, Tweed was eventually imprisoned for his misdeeds. The New York election was a watershed event for Lloyd, proving that, as he had been taught at Columbia College, a mobilized upper class could retake government from the opportunists. Basking in the glow of their success, Lloyd and his colleagues turned to other reforms and forgot about New York City.

The anti-Tweed effort also revealed how important publicity was to reform. One of the movement's leaders, New York Governor Samuel J. Tilden, observed that reformers typically fought two battles. One involved the corruption itself but the other was the "indifference and discouragement" of the public. It was that latter battle that Lloyd eventually joined and championed through his writings.[9]

In the wake of the Tweed victory, some of the reformers turned their attention to the corruption-riddled national government and began making plans to deny Ulysses S. Grant a second term as president. When it became clear that the overwhelming majority of Republicans supported the Civil War hero regardless of his many transgressions, the reformers formed a new party called the Liberal Republicans. A national convention was convened at Cincinnati in May 1872 to organize the anti-Grant effort and choose an alternative presidential candidate.[10]

Lloyd's American Free-Trade League embraced the new party, but for less than altruistic purposes. Frustrated that neither of the other major parties seemed interested in tariffs, the group hoped to force free trade onto the Liberal Republicans with the idea that the other parties would then have no choice but to accept it as well. To that end, Lloyd and his colleagues joined with a group of Missouri Liberal Republicans to form an organization called the National Tax-Payer's Union. The Union's goal was to oppose all tariffs and taxes, or as their slogan read, "He that removes a needless tax feeds multitudes." Financed by the Free-Trade League, the Union established its headquarters in St. Louis, largely to distance it from the free trade organization in New York.[11]

Lloyd eagerly embraced Liberal Republicanism, not just because of his job. He viewed the new party as a tangible expression of growing opposition to the corruption and opportunism in government he had learned about at Columbia. He recognized that the Liberal Republicans were in a unique position to woo both disenchanted Republicans and the many Democrats who had been shut out of national politics since the election of Abraham Lincoln in 1860. He wrote his brother David:

The times are ripening. A new party must be formed to unite those elements which Grant has driven out of the Republican party and which fear of Tammany and remembrance of Repudiative Copperheadism have cut away from the Democratic Party. That body of men which today is neither Republican nor Democratic is the largest and best in the country.[12]

The Tax Payer's Union needed a newsletter to publicize its views and Lloyd was the logical choice as editor. The first issue of the *People's Pictorial Tax-Payer*, which had an appearance reminiscent of *Harper's Weekly*, featured articles and commentaries critical of taxes and tariffs written in an advocacy style. One Thomas Nast-like cartoon showed a pig labeled "Horace Greeley" sleeping in the mud and contentedly nursing several tiny piglets labeled "American industries." Such unsophisticated humor met with the approval of Union members and supporters, especially in the West. *Chicago Tribune* editor and Free-Trade League member Horace White "laughed harder at the humorous cartoons than he has since the [Chicago] fire," it was said. An Illinois news dealer ordered five thousand copies of the publication, observing, "With two or three good commentaries each month there is no reason that I can see why the paper should not have a general sale through the trade." Lloyd used the *Tax-Payer* to build interest in the 1872 Liberal Republican convention. In March he proclaimed, "It is now time for advocates of reform, whether Republican or Democrats, to consider what may be expected from the independent movement to take form at Cincinnati. Undeniably this movement strikes more sharply and boldly at existing evils of the tariff, and at the very root of the whole monopoly system, than any party we have seen for twenty years."[13]

Although Lloyd and the Free-Traders knew it would not be easy to convince Liberal Republicans to adopt their issue, they did not count on their longtime nemesis, *New York Tribune* publisher Horace Greeley, winning the fledgling party's presidential nomination. Greeley was one of the most unlikely major party presidential candidates in American history. He stalked about the Cincinnati gathering in crumpled clothes and an old, white broad-brimmed hat, glad-handing delegates and often looking lost and out-of-place. Behind the scenes, he had hired the best political handlers money could buy, and they were busily promoting him as a compromise candidate among the widely disparate delegates.[14]

Greeley's supporters did everything they could to embarrass or discredit

the free traders during the Cincinnati convention. The two factions paired off
over seating arrangements, putting Lloyd in the middle of the fray. He had
been elected as a delegate as an honor by the Young Men's Municipal
Association, and the Greeley forces allowed him to sit for that reason alone.
His League employers were denied their seats, however, in retaliation for their
long-standing Greeley opposition, particularly Lloyd's stinging "No Monopoly"
New York Evening Post letters. Lloyd valiantly defended his colleagues from
the floor, but was hopelessly outnumbered and eventually forced to resign his
seat in protest. He watched the remainder of the proceedings as an embittered
spectator, his recollection of the events belying his emotions.

Then came the spontaneous rally which had been carefully planned the night before. The
hall was filled with a mechanical, preordained, stentorious bellowing. Hoary-haired,
hard-eyed politicians, who had not in twenty years felt a noble impulse, mounted their
chairs and with faces suffused with a seraphic fervor, blistered their throats hurraying
for the great and good Horace Greeley. The noise bred a panic. A furor, artificial at
first, became real and ended in a stampede.[15]

The Greeley nomination tarnished the Free-Trade League and depressed the
emotional Lloyd. Of the former, one newspaper explained, "Their day had
passed." Lloyd returned to his publicity job but his heart was no longer in his
work. He spoke with former League president and *New York Evening Post*
publisher William Cullen Bryant at a free-trade rally after the Cincinnati
convention and helped organize a Liberal Republican unity rally in June but his
enthusiasm had disappeared. The *New York Herald* wrote of the latter event,

Henry Demarest Lloyd, the juvenile representative of the whole free trade sentiment of
the nation . . . here found a chance to ventilate his somewhat immature opinions. He
sagely observed that it was his conviction that a platform was needed that represented the
convictions of the people. . . . The young agitator then sat down, rubbing his nearly
invisible mustache with the consciousness that if worth and importance came only with
years, that mustache ought to be gray.

The once friendly *New York Times* opined that the twenty-five year old Lloyd
appeared to be "under the delusion that he was carrying the nation on his
youthful shoulders."[16]
     The reality was that Lloyd's overwork habit had caught up with him as
much as the Liberal Republican fiasco. He was seriously ill after the
convention, perhaps with an ulcer, and suffered from insomnia and other stress-
related disorders. Both his family and friends agreed that a change in work was
in order. Lloyd's editorial work on the *Free-Trader* and *People's Pictorial Tax-
Payer* suggested newspapering. Unfortunately, Lloyd left no letters or
documents detailing his reasons for quitting the Free-Trade League and
becoming a journalist, or even his conceptions of mid-nineteenth century

journalism, but there could have been a number of reasons. Journalism was an attractive calling at the time. A surprising number of attorneys quit their "beggarly profession" for newspapers, including William Cullen Bryant, the publisher of the *New York Evening Post*, and Lloyd's future employer, *Chicago Tribune* editor Joseph Medill. The aura of journalism as a dignified calling still persisted in mid-century New York, nurtured by respected antebellum newspapers such as the *Evening Post* and the *Journal of Commerce*. Many saw newspapers as a stepping stone to politics or other more lucrative careers. One Chicago magazinist wrote, "At the present time there is no road to fame and political success so sure as the path of journalism, provided only the aspirant have the ability to excel, and a cunning in following up advantages. In politics, the 'corner' so long kept up by the lawyers may henceforth be talked of among the bygones." Or, Lloyd's younger and successful *New York Tribune* reporter brother David Demarest may have been an inducement.[17]

Whatever the reasons, Lloyd's decision was influenced as well by a friendship with another *New York Tribune* reporter, Henry Francis Keenan. The two roomed together and became friends during the Cincinnati Liberal Republican convention in May. Within weeks, Lloyd applied for a *Tribune* job. Whitelaw Reid, the acting editor of the paper while Greeley ran for president, interviewed Lloyd and Lloyd postponed a desperately needed vacation waiting for a reply. At the height of his anticipation, Lloyd wrote Keenan:

I can think of no profession which offers to the ambition a greater career than that of a man like [*Springfield Republican* editor Samuel] Bowles or [*Chicago Tribune* editor Horace] White or [Horace] Greeley or [*New York Herald* editor James Gordon] Bennett. I had rather be one of those men than the most successful lawyer or richest merchant or most brilliant author in America. I had rather raise myself to their height than be raised by others to the Presidency.

Unfortunately, Reid knew Lloyd only too well. Recalling his "No Monopoly" letters and his vehement opposition to protectionism, Reid probably laughed off the application as soon as Lloyd walked out of the office, even though Lloyd's brother worked for the newspaper. When it became clear that Reid had no intention of hiring him, Lloyd poured out an uncharacteristic wrath at him, writing, "I damned Whitelaw Reid and hereby do it again," to Keenan and others.[18]

Lloyd turned next to a fellow Free-Trade League member, Horace White, editor of the prestigious *Chicago Tribune*. White had seen Lloyd's *Free-Trader* and *People's Pictorial Tax-Payer* work, knew he was a good writer, and respected him for his stand against the Greeley forces at the Liberal Republican convention. Lloyd was troubled with the thought of leaving New York for Chicago, wondering aloud to Keenan if it was "judicious" for him to leave the city of his birth, but Chicago and the West were symbolic of the change that Lloyd needed in his life. He wrote to Keenan, "I want power, I must have power, I could not live if I did not think that I was in some way to be lifted above and upon the insensate masses who flood the stage of life in their passage to oblivion." David Lloyd observed of his brother and the West, "Anyone who seeks that enchanted land seems incapable of leaving it or of remaining long away from it."[19]

Lloyd traveled to Chicago in August 1872, ostensibly on free-trade business, but scheduled an interview with White. To save money, he stayed with Keenan, who was covering the aftermath of Chicago's 1871 fire for the *New York Tribune*. The two walked the still fire-ravaged streets of the city, watching the frantic efforts at reconstruction, and met with White in his temporary *Tribune* office. White responded by promising Lloyd his first editorial vacancy. While in Chicago, Keenan also introduced Lloyd to the city's social set, including the twenty-seven year old daughter of *Chicago Tribune* co-owner William Bross, Jessie. Lloyd was preparing to return to New York a few days later when the *Tribune*'s night editor died and White offered Lloyd the job. Elated beyond belief at his good fortune and substantial salary increase, Lloyd hurried back to New York to quit his free-trade job and pack his belongings. David Lloyd was so impressed by the *Tribune*'s offer that he told Keenan, "I agree with you that Henry's opportunity is a magnificent one. . . . It is about as unexpected as if some old gentleman should die and leave him $10,000 a year because he had once seen him in the street and admired him."[20]

Lloyd's journalistic career began in early September 1872 in much the same style as his collegiate and free-trade years. Recognizing that he knew little about daily newspapers, White took Lloyd under his wing and taught him the business from the beginning. Lloyd came in early and worked late even though he was still recovering from his possible ulcer and other stress disorders. White became so alarmed at his overwork habit that Lloyd told Keenan it was White who made him stop working overtime because "he seemed appalled when I told him that I did not get to bed till four [A.M.]." Still, such hours helped Lloyd learn the newspaper business.[21]

At the same time that White was worrying about Lloyd's health, Lloyd was testing his own mettle. Without White's knowledge or permission, Lloyd inserted an editorial called "Butter and Wells" into the *Tribune* one night after White had gone home. The editorial condemned Horace Greeley, in sharp contrast to the paper's stated editorial policy, and advocated free trade in a way that the *Tribune* had never done before. Angered more by Lloyd's impudence than by his words, White summoned his protege to his office. As Lloyd recalled, White told him in a "bone-chilling" voice, "Mr. Lloyd, I have decided that you have not sufficient experience to fill the position you now occupy." As punishment Lloyd was demoted to literary editor, White observing that he needed more "practice in the lower walks of the profession."[22]

An experienced newspaperman would have quit over such a rebuff, and Lloyd considered applying to the rival *Chicago Times*, but he ultimately decided

to bide his time. His decision was based on his desire to learn how to be a
journalist and another, unanticipated factor. Upon their first meeting, Lloyd had
become infatuated with pretty Jessie Bross, and he recognized that his *Tribune*
job was his only excuse to see her on a regular basis. Jessie rewarded his
fortitude with tiny encouragements, including the admonition that "[White] can't
live forever." Lloyd responded by swallowing his pride, taking the job as
literary editor, and boasting to her that he would "yet show [White] how to
write and run a newspaper."[23]

Lloyd courted Jessie with the same single-mindedness that had marked his
free-trade work and would figure in his various writings and reforms. He had
loved once before, but blinded by shyness and his preoccupation with his work,
he had lost the woman. He did not intend to suffer the same fate again. Jessie
was less sure of her attraction to Lloyd. Her decision was complicated because
she was the sole heir to her father, William Bross, and stood to gain his entire
fortune and control in the *Chicago Tribune* only if she remained unmarried.
Under Illinois law, a married woman was considered a person *sui juris* and
could not control a business partnership like the *Chicago Tribune*. Nineteenth-
century courtship historian Ellen K. Rothman has observed that "in order to
assume her position in the home, a woman relinquished her ambition for worldly
achievement while a man had to loosen—without ever cutting—his ties to home
in order to succeed in the world." Although Jessie was not categorically
opposed to marriage, it was a decision that she could not take as lightly as
Lloyd.[24]

To stall for time, Jessie embarked on an extended visit to Boston in late
October 1872. The couple's parting was a memorable event for she wrote in
her diary a year later, "Our first anniversary. A year ago today my king first
crowned me." Lloyd was disappointed but not without hope. He wrote to
Keenan, "I can not be downcast or find drudgery in a path which is lit by the
hope which is now my life. . . . All my paths—of pleasures, work, memory and
hope, lead, please God, to Jessie."[25]

Their separation came to a temporary end in February 1873 when Lloyd
visited Jessie on his return from attending his maternal grandfather's funeral in
New York. The couple attended church together, dined, walked along Newark
Bay, and went to a reception for abolitionist Wendell Philips. A month later,
Lloyd invited Jessie to meet his family and friends in New York. The two week
visit provided Jessie with "the happiest life I know" but forced her to reject a
Lloyd marriage proposal until it was clear to her that it was "God's leading and
His will" that they should marry. What that sign was was not specified.[26]

Her opposition melted over the summer of 1873. Jessie returned to
Chicago in June to help her parents move, and Lloyd became an almost daily
fixture on her doorstep. Together they picnicked along the sandy shores of Lake
Michigan, walked the rebuilt city, read to each other, sang, and did the other
things courting Victorian couples did. As their relationship became more

serious, William Bross traveled to New York to investigate Lloyd's background. He met with David Lloyd, who still worked for the *New York Tribune*, and inquired into the Lloyd family and its financial circumstances. Satisfied that Henry was not a gold digger, he gave his blessing to their engagement in September 1873. To celebrate, Lloyd took his fiancee for a horseback ride along the Lake Michigan shoreline. She wrote in her diary, "The great breakers rolling in . . . and the brightest glory in our hearts."[27]

They were married on Christmas evening 1873 by the Reverend Aaron Lloyd at a simple ceremony in the Bross's new Chicago home. The Jay Cooke financial panic had frozen both Lloyd's and Bross's bank accounts in the fall, making more elaborate arrangements impossible. Whitelaw Reid, who had become the *New York Tribune* publisher upon the death of Horace Greeley and who had once courted Jessie, sent his congratulations to his old nemesis Lloyd, writing, "Among the friends who surround you now with their felicitousness there can be none more earnest in their sincere good wishes than [this] old and distant one." The couple honeymooned in a small Chicago apartment that Lloyd had located in a *Chicago Tribune* classified advertisement and Jessie wrote in her diary the day after their marriage,

Awaken in the very early light. We awake together and I go into my dear husband's room. Our first happy meal together. We are as glad as we are shy. Received our friends and family in the afternoon. They linger rudely. Harry and I tuckered out. We go to sleep and wake up to cold prairie chicken eaten on the tray in bed. We are two really good fellows.[28]

In contrast to the years after Haymarket, Lloyd had little qualm in accepting the advice or gifts of his father-in-law in the first years of his marriage. William Bross's most generous wedding present was one-hundred shares of *Chicago Tribune* stock worth an estimated $30,000 to $50,000 in 1873. As part of his gift, Bross stipulated that Lloyd could not sell the stock without Bross's permission, but it was listed under Lloyd's name in the *Tribune*'s records, Lloyd could use it as collateral for loans, and Lloyd and Jessie received the dividends. The gift from Bross, one of seven *Chicago Tribune* stockholders, meant that Lloyd was no longer a mere employee of the *Tribune* but one of the owners. No other stockholder was as powerful as Bross in 1873 and all Lloyd needed to do was keep his wife and father-in-law happy, learn the business of big city newspapering, and be patient and he stood an excellent chance one day of becoming an editor or publisher of the *Chicago Tribune*.[29]

Beyond the *Tribune* stock, Bross took Lloyd under his wing and introduced him to the intricacies of Gilded Age Chicago business. Chicago was a mecca for quick-money entrepreneurs in the late nineteenth century, and its reputation for mammonism was worldwide and well deserved. In contrast to most of the city's businessmen, Lloyd was a prudent, conservative investor, always mindful of the money his father had lost in land speculation during the recession of the 1850s. Bross showed Lloyd his sizable real estate holdings, including a large section of Chicago's near north side, and a number of tracts in suburban Lake Forest that were certain to increase in value as the years passed. He introduced Lloyd to the fabled Chicago Board of Trade, the most unregulated commodities trading market in the world. As much as land speculation scared him, Lloyd cared even less for commodities trading, and the immorality of speculating in food and other necessities of life eventually led him to criticize the C.B.O.T. in a *North American Review* article. For his part, Bross admonished his son-in-law to be careful in commodities trading, for fortunes were won and lost daily at the C.B.O.T.[30]

Bross introduced Lloyd to Chicago's old-line business and political network. Most, like Bross, had moved to the city before the Civil War and kept the wheels of government and business from newer, even more unscrupulous opportunists. Like Lloyd, they distrusted the new money that had poured into their city as a result of the war and the 1871 fire. Bross's contacts proved invaluable to Lloyd's *Tribune* work, giving him an edge over other, less connected newspapermen, but they also ultimately helped turn Lloyd away from laissez-faire capitalism.

One friendship was particularly influential. William F. Coolbaugh was the president of one of Chicago's largest banks and considered by many to be the most influential financier in the West, but he was a political liberal like Lloyd and the two became fast friends. What Bross did not know about finance, Coolbaugh did, and he taught Lloyd what he knew, especially the advantages of a free-floating monetary system that was not fixed to any predetermined gold or silver standard. In return, Lloyd repeated Coolbaugh's views in his *Tribune* articles, adding to the banker's prestige and influence. It was a sad day for Lloyd in 1877 when Coolbaugh committed suicide over charges of embezzled bank funds. His body was found at the foot of a statue memorializing former Illinois Senator Stephen A. Douglas on the near south side of Chicago. Coolbaugh's death hardened Lloyd to what he called the "little ring of banks and certain real estate operations" that controlled Chicago and, coupled with the Haymarket bombing, helped turn him away from political economy and toward a more socialistic perspective as expressed in books such as *Wealth Against Commonwealth*.[31]

In compensation for his gifts, Lloyd did what was necessary to please William Bross. He and Jessie presented her father with his first grandson and namesake in February 1875. In turn, the parents of young William Bross Lloyd were rewarded with their first house, a two-story structure located at 202 Michigan Avenue, the site of Bross's fire-damaged first home. Lloyd was determined not to repeat the errors of his overbearing father, but in doing so he left most of the child-rearing duties to Jessie, assuming a benign, almost spectator-like role in the upbringing of their children. He maintained, naively, that children were a blessing, not a burden, and were best instructed by their mother. His sister recalled him saying, "I remember once as one of our dear little babies was held over smiling to kiss us, I believe the day will come when every human being will look at every other in just that way." Such disinterested fathering may have been an improvement from Lloyd's over-regulated childhood, but it was detrimental to Lloyd's four sons in equally distressing ways that would become apparent with time.[32]

Lloyd attacked his new job as *Tribune* literary editor with his typical enthusiasm. Literature was important to nineteenth century Western newspapers because it filled space on slow news days and helped teach people how to read the other parts of a newspaper. Still, the position of literary editor had nothing to do with news or editorial opinion, and its occupant was excluded from any important decision making. Lloyd made the best of his situation, using his columns to pontificate on intellectual matters and review the latest novels, books, and magazines. Subscribers looked forward to weekly serial installments of popular books or Lloyd's discussions of the current magazines as a form of home education. Lloyd offered reviews of local books and magazines such as Chicago's *Lakeside Monthly* as well as national and international writers. George Eliot was his favorite, and each of her books received an enthusiastic reception from the *Tribune*. Lloyd proudly sent one of his reviews to Eliot and her literary editor and companion, George H. Lewes, responded appreciatively, noting that she did not read reviews but "perhaps because she refrains from reading the [London] *Times*, *Edinburgh Review*, *Saturday*, or *Chicago Tribune*, she is all the more cheered by hearing of their friendly sympathetic appreciation."[33]

Although Lloyd was not permitted to make any political comments, White allowed him to excise some of the religious demons that had haunted him from his childhood in a couple of *Tribune* editorials. Lloyd's first ever for the newspaper, "Christians Unattached," advocated a universal Christianity while another, "The Coming Christian," called for an end to the petty doctrinal disputes that flared between the various Chicago denominations. His words were especially inflammatory in mid-1873 because they coincided with a well-publicized heresy trial then underway involving a prominent local Presbyterian minister who had advocated similar ideas.[34]

Ultimately, Horace White underestimated the backlash to his and Lloyd's ecumenicalism, and it was a combination of religion editorials and White's politics that brought an end to his *Tribune* editorship in November 1874. White had been a good mentor for Lloyd. College educated, a proficient and talented writer, he had worked himself up from the bottom of the newspaper business to become editor of one of the leading Gilded Age newspapers outside of New York City. Unfortunately, he forgot one elementary rule of being an editor, to check on your newspaper even when out of town. White was on vacation in June 1874 when the *Tribune* outraged the nation by publishing the previously secret love letters of Mrs. Theodore Tilton and the country's leading Protestant theologian, Henry Ward Beecher. Although the affair between the two had ended in 1871, rumors of their "sultry ardors" had circulated for years. No one could provide hard evidence until *Chicago Tribune* reporter George A. Townsend obtained copies of the letters and quoted from them extensively in a series of articles. The *Tribune*'s circulation surged as the Gilded Age public was scandalized by the sensuous details. Believing that the Beecher revelations hurt all organized religion, the majority of Chicago's clergy blamed the messenger rather than the minister, accusing the paper of sensationalism at the expense of the popular minister. As the fallout from the Beecher-Tilton and other articles increased, Lloyd wrote in late October, "[Joseph] Medill has got back and the whole town is speculating about the object of his return. One rumor has it that he has bought a controlling interest in the *Tribune*—which is stuff; another that he has bought the *Times*, and the price is $300,000!"[35]

To Lloyd's everlasting dismay, the "stuff" turned out to be true. Joseph Medill regained majority ownership of the *Tribune* from William Bross and his allies in November 1874, aided by a loan from retailer Marshall Field. His first acts were to replace Horace White as editor and William Bross as publisher with himself, and to turn the paper away from White's more liberal political and religious path. In a signed editorial on November 9, 1874, Medill explained:

A political newspaper, to be of service to the public, must give one party or the other the preference. And while the Democratic party embraces many excellent and worthy members . . . the Republican party comprises a much larger proportion of the intelligent and educated classes . . . and therefore the Government of the country and the civil rights of the poor and weak can be more safely and prudently committed to its keeping. . . . The *Tribune* hereafter will be, as it formerly was under my direction, an independent Republican journal.[36]

As a result, it was Joseph Medill, not Horace White or William Bross, who ultimately decided Lloyd's fate at the *Chicago Tribune*. Bross was infuriated by Medill's coup d'etat, writing in his diary, "As [Medill] has commenced his administration by treating me very unjustly, it may have a marked effect on my whole future life." As an olive branch to Bross, Medill promoted Lloyd to financial editor, a welcome change from the literary beat, but Lloyd had little opportunity for advancement beyond that level. With two marriageable daughters of his own, Medill left no doubt that it would be his sons-in-law, not Bross's, who would succeed him as *Tribune* editor and publisher. He was true to his word, for it was his progeny, with surnames such as Patterson and McCormick, who became synonymous with the media conglomerate known as the Chicago Tribune. At its height in 1947, the Medill-Patterson-McCormick family-controlled *Tribune* represented what media historian John Tebbel called a "peak in potential power and influence rivaled in our time only by William Randolph Hearst." The family retained ownership of the newspaper until

Medill's enforced trust expired in 1974 and the Tribune company went public.[37]

Photographs taken during the 1870s portrayed Lloyd as a well-dressed, confident, proper, almost serene-looking young man but underneath his Victorian demeanor, he remained emotional and high-strung. His overwork habit and insomnia continued to hurt his career. Medill's coup d'etat and a failed Lloyd/Bross bid to buy another Chicago newspaper in 1876 brought on a serious relapse of the nervous prostration that had felled Lloyd after the Liberal Republican convention, nearly paralyzing him for a time, and it took Jessie's full-time nursing to bring him back to health. Aaron Lloyd learned of his son's condition and offered sympathy. He complained that nothing "casual of advantage" ever fell to him either, and warned "the tide of prosperity seldom flows in without interception—there are obstacles which check it."[38]

Fortunately for Lloyd, Joseph Medill gave his junior *Tribune* editors some latitude in non-political news matters. Under the guidance of his father-in-law and banker William F. Coolbaugh, Lloyd had learned enough about the intricacies of Chicago business to make his daily columns as financial editor authoritative, timely, and knowledgeable. He wrote on a variety of topics, from the corruption of the Chicago Board of Trade and the cheating of farmers by Illinois grain elevators to his favorite topic during the mid-1870s, bimetallism. In supporting free silver coinage, Lloyd was reflecting not only the editorial policy of Medill and the *Tribune* but the sentiments of the entire West. His words took on Populist overtones at times, especially when he called Wall Street speculators "Shylocks" and complained about their control of the nation's economy. Although Lloyd was never a true devotee of a fixed monetary standard, his bimetallism columns were so enthusiastic during the 1870s that they were reprinted, much to his chagrin, during the free-silver presidential campaign of William Jennings Bryan in 1896.[39]

Lloyd enjoyed newspaper work, and he quickly proved that he was good at it. He was especially adept at summarizing the dense, complicated financial news of the day into interesting, readable late nineteenth-century newspaper prose, a talent he had developed in graduate school. His work was no small task considering the scheming and secrecy that went into Gilded Age business decisions. Lloyd had learned the Pittman stenographic system at Columbia, and he used shorthand to take verbatim notes of the meetings and lectures he covered. He scooped the other Chicago papers in 1874 by writing a verbatim account of a speech given by a prominent British economist while the *Chicago Times* and the other dailies had to wait for transcripts of the speech. Lloyd's shorthand also helped him to take more accurate quotes, a habit which pleased his sources in contrast to the often slipshod journalism practiced by many other reporters.[40]

With the encouragement of Medill, Lloyd became an enthusiastic booster of Chicago business in his columns, harkening back to his days as a free trade publicist and his training as a legal advocate. The Garden City did not emerge as the West's leading commercial center until 1880, and Lloyd oversaw the difficult years of the 1870s when the city struggled to recover from the fire, two financial panics, and stiff competition from St. Louis, Detroit, and Milwaukee. During the 1877 recession, he tried to downplay the dismal times by calling them a "local" phenomenon. "With bounteous crops in hand, and an unmistakable revival of manufacturing in progress, there would seem to be no bar to returning prosperity, in which Chicago will take a full share," he maintained. Simultaneously, he was a strident supporter of the city's unpredictable real estate market, which collapsed following the fire and failed to recover for the remainder of the decade. On the first day of 1880, he proudly reported, "The history of [Chicago] since 1878, in an industrial and commercial sense, is practically the history of the Great West, with which Chicago is more and more widely, if not more closely identified with each succeeding year."[41]

Lloyd's growing proficiency at journalism was finally recognized, in a manner, by Joseph Medill in 1880. As a recognition of Lloyd's talent as a writer, the *Tribune* editor promoted him to chief editorial writer, the only staff member beyond Medill allowed to speak officially for the newspaper. Medill also placed Lloyd in charge of the newspaper's special publications division so that he could use his publicity talents to promote Chicago and the *Tribune* in other venues. As impressive as the two job title sounded, anyone who knew anything about the *Chicago Tribune* realized that only one man spoke for the newspaper when it was important, Joseph Medill. As first one son-in-law and then another were brought into the paper's inner-management circle, Lloyd could hardly avoid recognizing his diminishing role in the paper's future. What bothered him most in later life was not that Joseph Medill wanted to leave his newspaper to his progeny but that Medill never fully appreciated Lloyd for either his talents or intellect. In particular, Lloyd never forgot that in naming him chief editorial writer in 1880, Medill failed to give him a pay raise.[42]

When his career got him down, Lloyd looked to his wife and growing family as an escape. His attitude toward Jessie was similar to that of most other upper-class Victorian men, putting her on a pedestal as long as she maintained a strict separation of the sexes and kept out of his professional world. He jokingly wrote a mutual friend in 1874, "Jessie—well, Jessie is a good girl. We are, I believe, growing daily into a deeper and fonder love for each other. In fact, she has never discredited your recommendation, and as long as she behaves herself, I shall keep her in my family." Jessie's letters had a slightly different tone, suggesting that marriage may not have been all that she had anticipated. "When you come back," she told a friend in 1877, "I hope you'll be tolerant of my dull ladyship, and if you don't seem to find me tedious I'll try to convince you of the truth that Dr. Clark has so lately enunciated 'as good a brain is needed to govern a household as to command a ship; to guide a family aright as to guide a Congress aright.'" A second son, Henry Demarest Lloyd, Jr., was born in early 1878. Lloyd announced the birth to a friend, revealing something of his own precarious mental state at the time. "My life has no events," he wrote, "a few new books read, 365 columns a year written of financial slush, a very few cents saved against the old age that I may cheat Time out of, a new baby, no new friends, except the baby—the gradual extirpation of the, let us call them theories of my green days, a good many happy evenings at home—this is the romance of this poor, young man."[43]

With the birth of their second son, it was evident that the Lloyds needed a larger house than their Michigan Avenue location. After exploring a number of possibilities, they settled on Winnetka, a sparsely-settled lake shore suburb located about twenty miles north of Chicago. With the help of William Bross, they bought a rundown roadside house known as the Wayside Inn. In one way or another, the Wayside became the focus of the rest of Lloyd's life. It was, as his eldest son recalled, a "baronial castle," the complete retreat from the indignities and cruelties of everyday life.[44]

The irony of Henry Demarest Lloyd was that he did not become involved in reform until he had removed himself and his family from what he considered the dangers of city life. This was in contrast to Jane Addams, Ellen Gates Starr, and other reformers who not only survived but embraced the late nineteenth-century city. To Lloyd, there were troubling signs in postbellum Chicago. As early as 1871, one writer complained that personal wealth in Chicago had become concentrated in "the hands of a few individuals beyond all possibility of rational enjoyment, while countless thousands are suffering." William Bross recalled the panic that swept the streets of Chicago during the 1871 fire. "Everybody was in mortal fear that what remained of the city would be burned by the desperados who were known to be prowling about everywhere," he wrote. In the wake of the fire, hard economic times and an influx of foreign immigrants added to the anxieties of native-born residents. Horace White warned in the *Tribune*, "The workingman must be given comfort, mental and physical. . . . We cannot wash our hands of this matter. If we do, we sow the wind and leave our children to reap the whirlwind. 'After us the deluge' is a neatly-sounding phrase compared with 'After the Commune.'" Labor unrest in 1877 stoked the fears as strikes shut down the city's vital railroad and lumber industries. The *Chicago Tribune* chronicled daily confrontations between workers and capitalists with sensationalistic headlines such as "Red War" and "Pitched Battles." A *Tribune* editorial on a labor rally in 1879 noted:

Skim the purlieus of the Fifth Ward, drain the Bohemian socialist slums of the Sixth and Seventh Wards, scour the Scandinavian dives of the Tenth and Fourteenth Wards, cull the choicest thieves from Halsted, Des Plaines, Pacific Avenue and Clark Street, pick out . . . the worst specimens of female depravity, scatter in all the red-headed, cross eyed and frowsy servant girls in the three divisions of the city and bunch all these together and you have a pretty good idea of the crowd that made up last night's gathering.[45]

Winnetka, with a population of 584 in 1880, was the ideal refuge for Lloyd whether he believed the *Tribune*'s sentiments or not. It had a Chicago and Northwestern passenger rail line that made the city a short commute away, yet it was twenty miles from Chicago. From his financial contacts, Lloyd learned that Winnetka real estate had been seriously undervalued as the result of a land bust, so he bought and remodeled his two-story Wayside roadhouse, situated near a large grove of trees and a picturesque pond, and moved his family there for good in 1879. He found the cold, clear, Lake Michigan water, the rocky shoreline, and the dramatic lake sunrises a powerful catharsis to the disappointments of his career. His sister Caro Lloyd recalled him saying that "nothing but a strict sense of duty drives me to my desk every morning" from such pleasant surroundings. Jessie Bross Lloyd built a new world for herself in Winnetka. She invited an eclectic variety of guests—from Marshall Field shop girls, the children of Jane Addam's Hull House, or down-on-their luck strangers to artists, intellectuals, and national reformers—to visit and stay with her family at the Wayside. Among their guests were John R. Commons, Samuel Gompers, Eugene V. Debs, Florence Kelley, Booker T. Washington, William Dean Howells, and Charlotte Perkins Gilman. Jane Addams called the Lloyd's residence "an annex to Hull House." Reformer Vida Scudder wrote, "To pass from an atmosphere charged with incredulous perplexity to one full of friendly tranquil comradeship is an experience one does not forget; the Lloyd's house must, I should think, have afforded such a haven to many a solitary spirit." Another guest put it more simply. The Wayside was "a bit of nineteenth century heaven." With the move of his family to Winnetka complete, Lloyd could turn his attention to other matters.[46]

NOTES

1. Blatchford, *Class of '67*, 48–49; Edward Hazen, *The Panorama of Professions and Trades; or Everyman's Book* (Philadelphia, 1839), vii as quoted in Kett, *Rites of Passage*, 94–95; Rotundo, "Manhood in America," 136–162; Helene S. Zahler, *The American Paradox* (New York: E. P. Dutton and Co., 1964), 126–152; and CLS Journal, HDL, Wisc.

2. Ross, *New York City*, 276–277.

3. Browne, *New York*, 314–315, 356–359; Boyer, *Urban Masses*, 77–78; and Bender,
New York, 170–176.

4. Various New York City newspaper clippings dated 10 May 1871 in HDL, mf.; Benjamin L. Smith to CLS, 11 October 1906 and Maria Lloyd to David Demarest Lloyd, 15 May 1871, both in HDL, Wisc.

5. "Petition to Henry W. Beecher . . .", February 1872; Abraham S. Hewitt to Beecher, 5 April 1872; Beecher to Hewitt, 1 May 1872; Smith to CLS, 11 October 1906;

all in HDL, Wisc.; Beecher, *Libraries and Public Reading-Rooms: Should They be Opened on Sunday?* (New York: J. B. Ford and Co., 1872) and unidentified, undated newspaper clipping; both in HDL, mf.; William G. McLoughlin, *The Meaning of Henry Ward Beecher: An Essay on the Shifting Values of Mid Victorian America* (New York: Alfred A. Knopf, 1970), 170–173; CLS, *Lloyd* I, 20–22; and *New York Tribune*, 17 May 1872.

6. Alexander Callow, Jr., *The Tweed Ring* (New York: Oxford University Press, 1966), 257–262; Mohl, *New City*, 89–97; Leo Hershkowitz, *Tweed's New York: Another Look* (New York: Anchor Press, 1977), 177–181; Bender, *New York*, 176–191; Augustus Cerillo, Jr., "The Impact of Reform Ideology: Early Twentieth-Century Municipal Government in New York City," in Michael H. Ebner and Eugene M. Tobin, *The Age of Urban Reform: New Perspectives of Urban Reform*, ed. (Port Washington, New York: Kennikat Press, 1977), 68–85.

Also see Seymour J. Mandelbaum, *Boss Tweed's New York* (New York: J. Wiley, 1965) and Jon C. Teaford, *The Unheralded Triumph: City Government in America, 1870–1900* (Baltimore: The Johns Hopkins University Press, 1984).

7. *New York Tribune*, 22 January 1871, clipping in HDL, mf.; *New York Tribune*, 28 June 1871, as quoted in CLS Journal; and HDL to Hodgskin, 10 October 1871 in HDL, Wisc.

8. HDL, *A Manual for the Guidance of Voters in the General State Election to be held in New York City, November 7, 1871* (New York: Young Men's Municipal Reform Association, 1871) and "Ballot Box Agreement," October 1871, both in HDL, Wisc.; Callow, 261–262; and *New York Times*, 21 October 1871, clipping in HDL, mf.

9. Walker, *Reform* and Sproat, *Best Men*, 78–88.

10. Carl Schurz to David A. Wells, 9 October 1870, in David A. Wells Papers and Schurz to E. L. Godkin, 31 March 1871, Carl Schurz Papers, both in Library of Congress; Sproat, *Best Men*, 49–50; George Henry Payne, *History of Journalism in the United States* (New York: D. Appleton and Co., 1929), 328–331; Earle Dudley Ross, *The Liberal Republican Movement* (New York: Henry Holt and Co., 1919), 48–50; Jacqueline B. Tusa, "Power, Priorities, and Political Insurgency: the Liberal Republican Movement, 1869–1872" (Ph.D. diss., Pennsylvania State University, 1970); Michael C. Robinson, "Illinois Politics in the Post-Civil War Era: the Liberal Republican Movement" (Ph.D. diss., University of Wyoming, 1971); and Michael E. McGerr, "The Meaning of Liberal Republicanism: The Case of Ohio," *Civil War History*, 28(Fall 1982): 307–323.

11. Roeliff Brinkerhoff, *Recollections of a Lifetime* (Cincinnati: The Robert Clarke Co., 1900), 215–217; various 1872 letterheads in HDL, Wisc; and CLS, *Lloyd* I, 26–28.

12. HDL to David Demarest Lloyd, 13 March 1871, in HDL, Wisc. and Thomas, *Alternative*, 43–46.

13. W. M. Grosvenor to HDL, 1 February 1872; Edward Atkinson to HDL, 2 February 1872; John R. Walsh to Horace White, 3 February 1872; S. Thornton K. Prime to HDL, 5 February 1872; Peter Voorhis to HDL, 10 March 1872; and Charles H. Marshall to CLS, 28 April 1909; all in HDL, Wisc.; prospectus, *People's Pictorial Tax-Payer* in *The Free-Trader*, 4 (April 1871), Library of Congress; *People's Pictorial Tax-Payer*, 1 (March 1872): 20, 28–29 and 1 (April 1872): 38, copies in Destler papers; and HDL to Richard R. Bowker, 2 February, 22 April, 1872, in R. R. Bowker papers, New York Public Library.

14. *New York Evening Post*, 1 May 1872, clipping in HDL, mf.; George William Curtis to David A. Wells, 31 August 1871 and Charles F. Adams to Wells, 18 April 1872, both in David A. Wells papers, New York Public Library; "The Cincinnati Convention," *Nation*, 14(9 May 1872): 303; Brinkerhoff, *Recollections*, 216–217; and Joseph Logsdon, *Horace White, Nineteenth-Century Liberal* (Westport, CT: Greenwood Publishing Corporation, 1971), 243.

15. HDL speech at the Steinway Hall Conference, 30 May 1872 as reported in the *New York Tribune*, 31 May 1872 and quoted in Ross, *Liberal Republican*, 86–105; *New York Tribune*, 1, 2, 3, 31 May 1872; *New York Evening Post*, 2, 3 May 1872; *New York Times*, 3 May 1872; all clippings in HDL, mf.; and CLS, *Lloyd* I, 27–28.

16. HDL to William Cullen Bryant, 26 June 1872, in Bryant–Godwin papers, New York Public Library; *New York Times*, *Tribune*, and *Herald*, 31 May 1872, *New York Times*, 21 June 1872, *New York Herald*, 22 June 1872, all clippings in HDL, mf.; Isaac H. Bromley, "Political Outlook: The Conference: It's Origin and Its Significance," *New York Tribune*, 25 June 1872; and HDL to Richard R. Bowker, 20 November 1875, in Bowker papers, New York Public Library.

16. HDL to William Cullen Bryant, 26 June 1872, in Bryant–Godwin papers, New York Public Library; *New York Times*, *Tribune*, and *Herald*, 31 May 1872, *New York Times*, 21 June 1872, *New York Herald*, 22 June 1872, all clippings in HDL, mf.; Isaac H. Bromley, "Political Outlook: The Conference: It's Origin and Its Significance," *New York Tribune*, 25 June 1872; and HDL to Richard R. Bowker, 20 November 1875, in Bowker papers, New York Public Library.

17. Bender, *Intellectual*, 130–131; Elise D. Nordquist and Edward Caudill, "'. . . to leave this beggarly profession': A Study of Lawyers in Journalism," paper delivered to the American Journalism Historians Association, Coeur d'Alene, ID, October 1990; and Frank Gilbert, "The Coming Man is the Coming Editor," *Lakeside Monthly*, 8 (August 1872): 113–115.

18. HDL to Keenan, 11, 16, 19, 23 April, 6, 12, 24 July 1872, all in HDL, Wisc. and CLS Journal, HDL, Wisc.

19. HDL to Keenan, 11 April, 10 July 1872 and David D. Lloyd to Keenan, 29 August 1872, all in HDL, Wisc.; Andreas, *History of Chicago* III, 858; John L. Wright, "The Case for Chicago," in *Chicago: Past, Present, and Future* (Chicago: Horton and Leonard, 1868) quoted in Cook, *City Life*, 44–45; Everett Chamberlin, *Chicago and Its Suburbs* (Chicago: T. A. Hungerford and Co., 1874), 169–176; McCarthy, *Noblesse Oblige*, 81–82; John J. Pauly, "The Great Chicago Fire as a National Event," *American Quarterly*, 36(Winter 1984): 668–683; Louis P. Cain, "From Mud to Metropolis: Chicago Before the Fire," *Research in Economic History*, 10(1986): 93–129; Homer Hoyt, *One-Hundred Years of Land Values in Chicago* (New York: Arno Press, 1970, 1933): 119–125; Elmer A. Riley, "The Development of Chicago and Vicinity as a Manufacturing Center Prior to 1880" (Ph.D. diss., University of Chicago, 1911); Kenan Heise and Michael Edgerton, *Chicago: Center for Enterprise* (Woodland Hills, CA: Windsor Publications, 1982), 132–133; Christine Meisner Rosen, *The Limits of Power: Great Fires and the Process of City Growth in America* (Cambridge, MA: Cambridge University Press, 1986); John B. Jentz, "Class and Politics in an Emerging Industrial City: Chicago in the 1860s and 1870s," *Urban History* 17(May 1991): 227–264; Edward Bubnys, "Nativity and the Distribution of Wealth: Chicago 1870," *Explorations in Economic History* 19(1982): 101–109; and Wesley G. Skogan, *Chicago Since 1840: A*

Time-Series Data Handbook (Urbana: University of Illinois Institute of Government and Public Affairs, 1976): 24–26.

20. HDL to Keenan, 24 July, 25 August 1872, and David D. Lloyd to Keenan, 29 August 1872, all in HDL, Wisc.; Thomas, *Alternative*, 46–47; and S.V.R. Hickcox obituary, *C.T.*, 18 August 1872.

21. HDL to Keenan, 3 September 1872, HDL, Wisc.

22. HDL to Keenan, 3, 4, 9 September, n.d., and 14, 15 October 1872, all in HDL, Wisc. and "Butter and Wells," *C.T.*, 15 October 1872.

23. HDL to Keenan, 14 October 1872, in HDL, Wisc.

24. HDL to Keenan, 24 June 1872, in HDL, Wisc. and Richard Digby-Junger, "Praying for God's Help," *Chicago History*, 22(March 1993): 4–19.

25. Lystra, *Searching the Heart*, 166; JBL Diary, 25 October 1873, JBL, CHS; and HDL to Keenan, 29 October 1872, HDL, Wisc.

26. HDL to Keenan, n.d., circa February 1873, HDL, Wisc.; JBL Diary, 14, 17, 20 March 1873; and Rothman, *Hands and Heart*, 99–100.

27. JBL Diary, 13, 14, 21 June, 6, 12, 20, 23, 24 July, 2, 10, 16, 17, 20, 21, 23, 24, 30, 31 August, 13, 14 September 1873; Bross Diary, 14 September 1873, both in CHS; and Destler, *Empire of Reform*, 79–80.

28. JBL diary, 25, 26 December 1873, Keenan to JBL, 18 November 1873, and Whitelaw Reid to JBL, 22 December 1873, all in JBL, CHS; and William Bross diary, 24, 25 December 1873, CHS.

29. HDL to William Bross, 1 May 1880 and Bross to HDL, 17 February 1886, both in JBL, CHS; Bross Diary, 17 March 1874, CHS; Agnes M. Johansen to Chester M. Destler, 14 August 1942 and William Bross Lloyd to Destler, 14 August 1942, both in Destler papers, Wisc.; and Faw, "*Chicago Tribune* and Its Control," 4.

30. Bessie Louise Pierce, *A History of Chicago* III (Chicago: University of Chicago Press, 1957): 206–233; Bross diary, 4 January, 17 March, 28 August 1874, CHS; Destler, *Empire of Reform*, 82–84; Hoyt, *One-Hundred Years*, 88–127; and Charles A. Yount, *William Bross, 1813–1890* (Lake Forest, IL: Lake Forest College, 1940): 328.

31. Bross Diary, 28 August 1874, CHS; Destler, *Empire of Reform*, 82; and Pierce, *Chicago* III, 195–196.

32. HDL to Henry F. Keenan, 26 February 1875 and CLS Journal, both HDL, Wisc.; Bross Diary, 31 December 1875, CHS; Rothman, *Hands and Heart*, 90–94; and Ruegamer, *Women*, 62–68.

33. Frank Luther Mott, *Time Enough: Essays in Autobiography* (Chapel Hill: University of North Carolina Press, 1962), 146–149; Duncan, *Reid*, 5–6; William Allen White, *The Autobiography of William Allen White*, ed. Sally Foreman Griffith (Lawrence: University Press of Kansas, 1990), 115; *C.T.*, various articles in September, October, and November, HDL mf.; and George H. Lewes to HDL, 19 March 1873, HDL, Wisc.

34. W. Stanley Jones to HDL, 19 December 1874, in HDL, Wisc.; *C.T.* 8, 11 October 1874, HDL, mf.; Destler, *Empire of Reform*, 86; Thomas, *Alternative*, 73–74; and David S. Johnson, Francis L. Patton, and George C. Noyes, *The Trial of the Reverend David Swing Before the Presbytery of Chicago* (Chicago: Jensen, McClurg and Co., 1874).

35. HDL to Henry F. Keenan, 28 October 1874, in HDL, Wisc. *Chicago Times*, 4 August 1874; *C.T.*, 10 October 1872, HDL mf.; Destler, *Empire of Reform*, 86–89;

Horace White to Whitelaw Reid, 26 August 1874, Reid papers, Library of Congress; Waller, *Reverend Beecher and Mrs. Tilton*, 130–150; McLoughlin, *Henry Ward Beecher*, 92–94; and Logsdon, *Horace White*, 276–277.

36. *C.T.*, 9 November 1874, also in *A Century of Tribune Editorials* (Chicago: Chicago Tribune Company, 1947), 43–46; Bross Diary, 25 November 1874, CHS; Logsdon, *Horace White*, 268; and Andreas, *History of Chicago* 3, 695–704.

37. Bross Diary, 31 December 1874, CHS; John Tebbel, *An American Dynasty: The Story of the McCormicks, Medills and Pattersons* (New York: Greenwood Press, 1968, 1947), 4; HDL to Keenan, 31 March 1874 in HDL, Wisc.; Faw, "The *Chicago Tribune* and Its Control," 18–19; Rick Kogan, "Down to Business: The Tribune Company," *Chicago History*, 22(March 1993): 20–25; and Charles D. Mosher, "Centennial Historical Albums of Biography," unpublished MS, Chicago, 1876, 23, 26, CHS.

38. Aaron Lloyd to HDL, 10 July 1877 in JBL, CHS, and CLS, *Lloyd*, I, 50.

39. CLS, ibid.; Bross Diary, 13 December 1877 and 15 January 1878, CHS; *C.T.*, 12 December 1873, 23 November 1874, 14 January, 23 February 1878; Destler, *Empire of Reform*, 98–101; Wendt, ibid.; and Logsdon, *Horace White*, 350.

40. *C.T.*, 10 November 1874 and *Chicago Times*, 10 November 1874.

41. CLS, *Lloyd* I, 50; *C.T.*, 13, 24 December 1874; 1 January, 7 February, 11, 27 March 1875; 14 November 1877; 1 January 1878; 28 September 1879; 27 and March, 24 November 1880; Wendt, *Tribune*, 259–263; Thomas, *Alternative*, 76; Bross Diary, various entries, October 1879, CHS; and Harvey Wish, "Altgeld and the Progressive Tradition," *American Historical Review*, 46(July 1941).

Also see Carl Abbott, *Boosters and Businessmen: Popular Economic Thought and Urban Growth in the Antebellum Middle West* (Westport, CT: Greenwood Press, 1981), 126–147 and Pierce, *Chicago* 3, 209–214.

42. HDL to JBL, 25 February 1903 and Robert W. Patterson to HDL, 8 December 1895, both in HDL, Wisc.; Wendt, *Tribune*, 271; Kinsley, *Tribune* II, 332; Destler, *Empire of Reform*, 109–110; and CLS, *Lloyd* I, 52–53.

43. HDL to Henry F. Keenan, 28 October 1874, 11 February 1878 and JBL to Keenan, n.d., circa 1877, all in HDL, Wisc.; Bross Diary, 15 January 1878, CHS; and Rothman, *Hands and Heart*, 90–102.

44. William Bross Lloyd to Richard T. Ely, 23 December 1907, in Richard T. Ely papers, State Historical Society of Wisconsin (hereafter Ely Papers).

45. D. H. Wheeler, "Political Communism," *Lakeside Monthly*, 6 (July 1871): 26–30; "William Bross" in Lowe, *Fire*, 53–60; various articles and editorials, *C.T.*, 19–31 July, 1–4 August 1877; "The Chicago Communists," *C.T.*, 10 November 1878; and *C.T.*, 23 March 1879 as quoted in Nelson, *Beyond the Martyrs*, 79–101.

46. CLS Journal, Quincy L. Dowd to CLS, 6 April 1907, and Vida Scudder to CLS, 20 February 1906, all in HDL, Wisc.; CLS, *Lloyd* I, 166–169; Thomas, *Alternative*, 133–135; Destler, *Empire of Reform*, 209–212; Bross Diary, 11 April, 20 May, 5 June 1878, CHS; Michael H. Ebner, *Creating Chicago's North Shore: A Suburban History* (Chicago: University of Chicago Press, 1988), 83–88; Ebner, "Henry Demarest Lloyd's Winnetka," *Chicago History*, 15(Fall 1986): 20–29; Stephen Beal, *Wayside: The Henry Demarest Lloyd House in Winnetka, Illinois* (Chicago: Landmark Preservation Council and Service, 1977); Lora Townsend Dickenson, *The Story of Winnetka* (Dekalb, IL: The Geographical Publishing Co., 1956), 78–80; Caroline Thomas Harnsberger, *Winnetka: The Biography of a Village* (Evanston, IL: The Schori Press, 1976), 60–63; Thomas,

3

The Celebrity

Among its usual staid offerings, the November 1882 issue of the *North American Review* featured an article on "The Pretensions of Journalism." Usually disdainful of the less cerebral press, the Gilded Age's leading intellectual journal gave grudging recognition to the postbellum American press:

A few years ago thinking men were agreed in grouping the dominant forces of our civilization in three great estates—the Family, the Church, and the State. . . . Today a fourth estate asserts itself, journalism, and plants itself beside, if not above, the ancient three. . . . A latter-day parvenu, its ephemeral flutter, its perpetual coming and going, its very iridescence of transiency and unresting flux, constitute its *raison d'etre*.

While not new to America, newspapers and magazines experienced a revitalization and redirection following the Civil War. Five prominent antebellum-era publishers died between 1869 and 1878, including Lloyd acquaintances Horace Greeley and William Cullen Bryant. In their place, new lions emerged. Edward W. Scripps started his newspaper chain in Cleveland. Melville E. Stone introduced Chicago to the penny newspaper. A Hungarian emigre named Joseph Pulitzer experimented with his *St. Louis Post-Dispatch* before he moved to New York. Bryant's successor at the *Evening-Post* was an English-born journalist named E. L. Godkin.[1]

Henry Demarest Lloyd was another member of this post-bellum generation of American journalists. He was not so successful as Pulitzer or Scripps, nor as influential as Godkin, but then neither Pulitzer, Scripps, or Godkin ever wrote a book with the impact of *Wealth Against Commonwealth*. Lloyd saw the press as a way to reach the people, not as a means of enriching or ingratiating himself. He observed in his personal notebook in 1879, "The only hope of society is in the education of the masses, especially in the use of the power of the State." A few months later he wrote, "The one great social feature which distinguishes modern civilization from any other of which we have a record [is] the eventual supremacy of enlightened public opinion." These were his two goals as he welcomed the decade of the 1880s.[2]

Regardless of his personal feelings, Lloyd's first brush with fame came about through four nationally published magazine articles and a number of *Chicago Tribune* editorials and articles written between 1880 and 1884. The first magazine article, which was published almost as an afterthought, was especially influential. In chronicling an obscure economic war between Pennsylvania oil refiners and an unknown oil company, Lloyd was the first to generate mass public opinion against John D. Rockefeller's Standard Oil Company, a movement that would culminate three years later with the U.S. Supreme Court-ordered breakup of the company into thirty eight individual oil companies. Considered together, the block of writings Lloyd produced between 1880 and 1884 set him on a course that he was to follow for the rest of the life and proved the need if not the value of an advocacy journalism involving social reform in Gilded Age America.

Beginning with his inopportune "Butter and Wells" editorial in 1872, Lloyd continued to display at the *Chicago Tribune* the proclivity for editorial writing that he had developed at Columbia College. Horace White allowed him to contribute to the editorial page on a more regular basis as early as 1874, providing Lloyd with valuable experience and an opportunity to address what Lloyd believed were important public issues. The standard practice of the day was to write editorials in the third person, without the use of bylines or other identification of the author. It is difficult to distinguish Lloyd's earliest efforts from his *Tribune* colleagues but his penchant for advocacy writing began to show itself with time. His editorials were terse, fluid, inquisitive, and frequently biting, in contrast to the flat, unimaginative, political hack style of the other *Tribune* staffers, especially Joseph Medill. Lloyd's classical education also provided him with a host of mythological metaphors that were unknown to his less educated colleagues.[3]

In early 1878, Lloyd found a particularly interesting editorial topic in a *New York Sun* article, "The Company that Divides a Million a Month in Profits." He was probably aware of some of the many other, earlier anti-monopoly writings, most notably Charles Francis Adams's various *North American Review* articles at the time, but as with labor unions, Populism, cooperatives, and most other causes in his life, he paid little attention to them until something piqued his interest. The *Sun* article discussed the exploits of an obscure Ohio oil company, the Standard, and its one time produce clerk chief executive, John D. Rockefeller. Concerned at what he believed was a developing monopoly in the Illinois coal industry, Lloyd borrowed facts from the *Sun* article for two *Tribune* editorials, "A Giant Monopoly" and "The Oil Monopoly." Both introduced *Tribune* readers to the Standard and efforts then underway by the Commonwealth of Pennsylvania to limit the company's monopolistic practices. In particular, independent or non-affiliated Pennsylvania oil producers were alarmed at a secret plan hatched by the Standard to force the Pennsylvania Railroad to pay kickbacks or rebates to the Standard for any non-Standard oil shipped on the railroad. This business technique, known as a rebate, effectively taxed the independents, with the proceeds going to the Standard, and made their oil more expensive to sell. Lloyd called for a thorough investigation of the Standard, a firm he labeled the "monster of the monopoly" trend, and predicted that civil unrest would be the inevitable result in Pennsylvania unless the Standard was brought under governmental control.[4]

It was somewhat unusual that the Chicago based Lloyd would take such an interest in as arcane a business as the late nineteenth-century oil industry. Illinois then and now had coal mines but no oil wells, and the market for oil products was minor before the turn of the twentieth century, primarily as kerosene, or coal or lamp oil as it was sometimes called, for lighting. Lloyd saw the trend toward monopolization of all American industries perfecting itself in the oil business. Rockefeller was more than just another greedy capitalist, he was the epitome of what was wrong with the American Industrial Revolution. The power of money had created an oligarchy, a self-anointed ruling class of amoral, unprincipled men, which was gaining control of the country without so much as a word of complaint from either the public or the government. As he had learned at Columbia College, Lloyd saw ominous parallels with the Standard and the decline of previous civilizations. He observed in his 1879 notebook, "The oppressive rich of Rome and Greece were individuals in an aristocratic order, those of today are corporations. . . . See Standard Oil monopoly."[5]

Pennsylvania's probe of the Standard floundered in 1880 because of political pressure applied by the company, but Lloyd reported on a Congressional investigation into other secret compacts between the railroads and the Standard in his *Tribune* financial columns that year. His information came from a growing number of non-Standard oil contacts, and they provided so many details that Lloyd prepared a lecture on the Standard for the Chicago Literary Club, a public affairs group, that he delivered in January 1880. "The Cure for Vanderbiltism," his euphemism for monopolies based on the infamous career of railroad magnate Cornelius Vanderbilt, detailed the activities of the Standard and assailed the corrupting influence of the company and other monopolies on American democracy. In contrast to previous advocacy writers, especially Harriet Beecher Stowe's *Uncle Tom's Cabin*, Lloyd refused to use fictionalized characters, recreated conversations, or highly moralistic platitudes in his speech. Instead, he played the role of a legal advocate, arguing his case against the Standard and other monopolies with carefully researched and thoughtfully analyzed legal evidence. His proof came from a variety of sources, firsthand statements, published reports, court testimony, and a wealth of secondary-source documents. "The time has come," Lloyd proclaimed, "to face the fact that the forces of capital and industry have outgrown the forces of government." He continued:

Our strong men are engaged in a headlong fight for fortune, power, precedence, success. American as they are, they ride over the people like Juggernauts to gain their ends. The moralists have preached to them since the world began, and have failed. The common people, the nation, must take them in hand. In the end, it was the strength of Lloyd's factual case, not the beauty of his words or the pathos of his characters, that made his speech a success, sending his youthful, liberal audience to their feet in applause.[6]

One of his listeners suggested that Lloyd submit the speech for publication in a national magazine. Lloyd reworked his arguments, updating his information and strengthening his legal logic, and submitted the manuscript to the prestigious *North American Review* in late 1880. Editor Allen Thorndike Rice was intrigued by what he read, but the *Review* was conservative in tone and Rice rejected Lloyd's work as too politically risque for his publication. Lloyd then turned to William Dean Howells's *Atlantic Monthly*, which lacked the stature of the *North American Review* but had a reputation for challenging the status quo. Howells was a onetime Ohio newspaperman who was nearing completion of *The Rise of Silas Lapham* in late 1880. Over his ten-year editorial tenure, he had made the *Atlantic Monthly* into a forum for American social commentary in contrast to the anglo-phobic perspective of the *North American Review*. Even so, Howells had never attacked the popular culture of American business. He was impressed by what Lloyd had to say and wrote him in December 1880, just a month before he resigned as editor, "I accept your paper with pleasure, and will give it the first place in the *Atlantic* for March."[7]

The "Story of a Great Monopoly" was an unprecedented success for the *Atlantic*, selling out seven editions of the publication. Although the sixteen-page essay was aimed at all monopolies, it was Lloyd's case study of the Standard Oil Company that generated the greatest public sensation. Never before had readers been privy to the behind-the-scene details of a monopoly as revealed by Lloyd. The article contended that the Standard controlled the world price of kerosene even though it produced less than 7 percent of the product. Its primary tactics were intimidation or outright cheating. Using prevailing market data, Lloyd estimated that the average American family, burning a gallon of kerosene per day, paid the Standard $32 a year in extra, surplus, undeserved profits, or what Lloyd characterized as a "tribute" given to the company by itself in the fashion of a Roman emperor. Although it was Lloyd's characterization of the Standard as an "octopus," an animal with tentacles sucking consumers and competitors from around the world, that became synonymous with the company, it was his allegation the Standard routinely bribed lawmakers that forever enshrined him as an advocate journalist. As Lloyd put it, "The Standard has done everything with the Pennsylvania legislature except refine it."[8]

The *Atlantic* article made Lloyd an instant celebrity, especially among the liberal, upper-class elite that had long harbored fears against the growing influence of uncultured "self made" men such as Cornelius Vanderbilt, John Jacob Astor, and John D. Rockefeller. Former free trade colleague E. L. Godkin endorsed Lloyd's article in his *Nation*. The *Oil, Paint, and Drug Reporter*, an anti-Standard weekly, noted that Lloyd's article was "at once the most complete and the fairest review of the iniquitous growth and despotic rule of that corporation which has ever been published." The *Chicago Tribune* reprinted the entire article, as did other newspapers. Letters poured in to Lloyd, with more than one writer telling him, "In a word it is the most interesting as well as the ablest article I have ever read on the evils of the railroad system." The Standard unwittingly strengthened Lloyd's case by ignoring him, in yet another example of late nineteenth-century business disdain toward public opinion, and the "Story of a Great Monopoly" was allowed to stand uncontested. It was a mistake the firm would repeat thirteen years later with *Wealth Against Commonwealth*, and it was only after Ida Tarbell began writing her *History of the Standard Oil Company* in 1900 that the company finally recognized the advantage of presenting its side to the public.[9]

Historians have debated the validity of Lloyd's facts in "Story of a Great Monopoly," but few have doubted the article's impact on the public perception of the Standard. John B. Clark noted the article "became the starting point for every public investigation" of monopolies in the late nineteenth century. Hans Thorelli called it the "climax" of early antimonopoly attacks. Standard Oil Company historians Ralph W. and Mauriel E. Hidy credited Lloyd with being the first to project the Standard's octopus "image upon the national screen." Chester M. Destler argued that it "made a profound impression on the reading public." Literary historian Robert E. Spiller observed, "If any single piece of writing may be said to have inaugurated a new movement, this article did."[10]

The reception of a "Story of a Great Monopoly" was so sudden, strong, and unexpected that Lloyd did not come to fully grasp its impact until years later. Across the country, scores of young people discovered the evils of monopolies through his eyes and made fighting the trusts part of their life's work. A Stanford University professor wrote Lloyd in 1895 that he had been inspired to study economics by the article and it was still "frequently in my mind." The editor of the *Des Moines Daily and Weekly News* told Lloyd in 1897, "The magazine article interested me and others and I have always regarded it as one of the promptings of the antimonopoly movement." William T. Harris, the U.S. Commissioner of Education and the founding editor of the *Journal of Speculative Philosophy*, wrote Lloyd the same year, "Ever since your first article in the *Atlantic Monthly* on the oil trust I have considered your work a very important one to be done and the lesson you teach can not be emphasized sufficiently." An Australian scholar provided a vivid recollection of the article during a Lloyd visit in 1900. Muckraker Charles Edward Russell, who wrote a series on the trusts for *Everybody's* between 1904 and 1905, remembered reading Lloyd's article as an academy student in Vermont. "I knew then in a general way," he wrote, "something of the menace of accumulated wealth, but it had never been made clear, vital, and personal to me until I read that article, and from that time I could never question the author's own conception of what lay before us." The *Multitude* credited "Story of a Great Monopoly" with initiating "the antimonopoly movement in this country" in 1903. Karl Marx had a copy of the *Atlantic Monthly* containing Lloyd's article in his library. Fifteen years later, Lloyd admitted to a friend that he had not understood the power of the published word until the "Story of a Great Monopoly." It "opened a path to me," he said, "and I have followed the leading as the Shakers say, ever since."[11]

The success of "Story of a Great Monopoly" and his sudden fame pleased Lloyd but he was disappointed that his case study on the Standard had detracted from his intended monopolistic target, the railroads. As the largest industry in late nineteenth-century America, the railroads easily eclipsed the petroleum business in influence and corruption. Lloyd had noted at the beginning of "Story of a Great Monopoly" that "the movement of railroad trains of this country is literally the circulation of its blood." His interest in the railroads dated back to as early as the mid-1870s. By 1878, he was writing a weekly railroad column and contributing a number of *Chicago Tribune* editorials advocating national railroad regulation. He wrote in his notebook in 1879, "The forces struggling to control the destinies of the future of this country are the masses and the railroad kings, the poor and the rich. The grandest political mission to which any man or body of men can be committed is to organize this struggle."[12]

To build on the success of his first article, Lloyd prepared another speech, "The Political Economy of Fifty Millions," which he delivered to the Chicago Literary Club in April 1882. Thomas Bailey Aldrich, William Dean Howells's successor at the *Atlantic*, invited Lloyd to submit the speech for publication even before it was delivered. Lloyd did some additional research, added another $23 million to the title, and sent it to the magazine. Aldrich was less of a crusader than Howells and had some "legal light thrown on certain points" in the "brave paper" to avoid a libel suit, but ultimately accepted it and "The Political Economy of Seventy-Three Million Dollars" appeared in the *Atlantic* in July 1882.[13]

Lloyd's second national magazine article began as a recantation of Lloyd's prior beliefs in political economy and laissez-faire economics. In preparation for the article, he re-read the laissez-faire heroes of his youth and discovered how much he had fallen out of step with them. In their place, he embraced a new, more radical group of thinkers and writers, including John Ruskin, the young Ralph Waldo Emerson, Immanuel Kant, Georg W. F. Hegel, Auguste Comte, William James, and even Karl Marx.   One passage of "Political Economy" parroted Marx, complaining that political economists disregarded "the natural history of their subject."   Of his previous adherence to political economy, Lloyd wrote, "laissez-faire theories of politics and political economy are useless in the treatment of the labor question, in the regulation of the railroads, sanitary and educational government, and a multitude of similar questions. . . . By neglecting the other forces, from sympathy to monopoly, the abstract political economist deduces principles which fit no realities, and has to neglect those realities for which we need principles most."   He discarded such orthodoxies, writing that true political economy should concern itself with "the care and culture of men . . . [the] world of wealth is the world of soul, over-soul, and under-soul."[14]

Self-absolved of his ideological sins, Lloyd then became a verbal caricaturist in the remainder of "Political Economy," lampooning the life and success of railroad magnate Jay Gould.   Since few readers were interested in economic theory, it was the Gould passages that created the most public interest. As Lloyd told the story, Gould first came to public notice in 1853 when one of his inventions, an elaborate mousetrap, was stolen from him as he rode on a New York streetcar.   Instead of making more inventions, the "mouse-trap man," as Lloyd called Gould, turned his talents to the systematic defrauding of competitors, customers, employees, and the government.   His various financial schemes, including the abuse of the nation's bankruptcy system and a failed effort to control gold prices that precipitated the financial panic of 1873, netted him millions.   The result of such activities should have been prison, as Lloyd reasoned, not fame and "seventy-three millions, and more, accumulated by an enthusiast in competition in twenty-nine years of office work!"   Lloyd made extensive use of Charles Francis Adams' 1869 *North American Review* article "Railroad Inflation," the first serious investigation of Gould's "orgy of fiduciary harlotry" as a resource, but he wrote for readers who were not familiar with Gould or Adams as well.   He concluded, "It is the solemn truth, that of Ruskin's, that every man has to choose in this world whether he will be a laborer or an assassin.   There are men who murder for money, but there must be no science of assassination," a closing reference to political economy.[15]

"Political Economy" elicited a wider but less favorable response than the "Story of a Great Monopoly," especially among liberal laissez-faire political economists.   The *Montreal Gazette* excerpted it as did *The New York Times*, but the latter challenged Lloyd to offer "some sort of principle that might work better than that of free competition."   E. L. Godkin disputed Lloyd's contention that political economy was a failure, noting, "Gould is the product of corrupt courts and legislatures, and no economist of any school ever taught the principle of laissez-faire covered the right to bribe judges or gobble railroads, any more than it does the right to rob and murder on the highway."   Lloyd responded to

Godkin, "If the theories of laissez-faire and exclusive regulation by competition do not permit these men to rob and murder by retail on the highway, they cause society to leave them to rob and murder by wholesale, by all kinds of "corners" and combinations, and by legal methods of oppressing the people, betraying trusts, and deceiving the community." Godkin retorted, "We advise [Lloyd] to let it alone" and the two never saw eye-to-eye again. Others applauded Lloyd. Journalist, politician, and former Liberal Republican Carl Schurz cited the article in his 1882 Phi Beta Kappa address at Harvard University. Henry R. Gorringe, the eccentric navy officer who brought Cleopatra's Needle from Egypt to New York's Central Park, predicted that the article would "immortalize" Lloyd.[16]

Lloyd continued to criticize the railroads in his *Chicago Tribune* editorials, both before and after "Political Economy." "The American Pashas," which appeared in late 1881, compared Vanderbilt, Gould, and other railroad magnates to authoritarian Middle-Eastern dictators. Lloyd predicted a similar loss of liberties in the United States if such economic pashas were allowed to operate unregulated, warning, "In this concentration of the property of the many by the 'force and fraud' of the few no agency is more powerful than the delay, the expensiveness, and the maladministration of what is called 'Justice'." In a call for nationalization, Lloyd alerted *Tribune* readers in 1882 to what he believed was the impending formation of a railroad monopoly, writing, "The needs of the public and the needs of the railroad are both for the intervention of the government." His most famous *Tribune* railroad editorial, "King's Horses and King's Men," which appeared the same year, contrasted the lavish conditions of Cornelius Vanderbilt's horse barn to the hazardous state of his railroad:

A great many of Mr. Vanderbilt's passengers have been killed on his roads, but none of his pet horses have suffered death at his hands. No Vanderbilt horse is allowed to ride on a Vanderbilt [rail] road. He is too humane a man to subject helpless dumb animals to the risk of a system which sacrificed a score of lives.[17]

Lloyd's strongest criticism of the railroads, especially their usurpation of the democratic process, appeared in a unique 1883 *Chicago Tribune* article. "Our Land" filled two full newspaper pages, providing "the first full statement that has yet been made" on how the American railroads misused lavish state and federal public land grants to increase their corporate profits. Writing as an advocate again, Lloyd began as if he was presenting an opening statement to a jury:

The public are profoundly ignorant of the facts about the public land. They know, in a dim way, that it is passing out of their hands, and that huge monopolies are being created out of the lands which they meant should be the inheritance of the settler. . . . In the story recited below every element of human fault and fraud will be seen to have been at work in the spoilation of the land of the people.

Most of Lloyd's charges were documented with statistical data, illustrating how much public land each railroad had received and how little had been given or sold to settlers at intended prices to stimulate Western development. Most had been kept by the railroads or sold to land speculators like Lloyd's father at tremendous profit. To illustrate his argument, Lloyd devised the first full page graphic to appear in the *Chicago Tribune*, a United States map revealing the extent of the railroad's land fraud. Unfortunately, his monumental undertaking was published inside the newspaper, was not promoted on the paper's front page, and received little public notice outside of Chicago. At the center of the nation's growing rail industry, Joseph Medill and the *Tribune* were less than eager to criticize what was rapidly becoming Chicago's leading business. As a result, "Our Land" proved to Lloyd that late nineteenth-century newspapers were not the best way to reach readers. He made occasional use of newspapers after he quit the *Chicago Tribune* in 1885, but never for more than a few paragraphs.[18]

Beyond land fraud, which was epidemic in the industry, Lloyd criticized a particular railroad monopoly in an 1883 *Chicago Tribune* series. "California Cornered" described how the Southern Pacific Railroad had outmaneuvered everyone in the industry, even the Goulds and Vanderbilts. Its secret was to require all shippers to provide intimate financial data on themselves with their shipping orders. With such information, the rail line could customize its rates, charging each customer as much as it could extract. As a result, the Southern became the most profitable railroad in the country by the early 1880s, making more money per mile than any other road. Lloyd explained, "Nowhere else in the country is there a corner on transportation so complete as this." The Southern article suffered the same fate as Lloyd's earlier "Our Land" piece—generating little public reaction—and the firm continued its monopolistic ways into the twentieth century.[19]

Lloyd's otherwise universal contempt for the late nineteenth-century railroads had one glaring blind spot. Henry Villard's Northern Pacific was the most lavish abuser of federal land grants, absorbing and selling more than forty million acres of prime farm and timber land at inflated prices during the 1870s. In spite of this well-documented fact, Lloyd counted Villard as a friend, frequently expressing admiration for him, and even joined him on two press junkets during the 1880s. The first found Lloyd in the company of some four hundred other journalists and dignitaries as Villard drove the last spike of the first northern transcontinental railway in 1883. Lloyd was so moved by the event that he recalled the details for the *Seattle Daily Times* twenty years later. He told the newspaper, "Mr. Villard was a most wonderful man in many ways. So magnetic was he in person that it is even said that many men of wealth would not allow themselves to be left alone with him for fear that he might, by the power of his will and magnetic personality, be able to induce them to consent to financial undertakings and advance money in enterprises of which their judgment did not approve." Lloyd was taken in by Villard as well, for he never wrote anything unkind about the man during his life.[20]

Explanations vary as to this shortsightedness. In her 1912 biography of her brother, Caro Lloyd observed that the 1883 spike-driving trip had been a "delightful experience" for Lloyd but said nothing more on the subject. Fifty years later, Chester M. Destler blamed the infatuation on the *Chicago Tribune*'s well-known support of the railroads and "friendship for a fellow journalist." The latter statement was true, for Villard had been the editor of an antebellum Wisconsin newspaper, had served as a Civil War correspondent, and had purchased the *New York Evening Post* in 1881, hiring Lloyd's onetime mentor Horace White as his editor. However, Villard had a natural instinct for publicity in sharp contrast to his secrecy-obsessed business competitors. He liked associating with newspapermen, unlike John D. Rockefeller and other monopolists, and knew how to promote himself and his railroad through elaborately orchestrated pseudo-events such as the 1883 stake-driving ceremony. Overworked, underpaid Gilded Age journalists appreciated any newsmaker who could make their job easier for them, and it was only after the widespread adoption of professionalized public relations in the early twentieth century that the rest of American business began to copy Villard's publicity practices.[21]

Beyond the railroads, Lloyd next despised the immorality of speculating in food and other necessities of life. He particularly detested the Chicago Board of Trade, which had been founded in 1848 to encourage Chicago's commercial growth but had evolved into the most unregulated commodities trading market in the world. Lloyd had learned about the C.B.O.T. from his father-in-law William Bross and his late banker friend William F. Coolbaugh. The C.B.O.T. permitted transactions that boards of trade in other cities in and outside the United States limited, regulated, or prohibited. Lloyd cared little for the professional speculators who made and lost fortunes each day with their heavily leveraged transactions, but he was incensed that their greed influenced the price and supply of food. He was especially critical of two common C.B.O.T. practices. Long and short selling allowed unscrupulous speculators to conspire among themselves to profit on weather conditions and other natural price fluctuations at the expense of farmers or small grain elevator operators. Corners artificially controlled the price and supply of commodities for a time to the detriment of consumers. Beyond encouraging the C.B.O.T. to reform itself, Lloyd's *Chicago Tribune* business columns repeatedly agitated for city, state, and federal regulations.[22]

Lloyd received a letter from a friend in 1883 contrasting the frenzied pace of the C.B.O.T. to the more refined and regulated New York Board of Trade. The result was Lloyd's third nationally published article and his first contribution to the prestigious *North Atlantic Review*. "Making Bread Dear" was a return to the advocacy writing style of "Story of a Great Monopoly" and "Our Land" and featured elaborately researched data on the improprieties of the

C.B.O.T. Lloyd saw a connection between commodities speculation and the late nineteenth-century manifestation of monopolies in America:

The manufacture of prices, like other modern industries, is being concentrated into vast establishments, and these are passing under the rule of bosses and syndicates. The markets, like political parties, are run by the Machine. The people are losing the power of making prices as well as nominations.

He provided real life examples. According to Lloyd, a wheat corner in 1879 controlled seventy million bushels of the grain "so that no other wheat could be got to market by the farmers and dealers." This was in contrast to what laissez-faire economist Adam Smith had once proclaimed, that wheat would be the least liable of all commodities to fall into speculation because "its owners can never be collected in one place." Pork, corn, beef, and flour corners were also common in Chicago, for the impossible, as Lloyd wryly noted, "is easily done by the [Chicago] Board of Trade." "The jail, which was the habitat of the distrusted grain trader of [Adam Smith's] day has become his palace of exchange—capable of handling the world's surplus in an afternoon . . . bringing all the owners of the crop into one place, and then overcoming them by a combination of capital, banks, and the courts," Lloyd wrote. In concluding, Lloyd warned that a French-style revolution was possible in the United States unless proper trading regulations were enacted and people provided with enough to eat. "The Carlyle who hunts through the newspapers of this generation, for the history of its people," he wrote, "will dig the regraters of our Broads of Trade and Produce exchanges . . . to write against their names: "They made bread dear."[23]

The article elicited favorable reviews in newspapers ranging from the *Springfield* (Massachusetts) *Republican* and the *St. Louis Globe-Democrat* to the *New York Journal*. A Colorado reader told Lloyd, "You are doing a grand work in calling the attention of our people to the threatening Hydra of Monopoly." Fearful of offending its conservative readership, the *North American Review* offered a rebuttal to Lloyd's article two months later, with the writer labeling "the Chevalier Henry D. Lloyd" a "socialistic red rag." The most revealing compliment that Lloyd received came from a former Chicago business colleague who now threatened to sue him for libel. Lloyd countered that his information had come from court documents and was therefore protected under Illinois law. He considered it a mark of distinction that he was never sued for libel, equating the higher moral road he took in his writings as a sign of character in contrast to his immoral, unprincipled adversaries. Still, "Bread" set in motion his estrangement from the Chicago old-boy, business network that William Bross had introduced him to a decade earlier. It was a process that would be completed three years later with Lloyd's reaction to the Haymarket Square bombing.[24]

Lloyd continued to monitor the activities of the Chicago Board of Trade following "Bread." He ridiculed pork speculation and other forms of what he called "organized gambling" in several 1884 *Tribune* editorials, calling for government regulation of commodity trading. "If the [Board] directors touch with so gentle a hand an operator who pleads guilty to having abused his membership . . . to the free use of all his rights and privileges after a vacation of thirty days," he wrote, "they must not squirm if the public reiterates with a new emphasis the charge that the Board of Trade is a great gambling-shop." He also criticized the C.B.O.T.'s tolerance of bucket shops, shady, fly-by-night brokerage houses that profited by misadvising and speculating against small-time investors. In spite of Lloyd's and others efforts, the Chicago Board of Trade remained relatively free of governmental regulation until the Great Depression.[25]

The Standard reemerged as a topic of national interest in 1883 when the *North American Review* published an article in praise of the company and the concept of monopolies. Written by U.S. Senator Johnson N. Camden, a former West Virginia oilman who had sold his oil properties to John D. Rockefeller only a few years before he was elected to the Senate, the article lauded the Standard for its "unprecedented development of the American petroleum industry." Camden held that monopolies were beneficial to society because they economized production to the advantage of the consumer, a not unpopular view. Whatever extra profits they extracted were justified as a small price to pay for cheaper goods. The *Review* tapped John C. Welch, an Ohio congressman and the editor of the antimonopoly *Monthly Petroleum Trade Reports*, to respond to Camden instead of the more logical choice of Lloyd. Welch repeated many of Lloyd's assertions from "Story of a Great Monopoly," but his argument was weak and unpersuasive.[26]

Concerned over the credibility that such a prestigious defense gave Rockefeller and his fellow monopolists, Lloyd embarked on what he intended to be a definitive study of American monopolies. The result fell short of that ambitious goal, but "Lords of Industry," which appeared in the *North American Review* in June 1884, argued that "the expansive ferment of the New Industry, coming with the new science, the new land, and the new liberties of our era . . . all do something to raise prices, or hold them up, and [the monopolists] wind up with banquets for which we pay." Lloyd cataloged fifty-eight monopolies, trusts, combinations, and pools in his article, from the National Burial Case Association and the American Wall Paper Manufacturers' Association to the Western Cracker Bakers' Association and the Western Wooden Ware Association. He wrote:

They come and go, but more come than go, and those that stay grow. All are "voluntary," of course, but if the milk farmer of Orange county, the iron molder of Troy, the lumber dealer of San Francisco, the Lackawanna Railroad, or any other individual or corporate producer, show any backwardness about accepting the invitation to join "the pool," they are whipped in with all the competitive weapons at command, from assault and battery to boycotting and conspiracy.

Lloyd contrasted "the tendency to combination" and "the demand for social control" to the civic humanism he had learned at Columbia College. "The first is capitalistic, the second social. The first, industrial; the second moral. The first promotes wealth; the second citizenship," he wrote. Beyond his impressive list, he offered columns of statistics, including capitalizations and market shares, as evidence of his contentions. The article was a triumph of advocacy journalism, in sharp contrast to the poorly-researched generalizations and blatant moralizing of Thomas A. Bland's 1881 *Reign of Monopoly*, Cloud's 1872 *Monopolies and the People*, and most previous antimonopoly works.[27]

In retrospect, "Lords" was almost as important for what it said about Lloyd as what it said about monopolies. His first magazine and newspaper articles had been persuasive but they lacked the polish and confidence that Lloyd exhibited in "Lords." The effect was compelling, sweeping the reader into Lloyd's conclusions by a body of accumulated evidence and the passion of its presenter. Government cannot be expected to control monopolies through regulation, Lloyd held, because the plutocrats had already corrupted the democratic system. Instead, a popular, moral revolution was needed, a renewed commitment to the individualism that had guided Americans since the country's founding. "We cannot here-after, as in the past, recover freedom by going to the prairies," Lloyd wrote, a reference to the individualism that he seen and experienced in frontier Pekin, Illinois. "We must find it in the society of the good. . . . It may be that the coming age of combination will issue in a nobler and fuller liberty for the individual than has yet been seen, but the consummation will be possible, not in a day of competitive trade, but in one of competitive morals." Lloyd's vision of a responsible industrial society, one he would articulate more fully three years later in a speech he called "The New Conscience," involved the Golden Rule, not the rule of the jungle. Any society that allowed brute competition instead of just human reason was doomed to failure, Lloyd believed.[28]

Response was swift and predictable. Lloyd had timed publication to coincide with the 1884 Republican National Convention in Chicago, in which Jay Gould's handpicked candidate, James G. Blaine, was the overwhelming favorite for the party's presidential nomination. *Bradstreet's*, the influential finance journal, attacked the essay in a special five-column review, warning of a growing popular dissent in America against laissez-faire capitalism. The *New York World* quoted from it, fearing a return to "guild slavery." Labor journalist John Swinton observed, "The appearance of this article in the oldest and ablest of American reviews is, we trust, but the precursor of a thorough discussion of a topic which has been strangely overlooked or ignored by political economists." The *Pall Mall Gazette* reported that the article had stirred a virulent reaction in Great Britain.[29]

In the years since Theodore Roosevelt coined the term in 1906, a debate has continued over whether "Lords," "Story of a Great Monopoly," and Lloyd's other articles and books constitute muckraking. In particular, Louis M. Hacker termed Lloyd "the first and finest of the muck-rakers" in a 1933 encyclopedia article he wrote on Lloyd, Louis Filler labeled *Wealth Against Commonwealth* "the first muckraking book," and Richard Hofstadter called *Wealth* a "brilliant piece of muckraking" in his 1956 *The Age of Reform*. However, a more recent generation of muckrake historians, including Judson A. Grenier, Herbert Shapiro, John M. Harrison, Harry M. Stein, David M. Chalmers, and Robert Miraldi have all contended that muckraking did not begin until 1900 or so, years after "Story of a Great Monopoly" and *Wealth* appeared. Shapiro characterized Lloyd as "a gentleman radical whose writings were an extension of his personal involvement in social movements." Harrison and Stein called *Wealth* a "quasi-muckraking production" and Chalmers dismissed the book as a "nineteenth-century reform report." Categorizations and time periods are always subject to definition, and perhaps it can be argued that Lloyd was the "father" of muckraking as Warren T. Francke has termed him. Lloyd's greatest direct contribution to muckraking as most define the word came through the assistance he provided to Ida M. Tarbell in the preparation of her *History of the Standard Oil Company* two decades after "Story of a Great Monopoly" was written, not before.[30]

The publication of "Lords of Industry" in 1884 brought an abrupt, temporary end to Lloyd's advocacy journalism. His first nationally-published reform works, including the "Story of a Great Monopoly," had revealed true literary talent. A few years later, author Robert Louis Stevenson compared Lloyd to Francis Parkman, Henry James, and William Dean Howells, noting that there was "not a touch in Lloyd of the amateur" and that his prose was one of the "most workmanlike . . . of any man known to me in America." Unfortunately, the editor of the *Chicago Tribune* did not concur with such sentiments. The dispute between Lloyd and Joseph Medill that would lead to Lloyd's resignation from the newspaper in 1885 stemmed from egos and the changing nature of Gilded Age journalism.[31]

If nothing else, the Civil War established daily newspapers such as the *Chicago Tribune* as a part of American life. Few Chicagoans did not have some stake in the war and the *Tribune* and the other daily Chicago newspapers were a primary source of information for them on the battles and the political events surrounding them. The interest in war stories de-emphasized the opinion function in most newspapers and readers looked more to reporters for their information and less to an editor for his view or personality. News became the primary product of a newspaper, and reporters were the ones who provided it.[32]

These changes were personally irksome to Joseph Medill. He had lost editorial control of the *Tribune* during the war in part due to his disinterest in providing war news. Since his return to the editor's chair in 1874, he had never allowed the paper to stray too far from his Republican leanings in either the opinion or news columns. Medill believed that a good newspaper was obligated to stand for its party under all circumstances, even if that party was wrong. Newspapers needed to be profitable, but Medill was not consumed with a bottom-line, business mentality, as were other Chicago newspapers, especially the *Chicago Daily News*. In the end, the *Chicago Tribune* existed to promote Republicanism, and Medill believed that every other function of the paper was subservient to that cause.[33]

Many in the generation of postbellum reporters, including Henry Demarest Lloyd, objected to Medill's partisan view of journalism. They saw themselves as the rising stars of the newspaper business. To celebrate their growing influence, they, like Lloyd, demanded salaries rather than pay based on the number of stories or editorials written each week. They gathered together for mutual criticism and collegiality in Chicago during the 1870s and started their own press club in 1880. They also tried to define appropriate journalistic conduct. One standard was that editors should not censor experienced writers and reporters. Another was that partisanship should not be more important than facts in a story.[34]

Medill's failure to recognize Lloyd's rising literary star was bad enough, but their egos exploded when Medill began dictating what editorials Lloyd could or could not write at about the time "Lords" appeared. Medill supported the presidential bid of James G. Blaine, even though he had severely ridiculed the Maine Senator in previous campaigns. His erratic sympathies led a competing newspaper to call the *Tribune* the "leap year Republican sheet." Lloyd viewed Medill's endorsement as a professional and personal rebuke and began attacking Blaine in his editorials. Medill had given Lloyd the right to do so when he had named him chief editorial writer in 1880. Nevertheless, Medill retaliated by restricting Lloyd to business editorials for the duration of the political campaign in the hope that Lloyd would stay away from politics. Lloyd was so insulted that he determined to embarrass his employer's presidential candidate on the editorial page of the *Tribune* whenever he could until the November election. His thoughtfully crafted, articulate political editorials always began by discussing business conditions but then relentlessly condemned Blaine and the Republican party in the remaining paragraphs. Medill tried to counter Lloyd's attacks in his own editorials, but the opinion page of the *Chicago Tribune* had a split personality for the duration of the 1884 campaign.[35]

As irritating as this battle of editorial wills was for readers, it was even more stressful to the sensitive Lloyd. He complained about the distraction that the fight with Medill presented for his other writings in a letter to his mother in 1885:

I have gone to the edge of the abyss and I have not gone over. The battle has left me weak and sore. To whom should a man confess if not to his mother? Pray for me, and that the strength wasted on unnecessary temptation may somehow be given to me for my work.

Lloyd was still bitter about Medill's treatment of him eighteen years later. He wrote his wife in reference to the editor, "Pat him on the back, get everything out of him that was possible, but never advance him in pay or position." Emotionally and physically exhausted, Lloyd launched an indirect final volley at Medill in February 1885, assailing Blaine and all forms of privilege through the Vanderbilt family, which had recently lost a fortune speculating on railroad stocks. "The Vanderbilts got rich faster than any other family of modern times had done . . . but that was not enough," he wrote. "Fortunately . . . the judgment of the Vanderbilts has been as bad as their intentions, and they make a vanquished exit to their own loss and the profit of all the rest of us." A few days later, he made a quiet exit from the *Chicago Tribune* newsroom and never worked for the newspaper again.[36]

NOTES

1. George T. Rider, "The Pretensions of Journalism," *North American Review*, 135(November 1882): 471–483.

2. HDL, Small Notebook, 1879, HDL mf.

3. Nineteenth-century *Chicago Tribune* editorials did not have bylines and efforts to determine authorship are speculative at best. Chester M. Destler maintained that "Lloyd's numerous *Chicago Tribune* unsigned editorials can be identified by his peculiar style, October, 1872–February 26, 1885." However, E. Jay Jernigan observed, "I have found it impossible to identify with confidence any *Tribune* editorials as Lloyd's unless they were signed." A number of Lloyd editorials are identified as his in his papers but his college education and world view distinguish his writings from his less educated, more parochial colleagues. Although it is possible that some editorials attributed to Lloyd may be the work of others, those that have his style are attributed to him in this study. See Destler, "Henry Demarest Lloyd and the Empire of Reform Bibliography," unpublished MSS, Library of Congress, 25 and Jernigan, *Lloyd*, 151.

4. *New York Sun*, 12, 13 November 1878; HDL, "The National Black List," 4 January 1878; "Finance and Trade," 18 January 1878; "A Giant Monopoly," 23 November 1878; and "The Oil Monopoly," 26 November 1878, all *C.T.*

5. Elisha G. Patterson to HDL, 18 December 1879; G. Shiras, Jr. to HDL, 26 December 1879; Thomas P. Fowler to HDL, 7 May 1881; John A. Lemon to HDL, 17 May 1881; Roger Sherman to HDL, 15 March 1880, 21 March 1881, 23 May 1881; all in HDL, Wisc.; small notebook A, 1879, HDL, mf; and Roger Sherman to HDL, 2, 31 January and 18 July 1880, all in Roger Sherman papers, Yale University Library.

6. "The Cure for Vanderbiltism," a conversation delivered to the Chicago Literary Club, 12 January 1880, various Chicago Literary Club documents, Wisconsin Historical Society.

7. CLS, *Lloyd*, I, 58–60; William Dean Howells to HDL, 6 December 1880, in

HDL, mf; Robert Lee Hough, *The Quiet Rebel: William Dean Howells as Social Commentator* (Hamden, CT: Archon Books, 1968), 25–36; Gregory L. Crider, "William Dean Howells and the Gilded Age: Socialist in a Fur-lined Overcoat," *Ohio History*, 88(Autumn 1979): 408–418; and Robert William Chambers, "The Influence of Magazine Journalists on the Rise of Realism in America, 1870–1890" (Ph.D. diss., University of Texas, 1964), 56–62.

8. HDL, "The Story of a Great Monopoly," *Atlantic Monthly*, 47(March 1881): 317–334; CLS, *Lloyd* I, 61; HDL to Harper and Brothers, 19 February 1894, in HDL, Wisc; Sean D. Gashman, *America in the Gilded Age* (New York: New York University Press, 1984), 61–62; and Filler, *Crusaders*, 25–26.

9. *C.T.*, 22 February 1881; Thomas Powell Fowler to HDL, 7 May 1881; Roger Sherman to HDL, 21 March 21 1881; and Oliver F. Aldis to HDL, 20 February 1881; all in HDL, Wisc.; CLS, *Lloyd* I, 61; Destler, *Empire of Reform*, 130–133; *Oil, Paint, and Drug Reporter*, 19(3 March 1881): 230; Sproat, *Best Men*, 161–162; Frederick, *Knights of the Golden Rule*, 63; "The Fallacies of the Antimonopoly League," *Nation*, 32(24 March 1881): 199–201; and "Thurber vs. Fink," *Nation*, 32(21 April 1881): 273–274.

10. John B. Clark, *The Federal Trust Policy* (Baltimore: The Johns Hopkins University Press, 1931), 17–18; Hans B. Thorelli, *The Federal Anti-Trust Policy: Organization of an American Tradition* (London: George Allen and Unwin Ltd., 1954), 134; Ralph W. and Mauriel E. Hidy, *History of the Standard Oil Company (New Jersey): Pioneering in Big Business, 1882–1911* (New York: Harper Brothers, 1955), 203; Destler, *Empire of Reform*, 131; Thomas, *Alternative*, 137–140; and Spiller, *Literary History of the United States* (New York: Macmillan Publishing Company, Inc., 1974), 979.

Regarding the controversy over Lloyd's facts, see Allan Nevins, *John D. Rockefeller: The Heroic Age of American Enterprise* (New York: Charles Scribner's Sons, 1940); Chester M. Destler, "Wealth Against Commonwealth, 1894 and 1944," *American Historical Review*, 50(October 1944): 49–72; Nevins, "Communication," *American Historical Review*, 50(October 1944): 676–689; Destler, "A Commentary on the Communication from Allan Nevins in the *American Historical Review*, unpublished manuscript, April, 1945, in the collection of the State Historical Society of Wisconsin; Destler, "The Standard Oil, Child of the Erie Ring, 1868–1872: Six Contracts and a Letter," *Mississippi Valley Historical Review*, 33(June 1946): 89–114; Nevins, *Study in Power: John D. Rockefeller, Industrialist and Philanthropist* (New York: Charles Scribner's Sons, 1953); and Earl Lantham, ed., *John D. Rockefeller: Robber Baron or Industrial Statesman* (Boston: D.C. Heath, 1949).

Also see Jules Abels, *The Rockefeller Billions: The Study of the World's Most Stupendous Fortune* (New York: Macmillan, 1965); Bruce Bringhurst, *Antitrust and the Oil Monopoly: The Standard Oil Cases, 1890-1911* (Westport, CT: Greenwood Press, 1979); and Joseph Pusateri, "The Rehabilitation of the 'Robber Barons'," *Cithara*, 10(Spring 1969): 43–55.

11. Amos G. Warren to HDL, 14 April 1895; HDL to George A. Gates, 23 May 1895; John J. Hamilton to HDL, 17 July 1897; William T. Harris to HDL, 11 December 1897; and Charles Edward Russell, "Introduction," typed MS, 24 December 1911, all in HDL, Wisc.; *The Multitude*, n.d., circa 1903; and "History of U.S. in Marx's Studies," *Daily Worker*, 31 March 31 1938; all in HDL, mf.; and Charles Edward

Russell, *The Greatest Trust in the World* (New York: Ridgway Thayer, 1905).

12. Small Notebook A, 1879, HDL mf; HDL to Albert Fink, 20 December 1880, and Fink to HDL, 4 April 1881, both in HDL, Wisc.; and HDL, "Railroads," *C.T.*, 1 January 1878.

13. HDL to Gates, 23 May 1895; Thomas Bailey Aldrich to HDL, 10, 24 April 1882; all in HDL, Wisc.; and "The Political Economy of Fifty Millions," a conversation delivered to the Chicago Literary Club, 10 April 1882, various Chicago Literary Club documents, State Historical Society of Wisconsin.

14. HDL, "The Political Economy of Seventy Three Million Dollars," *Atlantic Monthly*, 50(July 1882): 69–81; various Lloyd notebook entries, 1879, 1880, and 1881, HDL, mf.; Frederick, *Knights of the Golden Rule*, 60–65; and Walter E. Houghton, *The Victorian Frame of Mind, 1830–1870* (New Haven, CT: Yale University Press, 1957).

15. Thomas K. McCraw, *Prophets of Regulation* (Cambridge, MA: Belknap Press, 1984), 1–56.

16. F. B. Thurber to HDL, 20 June 1882; Henry R. Gorringe to HDL, 20 June 1882; and George Iles to HDL, n.d., circa 1889, all in HDL, Wisc.; *New York Times*, 17 June, 2 July 1882; CLS, "Political Economy" MS, n.d., circa 1936; all in HDL, mf.; untitled commentary, *Nation*, 34(22 June 1882): 522; HDL, "Political Economy and the Goulds," *Nation*, 34(29 June 1882): 543; and Lee Benson, *Merchants, Farmers and Railroads* (Cambridge, MA: Harvard University Press, 1955), 115–132.

17. HDL, "The Railroad Pool," 3 November, "Pennsylvania Railroad," 5 November, "Vanderbilt's Will," 21 December, and "Jay Gould's Latest Scheme," 31 December 1877; "Railroad Legislation," 26 September, "Railroad Plunder–The Remedy," 4 October, "The Vanderbilt-Gould Combination," 28 November 1879; "Vanderbilt's Folly," 20 January, "Cheaper Passenger Rates," 27 March 1880; "American Pasha," 30 December 1881; "Kings's Horses and King's Men," 11 October 1882; "Suburban Railroading," 7 January, and "Railroad Annexation," 12 April 1883; "Mistake of the Railroads," 2 December; "Rights of Railroad Property," 4 December; "Beauties of Watered Stock," 8 December; "Railroads and the Farms," 9 December; "Nation and the Railroads," 13 December; "The Central Pacific Monopoly," 17 December; "How High Freights Affect Cities," 18 December; "Two Kinds of Railroad Men," 20 December; "Union Pacific," 24 December, all 1884; "Reagan's Writing on the Wall," 10 January; "The Union Pacific Stock Never Paid For," 12 January; "The Senate Railroad Bill," 14 January; "Railroads are not Private," 17 January; "Pacific Railroad Debt," 30 January; "Pools a Failure," 7 February; "A Railway Age," 10 February 1885; all in *C.T.*; Charles H. Van Wyck to HDL, 7 May 1884 and HDL to Van Wyck, 25 January 1885, both in HDL, Wisc.; Wendt, *Tribune*, 273–275; and Klein, *Gould*, 242–243.

18. HDL, "Our Land: The Story of the Dissipation of Our Great National Inheritance," 17 March 1883, and "Public Land Frauds," 16 November 16 1884, both in *C.T.* and Wendt, *Tribune*, 273.

19. "California Cornered," *C.T.*, 8, 13 October 1883.

20. "H. D. Lloyd letters in *Chicago Tribune*, July 1881"; "H. D. Lloyd letters in *Chicago Tribune*, 1883;" "Undoing Duluth," *Superior Times*, 16 July 1881; "What the Invited Correspondent of President Villard's Party Thinks of the Head of the Lakes," *Duluth Tribune*, 19 July 1881; "Villard as He Saw Him: Mr. Lloyd Recalls an Old Story," *Seattle Daily Times*, 12 October 1901; all in HDL, mf.; Richard McLeod, "The Development of Superior, Wisconsin as a Western Transportation Center," *Journal of*

the West, 13(Autumn 1974): 17–27.

21. H. L. Nelson to HDL, 24 July 1899, in HDL, Wisc.; CLS, *Lloyd* I, 54–55; Destler, *Empire of Reform*, 114; James B. Hedges, *Henry Villard and the Railways of the Northwest* (New York: Russell and Russell, 1930); Henry Villard, *Memoirs of Henry Villard: Journalist and Financier, 1835–1900* (Boston: Houghton and Mifflin, 1904); and White, *Autobiography*, 351, 366.

22. Untitled financial columns, *C.T.*, 29 November, 13, 16, 24, 27 December 1874; 7 February, 7, 9, 10, 11, 17, 18, 27 March 1875; Pierce, *History of Chicago* 3, 64–81; Andreas, *Chicago* 1, 581–586; and John Moses and Joseph Kirkland, eds., *The History of Chicago, Illinois* (Chicago: Munsell and Company, 1885, 333–351.

23. HDL, "Making Bread Dear," *North American Review*, 137(August 1883), 118–136; Charles Partridge to HDL, 8 May 1883 and L. S. Vetealy to HDL, 2 June 1883, both in HDL, Wisc.; and "Board of Trade Morals," *C.T.*, 19 December 1884.

24. Various clippings in HDL, mf.; Winton E. Scarritt to HDL, 12 October 1883; L.S. Metcalf to HDL, 2 June 1883; Van Buren Denslow, "Board of Trade Morality," *North American Review*, 137(October 1883): 372–387; and eight letters between HDL and Juno N. Jewet, 14–27 August 1883, in HDL, Wisc.

25. "New Rules on Your Board of Trade," 5 March 1875; "Options on the Board of Trade," 11 November 1877; "Board of Trade Gambling," 14 November 1877; "The Social Rage for Gambling in Grain," 28 September 1879; "Bucket Shops," 27 March 1880; "The Bucket-Shops Ought to be Suppressed by Law," 24 November 1880; "The New Board of Trade Building," 26 December 1880; "Sage's Puts and Calls," 18 May 1884; "Barreled Pork," 1 June 1884; and "Board of Trade Morals," 19 December 1884; all in *C.T.*; "Corners in Grain," *Nation*, 35(September 14, 1882): 214–215; Pierce, *Chicago* III, 81–92; Ewert, "*Inter-Ocean*," 65–66; Ann Fabian, *Card Sharps, Dream Books, and Bucket Shops: Gambling in Nineteenth-Century America* (Ithaca, NY: Cornell University Press, 1990); untitled editorial, *The Current*, 2 (October 1884): 226; and "Gambling and Business," *The Current*, 9 (December 24, 1887): 58–59, both in HDL, mf.

26. Johnson N. Camden and John C. Welch, "The Standard Oil Company," *North American Review*, 136(February 1883): 181–200; and Hidy, *Standard Oil*, 211–213.

27. HDL, "Lords of Industry," *North American Review*, 138(June 1884): 535–553 and Thorelli, *Antitrust*, 133.

Also in HDL, *Lords of Industry* (New York: G. P. Putnam's Sons, 1910), 116–147.

28. HDL, "Lords of Industry," 553, and Frederick, *Knights of the Golden Rule*, 63–64.

29. *Age of Steel*, 4 (24 May 1884); *Bradstreet's*, 9 (24 May 1884); *John Swinton's Paper*, 25 December 1884; all in HDL, mf.; *Pall Mall Gazette*, as cited in William Clark to HDL, 23 May 1884, HDL, Wisc.; and Destler, *Empire of Reform*, 138–139.

30. Louis M. Hacker, "Henry Demarest Lloyd," *Encyclopedia of Social Sciences* (New York: Macmillan, 1933), 554–555; Louis Filler, *Crusaders for American Liberalism* (New York: Harbourt, Brace and Co., 1939), 26; Richard Hofstadter, *The Age of Reform: From Bryan to F.D.R.* (New York: Alfred A. Knopf, 1956), 186; Judson A. Grenier, "The Origins and Nature of Progressive Muckraking" (Ph.D. diss., University of California-Los Angeles, 1955), 25; Herbert Shapiro, ed., *The Muckrakers and American Society* (Boston: D.C. Heath, 1968), v; John M. Harrison and Harry H.

Stein, eds., *Muckraking Past, Present, and Future* (University Park: Pennsylvania State University Press, 1973), 27; David M. Chalmers, *The Muckrake Years* (New York: Van Nostrand, 1974), 8; Warren T. Francke, "Investigative Exposure in the Nineteenth-Century: The Journalistic Heritage of the Muckrakers" (Ph.D. diss., University of Minnesota, 1974), 246; and Robert Miraldi, *Muckraking and Objectivity: A Journalism's Colliding Traditions* (New York: Greenwood Press, 1990), 28.

31. Robert Louis Stevenson to George Iles, 14 December 1887; Iles to HDL, 19 December 1894, 4 August 1896; and HDL to Iles, 6 September 1896; all in HDL, Wisc.

32. Summers, *Press Gang*, 2–5; Dicken-Garcia, *Journalistic Standards*, 51–62; Schudson, *Discovering the News*, 66–87; Edward L. Carter, "The Revolution in Journalism During the Civil War," *Lincoln Herald*, 73(Winter 1971): 229–241; and Louis M. Starr, *Bohemian Brigade: Civil War Newsmen in Action* (New York: Alfred A. Knopf, 1954).

33. Tebbel, *Dynasty*, 53–58; Harris L. Dante, "The *Chicago Tribune*'s 'Lost' Years, 1865–1874," *Journal of the Illinois State Historical Society*, 58(Summer 1965): 139–114; Tracy Elmer Strevey, "Joseph Medill and the *Chicago Tribune* During the Civil War Period" (Ph.D. diss., University of Chicago, 1930); Lloyd Wendt, *Chicago Tribune: The Rise of a Great American Newspaper* (Chicago: Rand McNally and Co., 1979); and Philip Kinsley, *The Chicago Tribune: Its First Hundred Years* (Chicago: The Chicago Tribune, 1946).

34. Schudson, *Discovering the News*, 66–71; Baldasty, *Commercialization of News*, 88–91; and Dicken-Garcia, *Journalistic Standards*, 175–222.

35. "Mr. Blaine and *The Tribune*," *C.T.*, 7 May 1884; "Dangerous Democratic Finance," and "Not Bad for Hard Times," both *C.T.*, 22 October 1884; untitled editorial, *C.T.* 27 October 1884; *Radical Review*, 2 (20 September 1884): 1; Sproat, *Best Men*, 118–141; Klein, *Gould*, 392–393; Destler, *Empire of Reform*, 138–147; Ewert, "Inter-Ocean," 67–75; and Wendt, *Chicago Tribune*, 272–275.

36. HDL to Maria Lloyd, n.d., circa 1885; William Clarke to HDL, 22 October 1884; and HDL to JBL, 26 February 1903; all in HDL, Wisc.; 1885 Notebook, HDL, mf.; JBL Diary, 28 February 1885 and Bross Diary, 23, 24, 28 February, 3 March 1883, both CHS; Andreas, *History of Chicago* III, 696; "Not a Merry War," 14 February 14, and "Abdication of the Vanderbilts," 15 February 1885, both in *C.T.*; and Wendt, *Tribune*, 273–275.

4

A New Calling

A few months before his death in 1903, a friend asked Henry Demarest Lloyd to reflect upon his career as a writer and reformer. Lloyd had many reasons to be cynical. He had seen the fledgling labor movement torn apart by the Haymarket Square bombing and Pullman Strike of 1894. He had been part of the Populist movement that flourished and then died with the failed 1896 presidential bid of William Jennings Bryan. He had watched the number of monopolies grow despite efforts such as "Story of a Great Monopoly," "Lords of Industry," and *Wealth Against Commonwealth*. In spite of such events, Lloyd remained an optimist, writing, "The reformer is a poet, a creator. He sees visions and fills the people with their beauty; and by the contagion of virtue his creative impulse spreads among the mass, it begins to climb and build."[1]

Part of that optimism was born in the ashes of Lloyd's resignation from the *Chicago Tribune* in 1885 as he embarked on a new career as a freelance advocate journalist and writer. Even the 1886 Haymarket Square bombing, which indirectly destroyed much of his personal life, did little to quell Lloyd's hope for a better future. He wrote his first book in 1889, the story of a northern Illinois labor dispute, as an answer to the Gilded Age social question, and an article on child labor. Wary of monopolies, he paid for most of the book himself and published the article in the alternative labor press. In 1887, he composed a response to Social Darwinism, the utilitarian philosophy of "root, hog, or die" as William Graham Sumner once described it, called "The New Conscience," and began the development of a personal philosophy that sought to reconcile his pragmatic and idealistic natures. The end of the decade saw him busy at work on his opus against monopolies, *Wealth Against Commonwealth*, which was published in 1893. Before any of these projects could be completed, Lloyd needed to settle some personal problems and regain his delicate health.

The Wayside remained the center of Lloyd's life during the 1880s. He basked in its tranquility, escaping the demands of his magazine-writing career and the disappointments of the *Chicago Tribune*. He and his wife Jessie walked along the rocky Lake Michigan shoreline or he and his father-in-law William Bross hunted deer and other game in nearby Hubbard Woods. The Lloyds' two sons thrived in their suburban setting and Jessie was a leader in Winnetka's upper-class social set. When Lake Michigan failed to properly cool the Wayside during the heat of the summer, William Bross sent his daughter and her family on expense-paid vacations to the Adirondack Mountains and the Rhode Island coast. Although not perfect, Lloyd's life was not bad for a man who always felt that he was operating at a disadvantage.[2]

As befitted his sensitive constitution, Lloyd was plagued by a number of health complications during the 1880s. A concern that he might have inherited a family propensity for migraine headaches sent him to a New York osteopath, but the headaches ceased on their own with time. He developed a "a high, fierce headache and backache" during an 1882 Colorado hunting trip and barely made it home to Winnetka. Jessie hovered over him for days, as he battled a fever of more than 104 degrees before he recovered. Bad plumbing gave Lloyd sewer gas poisoning, and he suffered from sciatica as well. To add to his troubles, Jessie's health declined. She bore their third son, David Demarest, named after one of Lloyd's two younger brothers, in 1883, but had to travel to New York for an operation in 1884. She experienced several miscarriages before delivering their fourth and final son, John, named after Lloyd's favorite grandfather, in 1886.[3]

Insomnia and related stress disorders bothered Lloyd as his conflict with Joseph Medill worsened. Stretched to his mental and physical limits, he embarked with his wife on an extended vacation to Europe in February 1885. Technically, Lloyd had not yet resigned from the *Chicago Tribune*, only taken a leave of absence. Still, Joseph Medill had made his return all but impossible. Lloyd could have his old job back, but from that point on either Medill or Alfred Cowles, another co-owner, would have to personally approve all of his editorials before publication. Medill's dictum was not only hurtful to Lloyd's professionalism, it was insulting because Lloyd was a stockholder in the paper and entitled to some influence in its management. Out of sympathy for his son-in-law in 1885, William Bross granted him control outright of the one hundred *Tribune* shares he had given him in 1874.[4]

Foreign travel was not a casual decision in the late nineteenth century. Both Lloyd and Jessie completed new wills, leaving their possessions and guardianship of their sons to Lloyd's sister Caro in case of the worst, and made additional provisions for the care and supervision of their children and the upkeep of the Wayside during their absence. In spite of such elaborate plans, Lloyd left Winnetka with an sense of guilt for abandoning his children. That was unusual because he had not taken an active role in their upbringing, leaving the chore to his wife and their servants. He admonished his oldest son Will to be careful in the use of "firecrackers and torpedoes" during the upcoming Fourth of July festivities. "We don't want to get any cable dispatches about blown-out eyes and blown-off thumbs," he wrote.[5]

In spite of such preparations, the trip proved to be a trial for both of the Lloyds. Jessie suffered from seasickness and spent most of the Atlantic passage in her cabin. Following brief rest stops in London and Paris, the couple enjoyed Italy for a brief period only to have Jessie contract a severe case of typhoid fever. Lloyd immediately took her to a hospital in the Swiss mountains and spent the rest of the summer of 1885 caring for her until she was well enough to return home. He was suffering from nervous prostration, and William Bross advised him to remain in Europe and "take appropriate expense and all the time you need to get perfectly well." After seeing Jessie off, Lloyd returned to England and journeyed about the island nation with his brother David, who was living in Paris at the time. They visited Parliament and met several members, including James Bryce, who was writing his influential *The American Commonwealth* at the time. Bryce recognized Lloyd's name from his articles and gave him letters of introduction to the "the best doors in Cambridge, Edinboro [sic], and Aberdeen." A side excursion provided a brief glimpse of the Prince of Wales, the future King Edward VII, whom Lloyd compared to "St. Nicholas' bowlful of jelly."[6]

The pair also met English artist and philosopher William Morris. Best known for his poetry and paintings, Morris shared John Ruskin's fascination for medievalism and was regarded as something of a reincarnation of the English critic. He was the founder of the Fabian Society, a utopian group that advocated a uniquely British, non-Marxist form of socialism. The Fabians were still organizing in the 1880s but were eager to share their ideas, including a belief in the natural evolution of socialism in contrast to Marx's class struggle theory, with their American guest. Lloyd was as attracted to Fabianism as he was repulsed by Morris. He found the latter to be a humorless "Norse God style of fellow, big, broad, hairy, [and] loud" and was alarmed by Morris's "[free love] doctrines which would reduce love to the miscellaneous intercourse that would keep mankind on the level of a herd of wild dogs." Nevertheless, Lloyd found much to admire in Fabianism, especially its more passive solution to class warfare. He told a correspondent several years later:

If I were in England I should certainly have affiliated with the Fabian Society. I have been revolted [in the U.S.] by the hard tone of the German socialists, who are about all we have, and by the practical falsity of the doctrine they constantly reiterate, that this crisis must be met by a class struggle, and that the working people alone are to be trusted.

Lloyd corresponded with the Fabians for the remainder of his life, serving as an American correspondent for the *Progressive Review*, a Fabian monthly started by John Hobson and William Clarke.[7]

As he traveled about England, Lloyd considered his future with the *Tribune*. The urge to pursue his own interests was becoming stronger than the need for the security of an everyday job. By September 1885, he confided to Jessie, "I doubt whether I will go back to the *Tribune*." The relatively small number of *Tribune* readers who responded to his editorials and articles also entered into his calculations, especially in comparison to the larger number of people who had seen his national magazine articles:

I think perhaps the time has come for me to devote myself to a larger constituency—a constituency I already have. I can not work for *both*. That did well enough when I was willing to burn my candle at both ends in my enthusiasm, but I must now choose one to serve and follow.[8]

In letters to Jessie, Lloyd pretended to be resting in England, writing of fleecy clouds, soft breezes, and bright sunshine, but he was hurrying about the island to see as many sights as he could. The odyssey finally came to an end in the fall of 1885 when Lloyd suffered a serious relapse of nervous prostration. An English doctor ordered him to bed for six weeks, and his brother David attended him until he was well enough to return home. En route across the Atlantic Lloyd made friends with Edwin D. Mead, a Boston magazine editor who would prove a valuable advisor in the years ahead. Their shipboard discussions reinvigorated Lloyd, as did a short stay in the Adirondack Mountains, and he appeared to have recovered his health when he returned to Winnetka. Unfortunately an unsuccessful bid to buy the *Chicago Journal* in late 1885 plunged him into another round of depression and he quickly relapsed. Jessie, who was pregnant with their fourth son at the time, wrote in her diary, "As day after day goes by and Henry has not yet been able to go back to work, but still has sleepless nights and terrible headaches by day, I don't feel sure that our hard pull is over yet. This year of sore trial, of nearness and separation has almost seemed to alter our life and thought."[9]

Lloyd spent the winter months of 1886 recuperating at the Wayside. It was there that his father-in-law expressed concern that he might be enjoying the fruits of his one hundred shares of *Chicago Tribune* stock more than he should. In words William Bross would soon regret, he admonished his unemployed son in law, "If [the stock] should prompt you to sit down at ease it will prove the worst possible curse for you. Only in reasonable and active exertion, both of mind and body, can you receive health and long life. . . . Of course I leave your work to be pursued at your own choice but I beg you to *choose* and to *act*."[10]

Lloyd took his father-in-law at his word. First, he traveled to Mexico with his father-in-law, returning home when the high altitude brought about a relapse of his insomnia. Next, he returned to England with a friend to finish the sightseeing that he had been forced to stop the previous fall. It was in England that he learned of the Haymarket bombing. Upon the completion of his English odyssey, Lloyd busied himself back home by investigating the situation of the eight Haymarket anarchists. He visited each one in their jail cells and attended their trial, which transpired over the summer of 1886. He became convinced that at least seven of the eight were being punished for the crimes of speaking out, being poor, and being foreign born. He was concerned that Haymarket was a turning point in American history, a time when the Plutocrats sought to extend their control beyond government and business to individual Americans. As he explained in a speech he delivered at about the time the anarchists were convicted, "Every student of history knows that advancing despotism has always moved along the lines of least resistance, and that when a people begins to allow the rights of the poor and unpopular to be sacrificed it ends by losing all its own rights, and with its rights loses its safety, its riches, everything."[11]

He monitored the anarchists' unsuccessful appeals to the Illinois and U.S. Supreme courts, and his efforts culminated in a pardon petition written and presented to the Illinois governor by Lloyd six days before four of the anarchists were executed in early November 1887. In an unpublished manuscript, "Let the People's Voice Be Heard," written days after the executions, Lloyd blamed the deaths on the Christian church, which Lloyd believed was under the control of the Plutocrats and had allowed and even condoned the executions. He called for a new church, one of deed, not of doctrine:

The love [this church] bears to the weak and lowly and oppressed will shake the new tyrants of the industrial world out of their vested rights as surely as the gentle words of Jesus and Socrates drove the lords of the political world out of their divine rights. Passion of the moment may once and again run blood, but the blood will only make the grass greener and the harvest more golden.

Two months later, Lloyd wrote an angry essay denouncing the judge who had presided over the Haymarket trial in Chicago. When Joseph Medill refused to publish it in the *Tribune*, Lloyd turned to the competing *Chicago Herald*. Although Lloyd managed to save the lives of only two of the eight anarchists, Haymarket historians have lauded him for his efforts. Henry David called him "one of the most able and admirable men of his time" while Paul Avrich observed that "none worked harder to save the defendants than Henry Demarest Lloyd." One hundred years to the day of the Haymarket bombing, a poem was read at the site of the bombing in Chicago, and Lloyd was one of those honored in the poem.[12]

The executions were only the beginning of the Haymarket affair for Lloyd. In the months following the executions, his status in Chicago society declined from celebrity to social persona non grata. Chicago's native-born upper class viewed the executions not only as due punishment to the anarchists who supposedly inspired the bombing but as a warning to the flood of foreign-born immigrants then sweeping into their city with their unusual customs and political ideas. Months before the bombing, the *Chicago Daily News* had observed that "socialism in America is an anomaly, and Chicago is the last place on the continent where it would exist were it not for the dregs of foreign immigration that find lodgement here." Lloyd's support of the defendants was considered a betrayal to his class and country of origin and his and Jessie's names disappeared from guest lists, formerly close friends shunned them on the streets, and the doors of Chicago society once open to them were closed forever. The malice lingered for years, even after the Lloyds had built a new set of friends and the remaining Haymarket anarchists had been pardoned. In 1903, Jessie received an anonymous letter in the wake of her husband's death, admonishing her "to let his evil deeds die with him," a reference she and her family understood to mean Haymarket.[13]

More painful than their social repudiation was Jessie's estrangement from her father, William Bross. She had been warned of his anger in advance of the executions. She chanced upon Joseph Medill on a Chicago street corner one day in early 1887, and the editor tried to explain to her how distraught her father was over Lloyd's and her support of the defendants. Medill asked her, "Do you realize what you are doing, have you and Mr. Lloyd considered how this will influence your future?" Jessie looked at him and replied, "Do you suppose that any such consideration will stop Henry Lloyd from doing what he believes is right?" True to Medill's prediction, Bross disinherited Lloyd after the executions and never spoke to him again. He left his remaining estate, including four hundred shares of *Chicago Tribune* stock and his valuable real estate holdings, in a trust for the four Lloyd sons when they grew up. Jessie was granted a yearly annuity of $10,000 and the boys collectively received $11,000 a year for their support and education. The Winnetka land occupied by the Wayside was deeded to Jessie alone. Bross continued to visit his grandsons but never mentioned either Lloyd or Jessie in his personal diary again.[14]

Bross's decision had a variety of ramifications for the Lloyds. In Jessie's case, pride ran deep and she made no effort to reconcile with her father, writing in her diary the day of his death in 1890, "Why did I not go to him?" Deprived of her social connections, she became obsessed with her husband's career, directing his efforts and forbidding anyone to criticize him or his work in her presence. Children and friends were not allowed to interrupt or disturb him without her permission. Her chief goal in life became to nurture his career, and she lived vicariously through his activities. Only in passing references in her letters and writings is there a hint of the resentment she felt for the life that had denied to her by her gender and marriage.[15]

Bross tried unsuccessfully to alienate Lloyd's oldest son and his namesake,

William Bross Lloyd, from his parents. Will became impossible for anyone to control, and he was plagued by a similar lack of self-discipline throughout his life. He avenged himself on his grandfather by using his inherited money to espouse pacifism and other radical liberal causes. During World War I, a competing Chicago newspaper gloated that "One of the Owners of Tribune Attacks War," a reference to Will's pacifism. Will was dubbed "Chicago's Millionaire Communist" by another newspaper for his open support of the Industrial Workers of the World and the Communist Labor Party during the 1920s. Part of Will's pacifism was due to his first wife, but it can be said that one result of William Bross's anger over Haymarket was that the Bross and Lloyd family names became linked in the twentieth century to radicalism.[16]

For Lloyd, the security that had been so important to him as an adolescent and young adult eroded during the remainder of his life. By the early 1890s, the yearly allowance that William Bross had provided for Lloyd's children was being consumed by the cost of their private-school education. At the same time, the Medill family began diverting *Chicago Tribune* dividends into a new building, dramatically reducing the return on Lloyd's stock. Unable to survive on his wife's annuity alone, Lloyd started charging for speeches and became increasingly more prudent with his money. Friends with charitable requests were told he would get back to them when he had finished his "forty years in the wilderness," but the forty years was never completed, and Lloyd died a man of more modest means than most of his relatives and friends imagined.[17]

The Lloyds did not remain outcasts forever. Chicago's social set was replaced at the Wayside by an eclectic assortment of independent thinkers and fellow outsiders. Lloyd joined the Chicago Ethical Culture Society, a group that sponsored philosophical lectures and readings. He began a correspondence with a onetime *Tribune* colleague, Henry Huntington, that extended for years. He and his wife invited local and national social reform figures, people such as Jane Addams, Clarence Darrow, John R. Commons, Samuel Gompers, Eugene V. Debs, Florence Kelley, Booker T. Washington, William Dean Howells, and Charlotte Perkins Gilman, to stay with them at the Wayside. During the summer of 1889, the Lloyds built a summer cottage near Newport, Rhode Island, and developed a set of Eastern friends including Edward Everett Hale, Social Gospel minister B. Fay Mills, *Springfield* (Massachusetts) *Republican* publisher Samuel Bowles, Sylvester Baxter of the *Boston Herald*, and naturalist Margaret Morley. Still, Lloyd never completely recovered from the ostracism he had experienced in Chicago. Caro Lloyd recalled that he "once told me about how hard he found it not to have the companionship in the beaten track of humanity . . . he said he thought of moving to London, he ought to, there he would be free from personal opprobrium; that shortly before he had met an old friend on the streets of Chicago, and he had given him a look of the most intense human hatred which was possible." He evoked something of the hostility he felt for his adopted home town in a manuscript called "Chicago" that he wrote during the 1880s:

> Like a great, lank, sordid, stoop shouldered country boy.
> Possibilities immense or nil. . . .
> All lines of caste are thrown away; nothing but money counts in real social life, and
> money is quite as good as any other snobby reason for exclusiveness. . . .
> A happy go lucky town where everyone steals for himself and forgets that his neighbor
> has stolen in his turn. . . .
> Honesty is admired if possible come to think about it but it is ordinarily considered a
> mild or noxious form of insanity. . . .
> And it's all a matter of course. It's all a grab bag and if you can bribe the sunday
> school superintendent you get back more than your stake.[18]

Beyond Haymarket, Lloyd had at least one other, external push toward an outside career as a writer. One day in 1884, two years before Haymarket, a twenty seven-year-old coffin maker named Ethelbert Stewart walked into Lloyd's *Chicago Tribune* office and gave him documentary evidence of a coffin monopoly that had destroyed forty-thousand coffins the previous year to raise prices. Lloyd used the information for a *Tribune* editorial, "A Corner in Coffins," and his "Lords of Industry" article, and formed a lifelong friendship with "Bert" Stewart. In return for his information, Lloyd helped Stewart, who was handicapped by a speech impediment, to better employment. He recommended him as editor for the Chicago-based *Journal of the Knights of Labor*, the official organ of the largest nineteenth-century labor organization. Stewart was so radical in his *Journal* pronouncements that Joseph Medill warned him that the Haymarket defendants had been hanged to "show such fellows as you to keep your mouths shut." During the administration of Illinois Governor John Peter Altgeld, Stewart was hired as a field worker for the newly founded Illinois Bureau of Labor. From Illinois, Stewart went on to work for the U.S. Department of Labor, and became U.S. Commissioner of Labor Statistics from 1920 to 1932.[19]

Stewart's most valuable service to Lloyd came a few months after the coffin editorial. Irritated by Lloyd's oft stated social concerns, one of his coworkers challenged him to visit an actual working class neighborhood, something Lloyd had never done in all the years he had lived in Chicago. With Stewart as his guide, Lloyd walked the length of Archibold Avenue, one of the city's poorest and dirtiest immigrant slums. They stopped at one house, knocked on the door, and asked the nine-year-old boy who answered if his parents were home. The child replied that he was babysitting a younger brother while his mother visited their father in the hospital. Otherwise, he explained, he would have been out scavenging coal on railroad tracks to heat the family's shabby home. Stewart recalled:

Mr. Lloyd put his hand in his pocket and said to the boy, "what would you do if I gave you fifty cents?" The boy's face brightened, and he exclaimed, "Oh, fifty cents, I would go out and buy some beefsteak and then the whole family could have beef." Mr. Lloyd asked him if he did not want candy, but he said, "no, beefsteak" with a real relish of the taste of it.

Stewart explained to Lloyd that meat was a rarity in the slums of Gilded Age Chicago even though they stood just blocks from the busiest livestock yards in the world. Lloyd was so emotionally overcome by the encounter that he sat down and cried. In subsequent years, he continued to study the poor, obtaining a permit from the Chicago police that allowed him to enter slum dwellings at will. In contrast to Jane Addams and Ellen Gates Starr, who built their Hull House based on similar sights, Lloyd did not become a social worker, but his research did influence his writings.[20]

A result of Lloyd's slum visit was "The Political Economy of Child Labor," an article he wrote for Ethelbert Stewart's alternative press *Journal of the Knights of Labor* in 1887. Lloyd depended too much upon moral platitudes to discredit childhood labor, an unpopular late nineteenth-century practice that even President Rutherford B. Hayes considered "a blind folly." The secrecy of employers who used children on the job made it difficult for Lloyd to provide the statistical veracity that made his earlier advocacy writings convincing, so he took moral aim at the Social Darwinists who justified their abuse of children in the workplace as a logical extension of natural competition. "Under their gospel," Lloyd wrote, "the survival is not of the fittest, but of the fightingest." Lloyd contended that there could be no moral justification for child labor, noting, "By his treatment of the helpless we can infallibly tell how good a man is, and the same test will measure the virtues of a community. So judged, our industrial civilization is industrial savagery." Unfortunately, such attacks often had a negative effect, driving the practice further underground, and child labor was not effectively ended until the federal government enacted legislation around 1916.[21]

Lloyd's new free time also gave him an opportunity to reflect that had been denied to him by his job. He had always been an empiricist, preoccupied with the practical concerns of life such as financial and personal security. He enjoyed reading Emerson, especially Emerson's belief in the divinity of the individual and his rebellion from the Christian Church as an outmoded institution, but he found little else in Emerson or other social philosophers other than their general ideas about advancing public good. That began to change around the time that Lloyd met William M. Salter in 1886. Salter was a Unitarian theologian and a member of Felix Adler's ethical culture movement. He headed the Chicago ethical culture branch which Lloyd joined, lent him books on Kant and Hegel, and also shared with him his own *The Problem of Poverty*, which argued that poverty was neither necessary or inevitable and that employers needed to practice a "new morality." As the two became better friends, Lloyd learned that Salter believed the Haymarket anarchists innocent and shared his aversions to orthodox Protestantism and Social Darwinism. Beginning in 1886, Lloyd's personal notebooks showed a new intellectual direction, away from utilitarian thoughts about monopolies and his other writings, and more toward the creation of a personal social philosophy. "The moral sense of mankind has reached a stage of revolt which demands a wide, sweeping, radical change," Lloyd wrote in 1886. "If we wish the morally, socially fittest to survive we must provide the moral, social environment needed."[22]

Lloyd was also inspired by a nineteenth-century Italian revolutionary named Giusepe Mazzini. He first learned of Mazzini from the English Fabians in 1885 and read several of his essays while he was recovering his health the following year. Mazzini's best known work, *The Duties of Man*, published in 1844, held that all mankind, not just a particular messiah, were the children of God and had a right to a decent life. "Earth, matter, is the embodied thought of God, and sacred," Lloyd wrote. "All men are free to declare the thought of God, or what they think to be the thought of God, as it flows into their minds." Mazzini's contention was in contrast to Social Darwinists such as E. L. Youmans who argued that the poor were the inevitable result for those who could not compete and deserved to die. To Social Darwinists, well-meaning reforms such as settlement houses, public education, child labor laws, and government regulations contradicted natural law and had to be avoided to allow those fittest to survive and prosper. "Perhaps in four or five thousand years," Youmans observed, "evolution may have carried men beyond the [present] state of things." Lloyd was distressed by such thoughts, especially after his talks with the Haymarket anarchists and his walks through Chicago's ghetto. He held conventional Christianity largely to blame for condoning Social Darwinism and not becoming more involved in the lives of the poor. "Talk to the working people," Mazzini had written, "not in doctrines which they are too tired to follow, but in acts. These they can understand." Lloyd explained in a speech on Mazzini he delivered to the Chicago Ethical Culture Society in 1889, "A truth uttered was to Mazzini but half the truth: the other half was to execute it." His efforts on behalf of the Haymarket anarchists, labor unions, the poor, and others became his living testament to Mazzini's ideals.[23]

He articulated his evolving new philosophical thought first in a *Chicago Tribune* letter to the editor written three weeks before the Haymarket executions. In the letter, he argued that "Instead of showering smiles on the vice of spending money . . . why should we not teach that under the golden rule any one of us is worse than an infidel if we spend our money for laces and jewels and ermine, when but a few minutes walk distant our brothers [are] rotting day and night for want of decent houses which this same money would build?" In the months after the executions, he pondered possible solutions to the question he posed, writing in his notebook, "New Conscience—we must be economically fraternal and paternal, economically patriotic, economically religious. The individual alone can not fabricate the new conscience, nor obey it, alone."[24]

A more comprehensive answer was provided in "The New Conscience, or the Religion of Labor," a speech presented to the Chicago Ethical Culture Society in February 1888 and published a year later in the *North American Review*. The heart of Lloyd's new religion was the Judeo-Christian Golden Rule, but he went beyond simple platitudes. He argued that "The New Conscience" meant that all people, including the poor, were God's chosen, and that the much-feared organization of labor epitomized by the Haymarket bombing was not revolution but a remedy for revolution. Lloyd offered a religion of labor as an answer to industrialization and the Christian virtue of love as the religion's instrument of social change. "A new conscience takes its stand before all our institutions," Lloyd wrote, "and says to them: Labor shall not be a commodity, for the labor is the laborer." Evoking the legacy of abolitionism, Lloyd contended that "monopoly is force, and force is slavery, and slavery must be abolished." With a prediction that his new religion would end the impending class war before it started, Lloyd concluded his speech with a fitting nineteenth-century rhetorical flourish

In the sight of the new conscience wherever man walks, there is the Holy Land, and it raises the cross of the new crusade which shall deliver it from the infidels who deny the divine right of the people that the will of God shall be done on earth as in heaven. It insists that every question between men is a religious question, a question of moral economy before it becomes one of political economy . . . a church of the deed as well as the creed—a church that will not only preach Christ, but do Christ.

Lloyd's reference to Christ in his closing passage and his call for a new religion were revealing, for they indicated he was still operating within the intellectual framework of the Christianity he had known as a child even though he professed to be an atheist.[25]

As compelling as "The New Conscience" was in defining and analyzing the social question, it was naive and even counterproductive. Lloyd failed to explain how his new conscience would come about or to consider the coercive measures that would have been necessary to bring justice to late nineteenth-century workers. Without a more viable plan, his religion became another incomplete blueprint for Altruria. It was well received by left-wing ministers and reformers and it was widely reprinted both in the United States and outside. William M. Salter called it a "brilliant statement"; Henry George endorsed it, observing that his single tax concept fulfilled the spirit of Lloyd's new religion; and future Illinois Governor John P. Altgeld told Lloyd, "I would rather be the author of one such article than to hold any office in the gift of the American people." The English Fabian Society produced reprints and invited Lloyd to London to repeat his speech. Others were less encouraging. The *Chicago Tribune* criticized its former editorial editor for advocating what were termed useless "sentiments." The *Pittsburgh Telegraph* complained that the statement lacked a "concrete plan of relief." William Bross, who somehow made a habit of keeping track of the son-in-law he never spoke to, attended a reprise of Lloyd's speech delivered during the summer of 1888 at Chicago's Grand Opera House and noted in his journal that the proposal not "religiously sound." Lloyd's father Aaron read it and criticized his son for repudiating his more orthodox form of Christianity. As Charles Howard Hopkins observed, more moderate religious figures considered statements such as Lloyd's harmful because they were antagonistic toward organized religion and posited removing churches from any meaningful role in resolving the social question.[26]

Lloyd continued his intellectual development after "The New Conscience," filling more than twenty notebooks with wide-ranging, occasionally conflicting, and often haphazard philosophical thoughts before he died in 1903. He was never the "homespun realist" that Vernon L. Parrington portrayed him to be in *Main Currents of American Thought*. Instead David W. Noble described Lloyd's mature philosophy in *The Paradox of Progressive Thought* as a metaphysical "dualism between a real world that had to be conquered and an ideal that had to conquer." Mankind existed in a creative mediation between the ideal and real, theory and practice, passive and active, Lloyd believed. Society had ethical standards by which men could judge themselves, but individuals were still free to transcend society, to learn through inspiration what society should become, and then return to reform it according to their vision. Lloyd continued his studies of both Emerson and Mazzini, delivering speeches on each during the 1890s. He believed with Emerson that the material form could be conquered by spirit through the process of striving and creation. God neither knew nor controlled the future, existing only as the creative power within each individual, and it was man's responsibility to be the creative agent of God, the creator of himself and society. Lloyd remained a pragmatist at times. He quoted Emerson that "The highest virtue is always against the law. . . . To consecrate oneself to the right is always to move on a little in advance," writing, "Liberty is not escape from law, but the use of law. . . . the more law the more liberty." He continued to clothe "the ideals of labor with the highest religious sanctions," as James Dombrowksi observed. Still, his idealism was always present, even as just a few months before his death he toyed with but refused to join the Socialist Party. He wrote, "In the masses stirs a new born creative social consciousness with its message that all the reforms are one reform, and that that reform is the self-creation of a better individual by putting him to work as his own God at the creation of a better society."[27]

Lloyd's new belief in action led him to volunteer his efforts to alleviate the suffering of some one thousand Illinois coal miners and their families in 1889. Spring Valley was a coal town established in the early 1880s and located about eighty miles southwest of Chicago. In 1888, southern Illinois mine owners started a price war and the Spring Valley mines, along with their northern counterparts, were left with a surplus of higher-priced coal. The rest of the northern coal companies met the competition by cutting prices or wages, but the Spring Valley operators decided to stop production until the surplus was sold at their price. In the spirit of true Social Darwinism, no thought was given to the welfare of the miners or their families. As Lloyd wrote:

They had not struck; they had not asked for any increase in wages; they had made no new demands of any kind upon their employers. . . . The men were simply told to take out their tools at the close of the day, and not come back until they were bid. They were locked out. It was a strike, but it was a strike of millionaires against miners.[28]

The wage reductions touched off strikes at the other northern mines, and the governor appointed a special commission to investigate the situation. The commission reported that it had found no "actual cases of starvation" as a result of the strikes, but it had overlooked the town of Spring Valley because no strike had been called there. In reality, there were numerous cases of starvation, mainly among women, children, and the elderly, who had little or nothing to eat. Not only had the Spring Valley Coal Company laid off its work force, it had closed its company store, the only store that gave the miners credit. Even hurriedly planted crops were not enough to stem the slow death toll, and the coming of winter in 1889 offered the town's population little chance for hope.[29]

The Spring Valley situation was noteworthy because the company had enticed its workforce to Spring Valley with lucrative wages. With the workers captive, the company systematically reduced their pay and forced most into debt with exorbitant prices for food and rent. This made it impossible for them to quit. As Lloyd explained, for this particular form of wage slavery, the Spring Valley Coal Company was not condemned by the public but honored. Not only did its investors receive magnificent dividends, but corporate America congratulated it for its parsimony.[30]

Lloyd learned of the Spring Valley situation at his summer home on the coast of Rhode Island in August 1889, and he returned to investigate the situation. Expecting that he would support them, the company put on its best appearance for his visit, but Lloyd was appalled by the suffering he saw and the callousness displayed by the company. Unable to resist the miner's entreaties, he declared that the company deserved to be made an example for its violating of his "New Conscience" Golden Rule philosophy. He also saw the situation as an opportunity to practice his advocacy journalism to the betterment of the miners and their families, offering to provide "merciless exposure and just criticism" of the company.[31]

The Chicago press tried to ignore the lockout over the summer of 1889, but most of the newspapers, even the antilabor *Tribune*, came out against the company in the fall. Lloyd was ahead of them because he was living in Spring Valley, not sending reporters to visit. He began his campaign in October 1889 with a letter to the editor of the *Chicago Inter-Ocean* that was published under the headline "The Crisis at Spring Valley." He reported that the poverty in the area was so bad that even the county doctor would not treat the miners or their families unless he was paid first. The company responded to his charges by blaming unspecified "professional agitators and a partisan press" but did nothing to improve the situation, offering to hire back its workers at 60 percent of their former salaries. Lloyd next wrote "To Certain Rich Men," a letter to the editor directed specifically at the managers and owners of the Spring Valley Coal Company. It was published in a number of newspapers including the *Chicago Herald* and *New York Sun*. He named each member of the board of directors of the Spring Valley Coal Company, warning them "that this sort of thing will be held to be conspiracy, gentlemen millionaires, is certain as soon as the public get to grasp the motive and the result of your concerted attack upon the lives and liberties of the people." This time the company labeled Lloyd a "conscientious liar" in a letter to *The New York Times*, but its response was too late. Newspapers across the country declared it guilty of cruelty to its workers in the court of public opinion, due in part to Lloyd's efforts. The *Chicago Herald* called Lloyd's letter "one of the most powerful appeals for justice and one of the most eloquent denunciations of wrong which have come under the public eye for many a day." The *New York Sun* observed that the company was "in a very unfortunate position before the American people."[32]

Lloyd mistook the reaction to his Spring Valley letters as an endorsement of his "New Conscience" philosophy, but it was his exposure of the company's cruelties that was most helpful to the miners. Friends suggested he preserve his letters in "a more lasting form" as a benefit to labor, and he edited his hastily written dispatches during the winter of 1890. The resulting manuscript was too long for a newspaper or magazine article so Lloyd submitted it to a small Chicago book publishing company in April. The firm rejected it at first, noting "The people most interested [in it] are not book buyers," but Lloyd offered to pay all composition and manufacturing costs and *A Strike of Millionaires Against Miners: The Story of Spring Valley or An Open Letter to the Millionaires* was published during the summer of 1890. To make such accusations in a late-nineteenth-century newspaper or magazine article was not uncommon, but it was unusual to do so in a nonfiction book. The Boston magazine editor that Lloyd had befriended on his way back home from England in 1885 contended that nonfiction books rarely found a reading public, with Gilded Age Americans preferring fiction. Edwin D. Mead showed Lloyd's manuscript to an editor at Houghton Mifflin, one of the nation's largest publishing houses, and advised Lloyd, "He thinks you would make a mistake to publish it in book form, that you would not secure anything like so wide a reading or stir up so much discussion in that way as if you put what you have to say into a magazine article, to print in say the *North American Review* or the *Atlantic*. He says that books of that kind don't 'go' or are more likely not to accomplish what is expected of them." Lloyd persisted in the face of such opposition, with the view that nonfiction would sell in books if it was well written and compelling. He also saw books as a more permanent, and therefore more meaningful form for his advocacy journalism than newspapers or magazines.[33]

In spite of such intentions, Lloyd eventually dubbed *Millionaires* "my first and worst book." He told a friend in 1897 that he had been naive in thinking that laissez faire capitalists would be shamed by seeing their names and actions in print. "I was younger then than I am now," he explained. In spite of its factual facade, *Millionaires* was some two hundred pages of thinly disguised sermonizing, permeated at times by a smug, almost self-righteous tone. Lloyd did not yet have a clear idea of who made up his readership. Much of the book was directed at the mines' investors, not the public, and they ignored it. The majority had nothing to do with the daily management of the mines and lived hundreds of miles from them. Still, Lloyd warned them all, "If you continue your war on the miners, if you pocket the profits that success will bring you . . . if you usurp for your private profit all these trusts and grants . . . you will but repeat the folly of your medieval exemplars whose castles now decorate a better civilization with their prophetic ruins."[34]

Lloyd's assessment notwithstanding, *Millionaires* received an enthusiastic response from the few newspapers that received review copies. Complimentary notices appeared in the *Chicago Herald*, London *Labor World*, *Dover* (New Hampshire) *Democrat*, and *New York Commercial Advertiser*. The latter noted, "If the story is true, and it bears every appearance of truth, the Spring Valley mine owners have been guilty of damnable treachery and cruelty to their fellow man." American Federation of Labor president Samuel F. Gompers called it as a "great way" to help the coal miners. Frederick Engels thanked Lloyd for a copy and predicted that lockouts like Spring Valley would soon cripple capitalism in America. One reader compared it to Emile Zola's *Germinal*. Others were less certain of its merits. The *Chicago Tribune*, which was beginning to make a habit of bashing its stockholder and former editorial writer, noted that the "laws of supply and demand are inexorable." Chicago naturalist writer Joseph Kirkland challenged Lloyd's facts. Another reviewer dismissed it as "a chivalric effort for the defeated and downtrodden."[35]

Still, Lloyd's efforts helped reinforce the miners' resolve and they managed to win concessions in early 1890. New strikes broke out at Spring Valley in 1891, 1897, and 1898—all in an effort to empower the miners. One of the participants in the original lockout was a young miner named John Mitchell. Over the next decade, Mitchell would emerge as the president of the new United Mine Workers of America and became one of the most influential labor leaders in the early twentieth century. Lloyd donated paperback copies of *Millionaires* to labor newspapers to be given away as subscription premiums, helping the newspapers grow as he built his own reputation. Altogether, more than fifteen hundred copies were sold or distributed. For Lloyd, the most welcome word on *Millionaires* did not come until a dozen years later. In 1903, he learned that an Indiana miners' convention had voted him a resolution of thanks for his

Spring Valley letters back in 1889, but word had been delayed.   "Better late" he told Jessie.[36]

In an 1888 letter, Ethelbert Stewart made a reference to "Lords of Industry" and asked Lloyd:

I suppose you have noticed how your article in *North American Review* for June 1884 is being used in Congress just now on the "trust" question. I notice in Weaver's speech he refers to it as the "best authority extant." Suppose you "extant" from the same source a fuller and more exhaustive statement. I don't believe you can afford to let that paper remain the "best authority extant."

Stewart's question struck a responsive chord in Lloyd.   Even as he was developing "The New Conscience" and his Spring Valley letters, Lloyd was formulating a more ambitious project in his mind, one that would again bring together his two favorite topics, monopolies and John D. Rockefeller's Standard Oil Company. His intention was to produce the definitive indictment, the coup de grâce to monopolies, an intellectual effort that would cap more than ten years of research and study of the subject. Although *Wealth Against Commonwealth* failed to incite public opinion as Lloyd desired, it became the "best authority extant" for a decade and remains the most significant achievement of Lloyd's career.[37]

NOTES

1. HDL as quoted in Beal, *The Wayside*, 9; Sproat, *Best Men*, 46–69; Bremner, *From the Depths*, 16–30; Garraty, *New Commonwealth*, 321–331; and Trachtenberg, *Incorporation*, 71–78.

2. Destler, *Empire of Reform*, 144–146.

3. JBL Diary, 15 October, 15, 16, 17, 21 November 1882, 19 February 1883, 7, 9, 10, 11, 12, 15, 22 May 1884; Bross Diary, 5 June 1878, 12 April 1879, 16, 20, 22, 24, 26, 30 November 1882; HDL to JBL, n.d., circa 1884; all in CHS; A. S. Richardson to JBL, n.d., circa 1882 and Maria Lloyd to HDL, 14 June 1886, both in HDL, Wisc.; HDL to Edmund C. Stedman, n.d., circa 1880s, Columbia University Library Special Manuscript Collection; Thomas, *Alternative*, 147; and Destler, *Empire of Reform*.

4. "Not a Merry War," 14 February and "Abdication of the Vanderbilts," 15 February 1885, both in *C.T.*; JBL Diary, 28 February 1885 and Bross Diary, 24, 28 February, 3 March 1885, both CHS; and Wendt, *Tribune*, 273–275.

5. HDL and JBL wills dated 22 August 1882 and 25 February 1885; JBL to "My Precious Boys," 15 April, 1 May 1885; HDL to Will, Hall, and Demarest Lloyd, 17 July 1885; all in JBL, CHS.

6. JBL Diary, 28 February, 2, 4–8, 12, 13 March, 11 April, 1 May, 20, 24, 27 July, 7 August 1885; JBL to "my precious sons," 15 April 1885; HDL to Maria Lloyd, 30 May 1885; and William Bross to HDL, 17 June, 22 July 1885, all in CHS; HDL to Huntington, 20 July 1888 and HDL to JBL, 1, 5, 7, 12, 22 August 1885, all in HDL, Wisc.

7. HDL to JBL, 5 August, 2 September 1885, both in HDL, Wisc.; HDL to George Gates, circa 1895, as cited in CLS, *Lloyd*, I, 303; R. N. Berki, *Socialism* (New York: St. Martin's Press, 1975), 78–81; Margaret Cole, *The Story of Fabian Socialism* (Stanford, CA: Stanford University Press, 1961); and Frederick, *Knights of the Golden Rule*, 58.

Lloyd's recollection of William Morris is in "A Day with William Morris," *Mazzini and Other Essays* (New York: G. P. Putnam's Sons, 1910), 42–70.

8. Bross to HDL, 22 July, 22 August 1885 and HDL to Bross, 26 August 1885, all in JBL, CHS; HDL to JBL, 2 September 1885, in HDL, Wisc.; and "The Political Machinery of Socialism," unidentified clipping, 4 December 1886, in HDL, mf.

9. HDL to JBL, 5 September 1885; HDL to Huntington, 20 July 1888; Mead to HDL, 30 October 1885, all in HDL, Wisc.; Bross Diary, 13, 15 October 1885 and JBL Diary, 27 September 1885, both in CHS; and JBL as quoted in CLS, *Lloyd* I, 79.

10. William Bross to HDL, 22 July 1885, in CHS, and HDL to JBL, 1, 5, 7, 12, 22 August 1885, in HDL, Wisc.

11. "Haymarket speech," n.d., circa 1886, HDL, mf; Bross to HDL, 17 February 1886, JBL Papers; Agnes M. Johansen to Chester M. Destler, 14 August 1942 and William B. Lloyd to Destler, 14 August 1942, both in Chester Destler Papers; and Frances A. Book to HDL, 4 June 1886, HDL, Wisc.

12. "Let the People's Voice be Heard," unpublished MS, HDL, mf.; "Anarchists-Bar Association Speech," n.d., circa late 1887 or early 1888; Adolph Fischer to HDL and William M. Salter, 4 November 1887; Robert W. Patterson to HDL, 31 December 1887; Samuel J. Fielden to CLS, 25 August 1905; and Jessie Dale Pearce to CLS, n.d., before 24 October 1907; all in HDL, Wisc.; Bross Diary, 24 March 1883, 10, 11 November 1887, CHS; HDL, "Labor and Monopoly," *Chicago Herald*, 3 January 1888; CLS, *Lloyd* I, 95–99; David, *Haymarket*, 396; Avrich, *Haymarket*, 301–308; Thomas, *Alternative*, 207–209; Destler, *Empire of Reform*, 160–170; Chamberlain, *Reform*, 67–73; and Harold V. Zlotnik, *Toys of Desperation: A Haymarket Moral in Verse* (Interlaken, NY: Heart of the Lakes Publishing, 1987).

13. CLS Journal; J. A. Hunt to HDL, n.d., shortly after 11 November 1887; Clarence Darrow to HDL, January 4, 1888; and W. P. Black to HDL, 6 July 1889; all in HDL, Wisc.; CLS anecdotes, n.d., HDL, mf.; Nicholas Kelley Oral History, Columbia University, 4; Avrich, *Haymarket*, 304; Destler, *Empire of Reform*, 167–170; Ruegamer, "Women," 164–165; and *Chicago Daily News*, 14 January 1886 as quoted in Nelson, *Martyrs*, 7.

14. William Bross's Will, Probate Court, Cook County, IL *Record of Wills*, 10:278–283 and CLS, *Lloyd* I, 93.

15. CLS Journal, HDL, Wisc. and Jessie Bross Lloyd, "Lucretia Mott," 18–19, "Literary Spinsters," 3, and "Relative Values," three undated speeches delivered to the Chicago Women's Club, circa 1890s, CHS.

16. JBL Diary, 26, 28, 30 January 1890, CHS; "Interview with Mrs. Zelda Stewart Chambers, Washington D.C., 28 December 1939," Destler Papers, Wisc.; Bernard K. Johnpoll and Harvey Klehr, eds., *Biographical Dictionary of the American Left* (Westport, CT: Greenwood Press, 1986), 248–249; and Tebbel, *An American Dynasty*, 200.

17. Destler, *Empire of Reform*, 211, 218–219; HDL to Edward W. Bemis, 3 February 1900; Bemis to CLS, 30 August 1906; JBL to Richard T. Ely, 8 January 1904; all in

HDL, Wisc.; HDL to Ely, 21 December 1895, in Ely Papers.

18. CLS Journal, HDL, Wisc.; Destler, *Empire*, 211–222; and HDL, "Chicago," undated MS, circa 1880s, HDL, mf.

19. HDL, "A Corner in Coffins," *C.T.*, 3 October 1884; Ethelbert Stewart to HDL, 15 September, 24 October, 15, 23, 30 December 1884, 6 February 1885, 27 November 1886, 14 January 1887; HDL to Stewart, 23 December 1886; all in HDL, Wisc.; "Interview with Zelda Stewart Chambers," Destler Papers, Wisc.; HDL to Stewart, 26 August 1887, n.d, circa 1887, and 3 January 1889, all in Ethelbert Stewart papers, Southern History Collection, University of North Carolina at Chapel Hill; Stewart to Richard T. Ely, 31 January 1921, Ely to Stewart, 25 February 1921, and Ely to Irvine E. Lenroot, 25 February 1921, all in Ely Papers, Wisc.; *New York Times*, 14 October 1936; Destler, *Empire of Reform*, 155; Frederic C. Howe, *Confessions of a Reformer* (New York: Charles Scribner's Sons, 1925), 254; *American Funeral Gazette*, 24 October 1884, copy in HDL, mf.; and Margo Anderson Conk, *The U.S. Census and Labor Change: A History of Occupation Statistics, 1870–1940* (Ann Arbor, MI: University Microfilms International, 1987).

20. Caroline Stallbohm to CLS, 9 February 1906; Ethelbert Stewart to CLS, 20 September 1909; and CLS Journal; all in HDL, Wisc.; and CLS, *Lloyd* II, 20, 84.

21. HDL, "The Political Economy of Child Labor," *Journal of the Knights of Labor*, 7 May 1887, in HDL, mf., republished in *Men, the Workers* (New York: Doubleday, Page, and Co., 1909), and Destler, *Empire of Reform*, 158–160.

22. HDL, small notebooks, 1886 and 1887, HDL, mf; Frederick, *Knights of the Golden Rule*, 31–37; and Destler, *Empire*, 171–185.

23. Giuseppe Mazzini, *An Essay on the Duties of Man Addressed to Workingmen* (New York: E.P. Dutton, 1892, 1844), 44–45, 88–89; William Roberts, *Prophet in Exile: Joseph Mazzini in England, 1837–1868* (New York: Peter Lang, 1989), 4–22; HDL, "Mazzini: Prophet of Action," and "The Scholar in Contemporary Practical Questions," both in HDL, *Mazzini And Other Essays* (New York: G. P. Putnam's Sons, 1910), 1–9, 147–152; various notebook entries, 1887 and 1888, HDL, mf; Thomas, *Alternative*, 81–82, 212–213, 355–357; Frederick, *Knights of the Golden Rule*, 28–77; and Destler, *Empire of Reform*, 171–198.

24. HDL, untitled letter to the editor, *C.T.*, 25 September 1887 and notebook 5, circa 1887–1888, HDL, mf.

25. Arthur D. Winslow to HDL, 20 April 1888, in HDL, Wisc.; "The New Conscience," *North American Review*, 147(September 1888): 325–339; 1893 New Fellowship Series in HDL, mf.; HDL, *Man, The Social Creator* (New York: Doubleday and Page, 1906); Charles Hopkins, *The Rise of the Social Gospel in American Protestantism* (New Haven: Yale University Press, 1940), 88 and 107 as quoted in Schiffman, "Edward Bellamy," 19–23; and Destler, *Empire of Reform*, 129.

26. Schiffman, "Edward Bellamy," 15–22; William W. Salter to HDL, 6 February 1888; Buchanon to HDL, 6 February 1888; *Labor Enquirer*, 11 February 1888; *C.T.*, 8 September 1888; David D. Lloyd to HDL, 21 September 1888; C. S. Jackson to HDL, 25 September 1888; CLS to HDL, 18 October 1889; John P. Altgeld to HDL, 3 June 1890; Josephine E. Hall to HDL, 27 March 1892; all in HDL, Wisc.; *Pittsburgh Telegraph*, 27 September 1888, *New York Post*, 16, 26 December 1896, all in HDL, mf.; Hopkins, *Rise of the Social Gospel*, 137; Dombrowski, *Early Days of Christian Socialism*, 121–131; and Thomas, *Alternative*, 210–218.

Also see Ira L. Mandelker, *Religion, Society, and Utopia in Nineteenth- Century America* (Amhearst, MA: University of Massachusetts Press, 1984); Joseph Schiffman, "Edward Bellamy and the Social Gospel," in *Intellectual History in America* II, ed. Cushing Strout (New York: Harper and Row, 1968), 10–27; and Henry F. May, *Protestant Churches and Industrial America* (New York: Harper, 1949).

27. Vernon L. Parrington, *Main Currents in American Thought: The Beginnings of Critical Realism in America, 1860–1920*, III (New York: Harcourt, Brace, 1930), 284–285; Dombrowski, *Christian Socialism*, 125–127; David W. Noble, *The Paradox of Progressive Thought* (Minneapolis: University of Minnesota Press, 1958), 138–156; and Jernigan, *Lloyd*, 106–111.

28. HDL, *A Strike Of Millionaires Against Miners or the Story of Spring Valley* (Chicago: Belford-Clarke Co., 1890), 51, and Joseph M. Gowaskie, "John Mitchell: A Study in Leadership" (Ph.D. diss., Catholic University of America, 1968), 4–5.

29. J. M. Gould and Fred H. Wines, *Report of the Coal-Miners' Strike and Lock-Out in Northern Illinois* (Springfield: State of Illinois, 1889), 10–22.

30. HDL, *Millionaires*; untitled scrapbook, n.d., circa 1869 to 1874, HDL, mf.; and HDL, "The Hocking Valley Conspiracy," *C.T.*, 6 December 1884.

31. See untitled editorial, *C.T.*, 10 September 1882; J. W. Gibboney to HDL, 31 December 1895; Sylvester Baxter to HDL, 24 April, 8 June, 8 December 1896, and Mrs. Briggs to Jessie Lloyd O'Connor, 19 June 1935, all in HDL, Wisc.; and "In New Applications of Democracy," *The Congregationalist*, 5 January 1901, in HDL, mf.

32. John F. Power to HDL, 7 October 1889; William Henry Smith to HDL, 2, 17 December 1889; and Henry C. Hullinger to HDL, 25 December 1889, all in HDL, Wisc.; *C.T.* 29 September 1889; *Chicago Inter-Ocean*, n.d., circa October 1889; *Rock Islander*, 12 October 1889; and "To Certain Rich Men," *Chicago Herald*, 13 November 1889; all in HDL, mf.; *New York Times*, 1 December 1889, as cited in CLS, *Lloyd* I, 131; and Destler, *Empire of Reform*, 226–232.

33. Edwin D. Mead to HDL, 29 October 1889; F. A. Eastman to HDL, 27 November 1889; M. L. Scudder to HDL, 5 December 1889; John Swinton to HDL, 16 December 1889; Aaron Lloyd to HDL, 22 December 1889; William Scaife to HDL, 31 December 1889; J. Clarke to HDL, 12, 14 April 1890, all in HDL, Wisc.; *Knights of Labor*, 28 December 1889; CLS, MS "A note on Mr. Lloyd's book . . .," March 1935; all in HDL, mf.; and CLS, *Lloyd* I, 122–132.

34. HDL, *Millionaires*, 247; Thomas, *Alternative*, 50; and HDL to Richard T. Ely, 27 August 1890, in Ely papers, Wisc.

35. CLS, *Lloyd* I, 131; Furnas, *Social History*, 719–723; Moritz Pinner to HDL, 17 December 1897; Samuel Gompers to HDL, 15 May 1890; Frederick Engels to HDL, 27 May 1893; E. H. Blair to HDL, 22 February 1894; Joseph Kirkland to HDL, 20 July 1888, 29 May 1890; Stuart Charles Wade to A. C. McClurg Co., 5 January 1894; C. B. Matthews to HDL, 26 May 1890; Walter M. Raymond to HDL, 17 August 1893; all in HDL, Wisc.; *C.T.*, 24 May 1890; undated book reviews from *New York Commercial Advertiser*, London *Labor World*, and *Chicago Herald* along with *Dover Democrat*, 18 June 1890, all in HDL, mf.

36. Gowaskie, "Mitchell," 6–12; Elsie Gluck, *John Mitchell, Miner: Labor's Bargain with the Gilded Age* (New York: The John Day Company, 1929), 18; Thomas, *Alternative*, 215–217; J. Clarke to HDL, 7 July 1890; HDL to JBL, 8 November 1902; John F. Power to HDL, 16 May 1890, 1 June 1892, 5 October 1899 and Power to CLS,

26 May 1905, all in HDL, Wisc.
   37. Ethelbert Stewart to HDL, 23 June 1888, in HDL, Wisc.

5

Wealth Against Commonwealth

Looking Backward, 2000–1887 was the surprise best-selling book of 1888. Edward Bellamy's novel of a man who slept for more than a hundred years only to awaken in a utopian world was a fictional attack on nineteenth-century laissez-faire capitalism and Social Darwinism. Why did such topics capture the Gilded Age public's fancy? It was as much the times as it is was the story, as Bellamy explained shortly after publication:

All thoughtful men agree that the present aspect of society is portentous of great coming changes. The only question is, whether they will be for the better or the worse. . . . true and humane men and women, of every degree, are in a mood of exasperation, verging on absolute revolt, against social conditions that reduce life to a brutal struggle for existence.

Henry Demarest Lloyd was cognizant of the same social conditions but his goal was to fan the winds of change with reality, not Bellamy's fanciful storytelling. As he explained to a friend, he wanted to be a "photographer of facts" rather than a writer of fiction. To Lloyd, truth overshadowed all inventions of the mind, no matter how ingenious or daring. His thinking was ahead of public tastes in the early 1890s, for neither muckraking nor literary realism caught on until the early twentieth century, but his goal was the same as Bellamy's. *Wealth Against Commonwealth* was his contribution to the debate over the social question.[1]

    Wealth remains significant today as an example of American advocacy journalism. It chronicles the exploits of John D. Rockefeller and his supporters as he endeavored to construct the most complete monopoly in the world's history. Lloyd used all of his skills as a reporter and writer in the research and writing of the book. It has been faulted for ignoring the Standard's version of events, but it was Lloyd's intent to tell his story from the perspective of the independent producers, in contrast to a more balanced historical perspective employed by Ida M. Tarbell in her *History of the Standard Oil Company*. The factual basis of *Wealth* also hurt its impact because Lloyd provided more evidence than he needed to make his point. Still, the overwhelming majority of Lloyd's assertions were correct. *Wealth* helped show the potential of realism as a literary device and put Lloyd at the forefront of the antimonopoly movement.

 Wealth might not have been necessary had Congress been more determined to regulate monopolies during the Gilded Age. In 1886, Illinois Senator Shelby M. Cullom cosponsored a measure to control the Standard Oil Company and other monopolies through federal regulation, but his measure faced determined opposition from vested corporate interests in the Senate. In a letter to Cullom, Lloyd applauded his bill, but expressed a concern that it had too many loopholes that would allow the railroads to continue their discriminatory rate practices and monopolistic tendencies. Cullom responded, "It is impossible to get everything in the first proposed act on the subject just as it perhaps ought to be," but promised to address Lloyd's concerns in subsequent legislation. Time proved Lloyd right, for the U.S. Supreme Court so gutted Cullom's weakened Interstate Commerce Act that the Interstate Commerce Commission became more of a friend than a foe to the monopolists by the early twentieth century. Not long after it came into being, Lloyd, as many others, discounted both the act and the I.C.C.[2]

 Two weeks after the Haymarket executions in 1887, several Pennsylvania independent oil producers asked Lloyd to testify against the Standard at one of the I.C.C.'s first hearings in Washington, D.C. They were seeking an order that would have required the railroads to quote rates by the barrel rather than the tank car, the Standard's preferred shipping method. As Lloyd feared, their cause was lost before it could be won. Even as he testified before the commission, the Standard was openly flaunting commission rules in the oil region. Lloyd found the hearings worthwhile, but for another reason. While waiting for his turn to talk, he saw and heard John D. Rockefeller for the first and only time in his life. His recollection was preserved in an unpublished essay, "Fanatic S. Oil," written upon Lloyd's return to the Wayside. The work was never published—for good reason because it would have provided grounds for an excellent libel suit. Lloyd employed a literary technique to describe Rockefeller, one he would use again with success in *Wealth*, casting him as a villain in an imaginary melodrama. His description of Rockefeller had a theatrical flavor: "A young man—48—brown hair—if any gray, invisible at a distance . . . a long, narrow, predatory, sharp nose, hawk arched; very clean;

his smile a relaxing of two Cerberus-like muscles on each side of his guarded, invisible mouth; and the appearance of a cold light, the moonlight on snow, out of his recessed eyes." Rockefeller seemed a nervous man to Lloyd, one who saw an "Indian behind every shadow . . . as if every pore was on picket duty. . . . A corporation cat, about to spring on its victim." Protestations that all Rockefeller wanted to do was to make oil cheap were according to Lloyd, transparent ruses to hide his greed:

He is not a neighbor, not a fellow citizen; he is depredator. He is not a subject of the United States of America, not a worshipper of liberty. He is a Czar of Plutocracy, a worshipper of his own Money Power over mankind. He will never sacrifice any of his plans for the restraints of law, or patriotism, or philanthropy. His only limitations are what he can do with money against money.[3]

Lloyd had a number of concerns in mind as he contemplated a response to Rockefeller. His primary goal was to prove that monopolies and trusts were detrimental to democracy, something he believed that previous antimonopoly writers had failed to do. As he explained, "It is easy enough to argue that cheapness can not be produced by these tactics of dearness, but that is not enough. It must be *proved* arithmetically, statistically, historically that oil has been made dear by the methods of monopoly." He wanted to make his case so strong that even the Standard, with all its resources, would not be able to refute it. Beyond the numbers, Lloyd wanted to use Rockefeller and the Standard's own words and actions to discredit them, to rely upon the "transcript of the record" as he said. To focus public opinion against monopolies, he determined that he needed to make his case understandable to all readers, even those who were not normally involved in public debates. He jokingly told a priest friend that he wanted to make his next book "so clear and plain that even ministers and women could understand it." He also wanted to avoid the generalizations of *Millionaires*, especially after one reader complimented the book but complained, "I should say it would be advantageous to put in all the documentary proof that you can get of the assertions which you had made."[4]

He wanted to avoid using the mainstream press as well. His 1883 "Our Land" article proved that no American newspaper could claim the same kind of national readership as magazines, not even Lloyd's own *Chicago Tribune*. At the same time, the magazines were changing. From a product consumed primarily by the upper class, they were evolving into a mass market commodity during the 1880s. New titles were cutting into the circulations of traditional stalwarts such as *Harper's*, *Century*, *Scribner's*, and Lloyd's two favorites, *Atlantic Monthly* and *North American Review*. To compensate for their losses, the older magazines reduced the fees they paid to their writers. In 1889, Lloyd complained to Allen Thorndike Rice, the editor of the *North American*, that the magazine had promised to pay him ten dollars for "The New Conscience," but sent him a check for only five. In his letter, Lloyd noted that the magazine had paid him five dollars *a page* for "Making Bread Dear" in 1884. Lloyd erroneously blamed the situation not on changing public tastes but on what he believed was a "magazine trust" that was seeking to censor writers such as himself. He stopped contributing to the magazines from 1887 until 1900 and included a magazine trust in his list of corporate monopolies in the United States published in *Wealth*. The best alternative press left to him, outside of pamphlets, was books. He determined that his Rockefeller study would be published as a book and that he would use his own money to help pay for the publishing process to reduce potential interference with his message.[5]

Caro Lloyd, who stayed with her brother's family in Winnetka periodically, insisted that Lloyd began writing *Wealth* on 15 July 1889, but the book began taking shape in Lloyd's mind the day he saw John D. Rockefeller in Washington, D.C. A printed handbill in Lloyd's papers, titled "Sins of a Trust: The Story of a Great Monopoly" and dated 6 March 1889, promised "a book of reference for all students of American Liberty, who believe that freedom in the State can not live without freedom in the markets. . . . A full, and absolutely and documentarily accurate" study. Lloyd intended his study to be part of a projected "Bad Wealth" series on the American economy, a title derived from Ralph Waldo Emerson's remark that "It is high time our bad wealth came to an end." Bert Stewart originally promised to contribute another title, but could offer nothing of the caliber of *Wealth*, and Lloyd's book became the first and only volume in the series.[6]

Lloyd researched *Wealth* between 1889 and 1891, in part as he was finishing the *Millionaires* book. His evidence came from existing collections of anti-Standard information, most of which were located in Pennsylvania. In 1871, the Pennsylvania legislature had granted a charter to a Standard backed venture called the South Improvement Company. In turn, the South Improvement Company entered into contracts with all of the major railroads in the state giving the company sizable rebates on all petroleum shipped by the company and rebates for any oil shipped by other companies. In other words, the Standard made money selling its own oil and the oil of its competitors. News of the arrangement leaked out, creating a massive public outcry in Pennsylvania, but the Standard genie was out of the bottle. In the first three months of 1872 alone, the Standard increased its capacity some 600 percent and gained control of over one fifth of the national refining capacity, and it continued to grow. New York's Hepburn Commission noted in 1880:

It owns and controls the pipe lines of the producing regions that connect with the railroads. It controls both ends of these roads. It ships 95 per cent of all oil. . . . It dictates terms and rates to the railroads. It has bought out and frozen out refiners all over the country.

By the end of the 1880s, the Standard owned or had thwarted almost every oil refining or shipping competitor in the United States and was in the process of dominating crude oil production, the last step to complete integration from well to consumer. As John D. Rockefeller explained to the United States Industrial Commission several years later, "The success of the Standard [is due] to its consistent policy to make the volume of its business large through the merits and cheapness of its product. It has spared no expense in finding, securing, and utilizing the best and cheapest methods of manufacture."[7]

Opposition grew to the company, mostly in the oil-producing regions of western Pennsylvania, but paled in comparison to the organizational genius of Rockefeller. Independent refiners and shippers filed a multitude of lawsuits against the Standard, most unsuccessful. Frustrated, these businessmen then turned to the states and federal government, which conducted their own investigations with few tangible results, or tried to fight the Standard's price-cutting tactics with their own. On another level, journalists and writers tried to call public attention to the excesses of the Standard. Most of these efforts were limited to western Pennsylvania, small newspapers in the oil region or, occasionally, the Pittsburgh press. The *Monthly Petroleum Trade Reports*, edited by John Collins Welch, acted as a print voice for independent refiners from 1874 to 1887 and the New York based trade publication *Oil, Paint and Drug Reporter* waged a campaign against the Standard from 1877 until it was silenced by the Standard in 1883. Big city newspapers ran occasional articles or editorials about the Standard. Lloyd's *Chicago Tribune* editorials and his "Story of a Great Monopoly" were inspired by an editorial in the *New York Sun*, and Joseph Pultizer's *New York World* had a reputation as an antimonopoly newspaper in the 1880s. As vocal as they were, these businessmen, bureaucrats, politicians, lawyers, and journalists knew much about the Standard but were unorganized in their attacks. Until Lloyd, no one had thought to thoroughly study and catalogue what was known about the Standard.[8]

Lloyd wrote to anyone he could think of connected to or associated with the oil industry who did not work for the Standard. Those who could not help put him in touch with others who did. He even contacted sources in Europe to learn about the Standard's activities there. The result was the most extensive oil industry bibliography then in existence. The list was so long that it could not be included even in the voluminous *Wealth*, but Lloyd printed it himself, put a copy in the Library of Congress, and made other copies available to fellow researchers including Ida Tarbell. The list remained the best oil industry bibliography into the twentieth century. Lloyd was so confident of his information that he boasted, "I doubt very much whether after the exhibit which my book gives . . . the great trusts are likely soon again to allow any important investigation to be made by Congress or the state legislatures."[9]

Of all his sources, the most valuable was the four volume study of the railroad industry conducted by the New York State legislative committee known as the Hepburn Commission in 1879. The Hepburn Report, as it was nicknamed, was the most comprehensive study of the early years of the

Standard. Its primary focus was the railroads, and it revealed that the New York Central had made more than six thousand secret rebate contracts in the first months of 1879 alone, but the Standard entered into the commission's purview as well, for as the commission observed, "The history of this corporation is a unique illustration of the possible outgrowth of the present system of railroad management . . . showing the colossal proportions to which monopoly can grow under the laws of this country." Rockefeller was so distressed by the Hepburn report and its conclusions that he reportedly purchased and destroyed most of the copies. Even for nineteenth-century government reports it remains rare today. Lloyd bought his own set in 1880 and made ample use of its information in his editorials, articles, and *Wealth*.[10]

Lloyd drew upon the extensive resources of an oil region attorney who had masterminded Pennsylvania's unsuccessful legal challenge against the Standard in 1879 and 1880. Following his courtroom defeat, Roger Sherman had worked briefly for Rockefeller, but he rejoined the independent cause during the mid 1880s and made available to Lloyd everything he had been able to collect on the company. His materials ranged from obscure court decisions and rare anti-Standard pamphlets to contacts and even some secret agreements. As a lawyer, Sherman knew virtually all of the leading independents, and put Lloyd in touch with those that he did not already know. When the documents and information proved too much for Lloyd to assimilate, Sherman gave him moral support and encouragement, and whenever Lloyd wavered in his determination, Sherman tried to keep him on track. He read the final drafts of *Wealth* for legal or factual errors, exclaiming, "I have no doubt of its success." For his efforts, Sherman refused any compensation, but Lloyd quoted him extensively in reference to several court cases.[11]

Lloyd was aided by several anti-Standard independents. George Rice was the leading late nineteenth-century Standard opponent. He built and operated a small refinery in Marietta, Ohio, in 1872 that was the price-cutting target of the Standard several times. In 1881, he published an anti-Standard pamphlet called *Black Death* and regularily advertised his petroleum products as "Anti-Standard" and "Anti-Monopoly." The Standard tried to buy his silence several times, but each time Rice upped his price to something the Standard was unwilling to pay, and he remained an anti-Standard gadfly and litigant until his death. Lewis Emery, Jr. was a Pennsylvania refiner who had sold out twice to the Standard but kept building new refineries and criticizing the company for its competitive practices. He helped form a competing company called the Pure Oil Trust during the 1890s. Charles B. Matthews operated a New York refinery called the Buffalo Lubricating Oil Company that would figure in one of Lloyd's vignettes and was also a Populist, running for governor in 1894. James F. Hudson was a reporter for the *Pittsburgh Dispatch* who wrote several critical newspaper stories on the company during the 1880s and an antimonopoly article for the *North American Review* in 1887 called "Modern Feudalism."[12]

Lloyd also read as much of the pro-Standard literature as he could find. He was well aware of the 1883 *North American Review* defense of the Standard provided by Senator Johnson N. Camden, which had argued that the Standard had been the instrument, if not the cause, of almost the entire development of the American oil industry. He read political economist George Gunton's 1888 "The Economic and Social Aspects of Trusts" and S.C.T. Dodd's 1888 *Combinations: Their Uses and Abuses, with A History of the Standard Oil Trust*. Dodd was the Standard Oil Company's solicitor, and his book was a reprint of testimony he delivered before the New York State legislature. Lloyd suspected that Dodd might have tampered with some the documents involving a conspiracy trial in Buffalo in which three Standard officials had been accused of conspiring to blow up another refinery, an incident he described in *Wealth*. He read a *Political Science Quarterly* article in defense of monopolies by Theodore W. Dwight, one of his Columbia law professors. He also had a newspaper clipping service keep track of the *Cleveland Herald*, which was partially owned by the Standard, and the *Oil City Derrick*, a western Pennsylvania newspaper that was not owned by the Standard but was considered to be its mouthpiece in the oil region.[13]

Research was the strong point of *Wealth*, but Lloyd's findings have been cited as one of the book's greatest weaknesses. The reason is simple. Not once during the preparation of *Wealth* did Lloyd officially or unofficially contact the Standard Oil Company to learn its side of the story or verify his sources' accounts or information. This seeming bias represents what lawyers call an ex parte or one sided prosecution. Lloyd's ex parte perspective has been cited as the most serious flaw of his book, especially when *Wealth* is compared to Ida Tarbell's *History of the Standard Oil Company*, but Lloyd had reason. The Standard Oil Company and other Gilded Age corporations were not required to provide the detailed financial information demanded of their twentieth-century counterparts, and most shunned publicity, especially in competitive matters, as a protection for their businesses. The Gilded Age public tolerated this behavior because corporations were viewed by many as allies of the public, not enemies. Andrew Carnegie summarized this attitude when he observed, "It will be a great mistake for the community to shoot the millionaires, for they are the bees that make the most honey and contribute most to the hive even after they have gorged themselves full."[14]

John D. Rockefeller was especially notorious in this regard. His obsession for secrecy was legendary in the oil industry. He told an interviewer some twenty years after *Wealth* appeared, "Good business men are not giving away their business secrets or publishing their advantages in any way. . . . I kept silent because it would not have been statesmanlike to speak." Under such circumstances, it would have been pointless for Lloyd to ask the company anything, and he did not. Instead, he turned to the only source of pro-Standard information he had access to, the company's sworn court testimony. He quoted extensively from the remarks of various company officials including Rockefeller. As an advocate for those people who were being cheated by the Standard, he felt no further compulsion to provide the other side of his story, assuming the company would eventually do so. Nevertheless, many refused to believe, as do scholars today, that the Standard would remain silent on such an important subject, and blamed Lloyd, not the Standard, for the one sided perspective of *Wealth*.[15]

The Standard's predilection for secrecy took on sinister overtones at times. Lloyd learned that some documents on monopolies prepared for Congressional committees in 1872 and 1876 had disappeared from official Congressional archives under unexplained circumstances, with no obvious culprit other than the Standard. Lloyd suspected that the Standard's lawyer had tampered with a court transcript in 1888 and was told that another Standard employee had thrown ledger books and other documents into a furnace in front of witnesses. Following the publication of *Wealth* in 1894, Lloyd discovered that several court documents cited in his book had disappeared. Ida Tarbell could still not find them a decade later, and she finally had to pay Lloyd and his family for certified copies. The U.S. Justice Department, which began prosecuting the Standard for antitrust violations in 1908, also turned to the Lloyd family for the same missing documents.[16]

His research completed, Lloyd found the task of writing *Wealth* arduous. He used a muckrake-like metaphor to describe the process in an 1891 letter to his mother:

I spend every morning at my desk working on a book about the trusts but my progress seems lamentably slow. However it "do move." The worst of it is the work is really so *distasteful*. It keeps me poking around and scavaging in files of filthy human greed and cruelty, almost too nauseous to handle. Nothing but the sternest sense of duty . . . drives me back to my desk every day.

He complained to an independent oil producer about the difficulty of writing nonfiction. "I could spin a yarn from my own inner consciousness ten times as fast," he said. He told a friend, "I feel . . . like the baby . . . would never get itself born, but would have to be carried about unborn for twenty years." He confessed to another friend, "facts are difficult things to harness."[17]

The text began to take a definitive form in 1892, revealing another defect in the book. As he developed his case, Lloyd was so determined to prove his case that he overdocumented his evidence. He wanted to avoid the generalization flaw of *Millionaires*, but in doing so he buttressed every allegation, argument, comment, and observation to the point of overkill. Lawyers are trained to anticipate all possible objections, and overpreparation is a part of their job, but journalism does not have the same standards of evidence as the law. As he wrote, Lloyd tried to guess which part of *Wealth* the Standard would attack first, and how they would do it. Since he could only anticipate, he protected himself beyond necessity. His anxiety to prove his case so thoroughly mystified his friends and supporters. They were convinced the Standard could provide no justification for its actions and would perish once the truth was exposed. Journalist James F. Hudson told Lloyd, "Answering such fellows would be like firing cannon at snipes." Nevertheless, Lloyd persevered, and when the Standard failed to even acknowledge the presence of his book after it appeared, the factual overkill made some readers suspicious of Lloyd's intentions. The situation could have been worse. Lloyd's publisher made him reduce his original thousand-page manuscript to less than six hundred pages, but there was still more evidence than required to make Lloyd's points.[18]

Beyond his distrust of the Standard, Lloyd engaged in overkill because he wanted all of his readers to understand and act upon his message, not just those who were normally involved in public issues. He wanted to reach women readers in particular because he believed they would be more sensitive to his moral undertones, but nineteenth-century women could not vote and many were unaccustomed to public debates. To test the clarity of his message, he read each chapter aloud to his German-born secretary, admonishing her to stop him if she did not immediately understand anything that was spoken. She recalled, "[Lloyd] wanted it so clear that women and clergymen could understand it, both being in a class unused to this line of fact." Another test reader might have been able to warn Lloyd of his overkill, especially a native born speaker, but the secretary apparently made Lloyd prove every assertion two, three, or even more times. Lloyd also sent his manuscript to two independent-affiliated lawyers, but they were even less objective about the writing than his secretary. One, Adelbert Moot, offered a few minor revisions and wrote, "It is remarkably well drawn, as interesting as a novel to me." The other, Roger Sherman, replied, "Have no fears of your book!"[19]

In its draft form, *Wealth* was the most thoroughly researched and written attack of a respected late nineteenth-century American corporation and its founder. It was clear from beginning of the book that parts were intended for the better educated even though Lloyd had cherished hopes that it would be read by the lower class. The very first sentence was modeled after French philosopher Jean-Jacques Rousseau's classic line that "Man was born free but is everywhere in chains." To Lloyd, "Nature is rich; but everywhere man, the heir of nature, is poor." Rousseau had argued that private property deprived men of their natural rights. Lloyd reasoned that monopolies were the inevitable consequence of private property ownership left uncontrolled, and their presence usurped the American dream, imperiled democracy, and hurt each and every American.[20]

The major thesis of *Wealth* was that John D. Rockefeller would have been a failure at business had he not been able to use the illegal, dishonest, and immoral business tactics that nurtured the growth of his Standard Oil Company. After relating Rockefeller's inauspicious start as a wholesale grocer in Civil War era Cleveland, Lloyd chronicled his three most duplicitous business techniques. First, he discussed the Standard's legendary ability to manipulate the railroads, reducing its transportation costs to the detriment of its competitors. The largest businesses in the country at the time, the railroads should have been able to ignore a petty criminal like Rockefeller, Lloyd wrote. Rockefeller, though, exploited the smaller railroads, the less affluent regional lines, to give him the secret rate reductions known as rebates. His first such attempt, the South Improvement Company of 1872, was discovered, and alarmed competitors convinced Pennsylvania officials to dissolve it before it could it could achieve its goal, but Rockefeller kept pressuring the smaller railroads, using even more duplicitous means in the process. Once ingratiated with the regional lines, he then managed to get either himself or his allies elected to the larger railroads' board of directors and elicited favorable treatment from them as a result. By the early 1890s, the relationships between the Standard and the nation's railroads were so intertwined that even the most determined governmental investigators could not untangle them. Whenever the Standard was publicly chastised for its railroad manipulation, as it was by New York State's Hepburn Commission in 1879 and by other public bodies in 1876, 1882, 1887, 1888, and 1892, it lied, distorted, or did whatever else was necessary to frustrate the criticism. Lloyd compared this strategy to economic warfare, noting, "The Pennsylvania Railroad, the New York Central, the Erie, and their branches and connections in and out of the oil regions, east and west, were as entirely closed to [the independents] as if a foreign enemy had seized the country and laid an embargo on their business—which was, indeed, just what had happened."[21]

Next, Lloyd examined how Rockefeller gained control of the nation's growing oil pipeline network. Beginning in the 1870s, pipelines of varying lengths were built by independent producers to bypass the Rockefeller-controlled railroads. The best example was the Tidewater, a pipeline conceived and constructed in 1878 by a group of independent producers to circumvent several Rockefeller railroads. As it was being constructed, the Standard used its influence with the railroads to stall and sabotage the pipeline project, especially whenever it crossed railroad property. When the line was finally completed and began shipping oil at a great savings to its investors, Rockefeller obtained control of the pipeline by secretly buying out several "plants" among the investors. To intensify his literary effect, Lloyd used colorful metaphors in his writing. As the company grew larger and larger, he likened the Standard to a massive, pulsating machine that was intruding itself upon the pastoral serenity of the American countryside:

This heart of a machine, beating at the headquarters in New York, and numbering its beats day and night, stands for thousands of hearts whose throbs of hope have been transmuted into this metallic substance. This heart counts out a gold dollar for every drop of blood that used to run through the living breasts of the men who divined, projected, accomplished, and lost.[22]

Finally, Lloyd related several case studies of how Rockefeller bullied, coerced, corrupted, sabotaged, and otherwise intimidated his competitors to sell to him at ridiculous prices. To make his tales of greed and misery as theatrical as possible, he created tiny melodramas, with the same kind of stereotypical good and evil characters that he had employed in his earlier "Fanatic S. Oil." One of his more touching cases involved the Standard's purchase of a refinery from a woman Lloyd called the Widow Backus. Backus's husband had died in 1874, leaving her his refinery business, and she had operated it at a profit for several years until Rockefeller allegedly forced her to sell to him for a fraction of what the business was worth in 1879. She tried to sue the Standard for its duplicity, but the Pennsylvania courts, at the Standard's bidding, ruled for the company. Lloyd added an ominous postscript to her case, noting that several incriminating documents had disappeared from court files when the company found out about his research in 1891. That the heroine of the story was a widow made it more heartrending, for Lloyd wanted readers to think of Rockefeller as an evil landlord, tricking the defenseless woman into selling and then throwing her out of her own home into the cold winter night.[23]

Another case study involved the alleged sabotage of an independent refiner by a Standard-paid agent. One of Lloyd's most cooperative sources, Charles B. Matthews, had operated the Buffalo Lubricating Oil Company since the late 1870s. Matthews's claim to fame was that he was able to beat the Standard at its own game by stealing customers and technology. When Rockefeller could not put Matthews out of business with his usual duplicitous techniques, he paid a young employee, Albert Miller, to bomb the Buffalo Lubricating Oil Company. Miller's effort failed, and he was caught and admitted his Standard connection to officials. However, when Matthews pressed criminal charges against Rockefeller and the Standard for the attack, only one minor executive was convicted, and he was fined an insignificant $250. Perhaps troubled by Matthews's own questionable business ethics, Lloyd centered his story on Albert Miller. He described how the Standard had promised to protect Miller only to abandon him and his wife after the unsuccessful bombing. Miller testified that in order to protect Rockefeller, he had spent his entire life savings to hide from authorities. At the trial, Lloyd recounted how cruel Rockefeller's attorneys were to their former coworker:

This hard-working and hard-living laborer and his wife had, by thirteen or fourteen years of toil and stinting, saved $6,000. The laughers had in the same time saved about $300,000,000, and somebody else had done all the work. The poor man and his wife had been afraid that the $300,000,000 would devour the $6,000. It said it would, and it had. Shall not they laugh who win?[24]

Such emotionalism may seem at odds with Lloyd's journalistic perspective in *Wealth*, but emotion was an important tactic of a skilled legal advocate. One legal textbook of Lloyd's day noted that "the sympathies of the jury are a proper subject to reach if the advocate can do it by the facts, and not by meretricious sentiment; this is a legitimate exercise of the art of advocacy and of the powers of eloquence; and the art consists in so presenting the facts that they will accomplish that which the advocate is forbidden to attempt." The text warned against direct "appeal[s] to their feeling[s]," but subtle plays were considered useful.[25]

Like any good prosecutor, Lloyd did not want to leave his jury of readers without a semblance of hope at the conclusion of his presentation. In spite of the manifest evils that the Standard Oil Company and other monopolies represented, Lloyd's final summation included two stories of how organized citizenry had overcome the Rockefeller octopus. The first involved a small Mississippi community where local merchants formed an cooperative association and priced the Standard out of their town. Lloyd compared them to the "Indians" of Boston who "emptied King George's taxed tea into Boston harbor." He also cited Toledo, Ohio, where residents had voted to build their own natural gas system rather than pay the Standard's inflated prices. The Standard tried to frustrate the effort through various legal challenges and a vicious publicity campaign, but the town eventually won, achieving energy independence in the process. Predictably, Lloyd ended Toledo's tale with a reference to the "passion of freedom of 1776," noting, "Defeat, final and irrevocable, crowned the unvarying series of defeats which the private companies had suffered everywhere and in everything—in public meetings, in the Legislature, in the gas-fields, at the polls, in the courts, in the sale of bonds, and in the competition with the city. The City Council of Toledo, advised by its lawyers that it could recover damages from those responsible for the losses brought upon the city by the opposition to its pipe line, has had suit brought for that purpose."[26]

The final two chapters of *Wealth* were the raison d'être for the book. Recognizing that not every reader would wade through his five hundred pages of evidence, Lloyd condensed his case into a fourteen-point "Bill of Particulars," much as Martin Luther had done in his ninety-nine theses some four hundred years earlier. The charges ranged from "freight rates to the general public have been increased" to "killing delay has been created in the administration of justice." He conceded that effective public regulation might be able to curb some of the abuses, but he argued that the basic necessities of life would still be controlled by selfish private interests until all monopolies were outlawed. As a solution, Lloyd envisioned an altruistic return to Rousseau's natural order of communal relationships, arguing that a blueprint to such a life existed in his "New Conscience" religion. Until the day that such a utopia would become a reality, Lloyd maintained that the right to life and liberty was at the mercy of monopolists:

We must know the right before we can do the right. When it comes to know the facts the human heart can no more endure monopoly than American slavery or Roman empire. The first step to a remedy is that the people care. If they know, they will care. To help them to know and care . . . this compilation of fact has been made.

Lloyd has been faulted for providing what others, including Ida Tarbell, thought was a socialistic solution to monopolies at the end of *Wealth*, but his economic philosophy, as was his personal, was always dualistic. Lloyd documented the real problems of monopolies in most of the book, and his final answer was as unique and impractical as any other of his philosophies, bearing as much direct resemblance to socialism as "The New Conscience" did to Christianity.[27]

Wealth has been dissected by a variety of reviewers since it was published in 1894, but only a handful have dealt with it in its entirety. This is not surprising considering that the 535-page book was and still is a daunting reading task. Still, it is an important book and deserves serious consideration as a precursor to Ida Tarbell's better-known *History of the Standard Oil Company* and the eventual dissolution of the Standard. There is a common thread of criticisms and compliments in most of the reviews.[28]

The most frequent criticism leveled against *Wealth* involves Lloyd's accuracy. Critics have faulted him for a variety of factual exaggerations, from the tearjerker tale of the Widow Backus to his characterization of the failed South Improvement Company. The veracity of most of Lloyd's allegations can be ascertained through the hundreds of footnotes that he provided throughout the text, in contrast to Ida Tarbell's un-footnoted book. The most exhaustive study of these sources was conducted by Chester M. Destler over a thirty-year period. Analyzing 420 of Lloyd's 648 reference footnotes, along with an additional 241 unsupported statements of fact, Destler found only fourteen assertions that he considered incorrect. A few involved major errors, such as serious exaggerations of the Widow Backus and Tidewater pipeline cases, but the bulk of Lloyd's factual statements were correct, a remarkable feat considering that Lloyd did not have available to him all of the documents that modern historians can consult. Although Lloyd never intended *Wealth* to be a historical document like *History of the Standard Oil Company*, it was largely accurate.[29]

In his research, Destler disputed another charge made against Lloyd by the Standard Oil Company and the first John D. Rockefeller biographer, Allan Nevins. Both claimed Lloyd was practicing a literary form of blackmail with the writing and publication of the book. In particular, Rockefeller, who was used to paying people to obtain their cooperation, assumed that Lloyd's primary motive for the book was to extort money, a charge Nevins subsequently repeated. The reality is that no surviving Lloyd document reveals any evidence of extortion or other torturous intent on the part of Lloyd. Beginning in the early 1880s, Lloyd committed himself to reform and rebuffed any attempts to influence him or buy him off. By the time he had published *Wealth*, he was independently wealthy and had no need for the Standard's money. If anything, his upbringing harkened back to a lost generation of character and honesty. Anyone accusing Lloyd of blackmail or extortion in *Wealth* is ignorant of

Lloyd's life and the high moral standards that he obeyed.[30]

One oddity of *Wealth* is that Lloyd mentioned John D. Rockefeller by name only once in his entire narrative, employing pronouns or other literary devices to refer to the monopolist throughout the remainder of the book. He did this because he wanted readers to concentrate on the victims, the unknown or lesser-known men or women who had been wronged by Rockefeller but did not have his public persona. He told a friend:

I wrote not to attack or expose certain men but to unfold a realistic picture of modern business. It so happened that the oil trust afforded in all ways the very best illustration for my purpose, but owing to the fact that it is the creation of but two or three men, if I had mentioned them they would have appeared on almost every page, and the book would have taken on the appearance to being a personal assault. No matter how much the assault was deserved, to have given the work that aspect would have been fatal to the usefulness which I hope for it.

Lloyd had also been instructed as a young man that naming names was a sign of poor character and bad breeding, a means of glorifying the guilty. Most early nineteenth-century journalists followed a similar practice, using pseudonyms, asterisks, or other devices to mask identities in their writings. Lloyd had deviated from that practice in *Millionaires* by naming the entire Spring Valley Coal Company board of directors and had been criticized for doing so. He hoped to avoid a similar dilution of his message in *Wealth*.[31]

Critics immediately charged that Lloyd had left Rockefeller out of his book to avoid a libel suit. Most of the criminal accusations made in the book would have been difficult or impossible for Lloyd to prove in court and were therefore potentially libelous even if true. Yet, few juries in the civilized world, much less the United States, could have failed to recognize Lloyd's unflattering description of the founder and chief executive of the world's largest oil company, and identification can occur in libel by either name or description. Further, Lloyd probably would have enjoyed defending against a Rockefeller libel suit, even if it cost him money, using the court proceedings to publicize what he believed was his irrefutable case against the Standard Oil Company. Only in his final years did Rockefeller admit how much Lloyd, Tarbell, and his other critics had hurt him. To have filed a libel suit against them would have given them the credibility and publicity that Rockefeller did not want to provide, and a court trial would have required him to discuss business tactics and decisions he did not want to publicize. He never sued Lloyd or Tarbell.[32]

Regardless, Lloyd's choice not to name Rockefeller had more of a detrimental impact on the book than if he had named Rockefeller on every page. *Wealth* became a roman à clef, with readers eagerly poring over every page in an effort the guess the identity of the various heroes and villains. Even Lloyd's supporters were unhappy with his seeming decision to spare Rockefeller. Roger Sherman complained, "The fact is about this man, and the people for whom he and similar characters work, that they are hired to lie, and it is useless to treat them with the usual courtesy of supposing that they mean what they say, or to argue with them." Lloyd defended his decision for the duration of his life as the honorable course. Even after his death, his sister Caro wrote, "I dare to prophesy that as time goes on [Henry's] self-restraint, self-control in *Wealth versus Commonwealth* [sic] . . . will become more and more a marked quality as others take up the theme and use other methods and the people grow revengeful."[33]

Beyond its contribution to advocacy journalism, *Wealth* was significant for providing a new perception of monopolies. Prior to the 1880s, economists considered monopolies beneficial to society because they made more products available and created new markets for goods. Efforts to restrict or outlaw them were viewed as detrimental to society. That orthodoxy was challenged in 1885 when Johns Hopkins economist Richard T. Ely and the American Economic Association argued that some monopolies were beneficial while others were labeled harmful. Capital intensive businesses such as the telegraph and railroad lines were defined as natural monopolies because they provided an essential service that would have been costly to duplicate and were therefore considered good. Labor intensive businesses such as the sugar and whiskey trusts were designated as artificial monopolies because they restricted production, kept wages low, and used legal loopholes to increase their profits. Ely and his followers had no problem with natural monopolies, which they believed could be controlled through effective governmental regulation. They were concerned that the growing number of artificial monopolies hurt the economy and were unnatural and immoral.[34]

Lloyd failed to make such a dichotomy in *Wealth*. He categorized all monopolies as harmful to society, "created by mere force of money" to the detriment of the middle and lower classes. Their ongoing "division of property," Lloyd's reference to a redistribution of wealth from the poor to the rich, would lead to a French-style revolution in America. His textbook case was the Standard Oil Company, which he argued had been built on the strength of its ties with what had become a monopoly in the 1890s, the railroads, and now operated as another, even more powerful monopoly. Lloyd was concerned that the "sheer financial strength" of the Standard would soon thwart any governmental effort to control it, likening it to a nation with "financial power [that] seems to me precisely like military power. If you have enough of it you can 'lick' the other fellow and get a monopoly, as William The Conqueror did with England."[35]

For better or worse, it was Lloyd's characterization of monopolies, as repeated by other writers, that shaped late nineteenth- and early twentieth-century public debate. The 1881 "Story of a Great Monopoly" sparked the process but *Wealth* fanned the flames. Historian Steven L. Piott equated Lloyd's influence to Ida Tarbell's a decade later. Louis Filler observed:

The classic criticism of business continues to be Henry Demarest Lloyd's *Wealth Against Commonwealth*. . . . It was answered at length in Allen Nevins's Study in Power, *John D. Rockefeller, Industrialist and Philanthropist* (1953), but not before Lloyd's book had influenced an entire generation of American social thinkers. The question of what the "facts" in the matter are is relevant. . . . However . . . much American social discourse has necessarily tended toward exaggeration, in order to underscore its points.[36]

Wealth is important for another reason as well, as a spiritual influence on fictional realism. As already indicated, Lloyd used literary devices such as *Wealth*. However, the preference among social reformers before Lloyd was to go further, fictionalizing concerns into made-up characters, situations, and conversations. Readers, it was assumed, would sympathize more effectively with imaginary than real people and events. *Wealth* relied on facts, some would say too many. Lloyd knew he was breaking new ground with *Wealth*, writing shortly before it was published, "One main purpose of this book will have been fulfilled if it succeeds in giving our novelists, dramatists, poets, and historians some hint of the treasures of new material that lie waiting for them in real life. Here are whole continents of romance, adventure and ungathered gold which have been *terrae incognitae* to our explorers of the pen." True to his prediction, an ever increasing number of writers, including the muckrakers, turned to realism in the years after *Wealth* with astonishing success. Unfortunately for Lloyd, by the time the reading public had become receptive to realism, he had become frustrated with the style.[37]

Lloyd completed what he hoped would be the final draft of *Wealth* in mid-May 1893 and celebrated his accomplishment by attending the newly-opened Columbian World Exposition in Chicago. Jessie wrote in her diary, "The most beautiful day of all this spring celebrated with Harry and the finishing of his four-year task by going to the fair. It is so blessed to be with my husband." Lloyd sent copies of his manuscript to five publishers and waited for their reaction. He was exceedingly disheartened when, one by one, all five rejected it over the summer. The result was a revision, shorter, but with publication, *Wealth* took on a life of its own.[38]

NOTES

1. Edward Bellamy, *A Letter from Edward Bellamy: The Rate of the World's Progress*, undated pamphlet, circa April 1888, State Historical Society of Wisconsin and HDL to Moritz Pinner, 17 December 1897, in HDL, Wisc.

2. HDL to Shelby Cullom, 10 December 1886 and Cullom to HDL, 18 December 1886, both in HDL, Wisc.; Ari and Olive Hoogenboom, *A History of the I.C.C.* (New York: Norton, 1976); and Balthasar H. Meyer, *Railway Legislation in the United States* (New York: Arno Press, 1973, 1903).

3. George Rice to HDL, 9 November 1887, in HDL, Wisc.; *New York Times*, 23 February 1887 and HDL, "Fanatic S. Oil," 26 November 1887, both in HDL, mf.

4. M. L. Scudder to HDL, 5 December 1889; HDL to George Rice, 20 November

1891; and John F. Power to CLS, 23 October 1907; all in HDL, Wisc.

5. David D. Lloyd to HDL, 14 November 1888 and 15 April 1889; HDL to Rice, 3, 9, 11, 13 March 1889; and Junius Henry Brown to HDL, 3 April 1889, all in HDL, Wisc.

6. CLS, MS note, n.d. and "Sins of a Trust" publicity notice, 6 March 1889, both in HDL, mf.; HDL to Charles B. Matthews, 20 May 1889; HDL to William M. Salter, 30 August 1894; HDL to Ethelbert Stewart, 7 October 1890; Stewart to HDL, 29 October, 12 December 1890, all in HDL, Wisc.

7. *Pure Oil Trust v. Standard Oil Company: Being the Report of An Investigation by the United States Industrial Commission Compiled from Private and Official Sources by the Oil City Derrick, 1899-1900* (Oil City, PA: Derrick Publishing Co., 1901): 68; Thorelli, *Federal Anti-Trust Policy*, 91–96; Hidy and Hidy, *Standard Oil Company*, 205-346-368; Harold F. Williamson and Arnold R. Daum, *The American Petroleum Industry: The Age of Illumination 1859-1899* (Evanston, IL: Northwestern University Press, 1959); and Ernest C. Miller, *Pennsylvania's Oil Industry* (Gettysburg, PA: The Pennsylvania Historical Association, 1974), 47-55.

8. Clark, *Federal Trust Policy*, 17–18; Thorelli, *Federal Anti-Trust Policy*, 134; Hidy and Hidy, *History of the Standard Oil Company*, 702-711.

9. HDL, Wisc. contains correspondence too extensive to cite regarding Lloyd's research for *Wealth*. Also see HDL to Warren M. Foote, 1 November 1898, in HDL, Wisc.; *Wealth Against Commonwealth* bibliography in HDL, mf.; and Destler, *Empire of Reform*, 293-294.

10. Alonzo Barton Hepburn, *Proceedings Before the Assembly Committee on Railroads on the Bill Entitled An Act to Regulate the Transportation of Freight by Railroad Companys* (Albany: Weed, Parsons and Company, 1880), 40–46; *Report of the Special Committee on Railroads Appointed Under a Resolution of the Assembly, February 28, 1879 to Investigate Alleged Abuses of the Management of Railroads Chartered by the State of New York* (Albany: Weed, Parsons and Company, 1880); *Testimony of George R. Blanchard Before the Special Railroad Committee of the New York Assembly Appointed to Investigate Alleged Abuses in the Management of the Railroads of the State, October 17-25, 1879* (New York: Marton B. Brown, 1880), 602–603; HDL to Simon Sterne, 23 September, 20 December 1879, in HDL, Wisc.; *C.T.*, 28 January, 13 March 1880; and S. M. Cullom to Simon Sterne, 8 September 1885 and 16 June 1886, in Simon Sterne papers, New York Public Library.

11. Roger Sherman, "The Standard Oil Trust: The Gospel of Greed," *Forum*, 13(July 1892): 602-615 and Chester M. Destler, *Roger Sherman and the Independent Oil Men* (Ithaca, NY: Cornell University Press, 1967), 223-228.

12. James F. Hudson, "Modern Feudalism," *North American Review*, 144(March 1887): 271-290; HDL to Carroll D. Wright, 16 January 1888; HDL to Ethelbert Stewart, 30 November 1893; James F. Hudson to HDL, 19 March 1892, 16 December 1893; and Hudson to CLS, 20 April 1906; all in HDL, Wisc.; CLS, "Directions left by Mr. Lloyd in 1896 or 1897 with regard to the publication of his writings," typed MS, both in HDL, mf.; Hidy and Hidy, *Standard Oil*, 713-714; and Destler, *Empire of Reform*, 292-295.

13. Johnson N. Camden and John C. Welch, "The Standard Oil Company," *North American Review*, 136(February 1883): 181-200; S. C. T. Dodd, *Combinations; Their Uses and Abuses; with a History of the Standard Oil Trust* (New York: G. F. Nesbitt &

Co., 1888); George Gunton, "The Economic and Social Aspects of Trusts," *Political Science Quarterly*, 3 (September 1888), 385–408; and Theodore W. Dwight, "The Legality of Trusts,'" *Political Science Quarterly*, 3 (December 1888): 592–628.

14. HDL to John Teagle, 29 March 1892, HDL, Wisc.; Edward Chase Kirkland, *Dream and Thought in the Business Community, 1860–1900* (Ithaca, NY: Cornell University Press, 1956), 1–28; Gerald F. Cavanagh, *American Business Values*, 3d ed. (Englewood Cliffs, NJ: Prentice Hall, 1990), 77–91; Saul Engelbourg, *Power and Morality: American Business Ethics 1840–1914* (Westport, CT: Greenwood Press, 1980), 12–49; and Michael J. Turner, "Henry Demarest Lloyd and Business Ethics in Late Nineteenth- and Early Twentieth-Century America," *Business History*, 36(October 1994): 53–78.

15. *John D. Rockefeller Interview, 1917–1920, conducted by William O. Inglis*, compiled and introduced by David Freeman Hawke (Westport CT: Meckler Publishing, 1984), 79a, 86 (hereafter JDR Interview); Kirkland, *Dream and Thought*, 147–167; "An Oily Interview: A Former Agent Discusses the Standard Oil Company's Methods," *Detroit Free Press*, 16 January 1891; Henry Campbell Black, *A Dictionary of Law* (St. Paul, MN: West Publishing Co., 1891), 446; Tarbell, *Day's Work*, 231–253; and various newspaper clippings on the Standard, HDL, mf.

16. CLS Journal; William W. Harkness to HDL, 8 July 1889; C. B. Fanwood to HDL, 14 May 1889; Lewis Emery Jr. to HDL, 4 April 1891; Congressman John H. Reagan to HDL, 6 May 1888; L. S. Saner to HDL, 23 December 1891; all in HDL, Wisc.; MS note on missing documents from Caroline Stallbohm, n.d., circa 1935, in HDL, mf.; CLS, *Lloyd* I, 238; and Tarbell, *Day's Work*, 209–210.

17. HDL to Maria Lloyd, 27 March 1891; HDL to C. B. Matthews, 2 October 1891; HDL to Father John Power, 1 June 1892; and HDL to William M. Salter, 30 August 1894; all in HDL, Wisc.

18. James F. Hudson to HDL, 26 October 1890, in HDL, Wisc. and HDL, "Song of the Barrel," *Wealth Against Commonwealth* (New York: Harper and Brothers, 1894), 128–151. All *Wealth* quotations are from the original, unabridged 1894 edition.

19. "A Talk With Fraulein," undated MS; Moot to C. B. Matthews, 30 April 1893; and Sherman to HDL, 15 May 1893; all in HDL, Wisc.

20. The comparison between Lloyd's opening line and Rousseau is discussed in Chamberlain, *Reform*, 54. Also see Staughton Lynd, *Intellectual Origins of American Radicalism* (New York: Pantheon Books, 1968), 4–7 and J. Herbert Altschull, *From Milton to McLuhan: The Ideas Behind American Journalism* (New York: Longman Press, 1990), 85–92.

21. Philip P. Robbins, "The Tarbell Papers and the History of the Standard Oil Company" (Ph.D. diss., University of Pittsburgh, 1966), 29–48, 104–124; Miller, *Oil Industry*, 47–52; HDL, *Wealth Against Commonwealth*, 94; and "A History of the Rise and Fall of the South Improvement Company," unpublished MS, n.d., circa 1870s, Destler Papers, Wisc.

22. HDL, *Wealth Against Commonwealth*, 117; Williamson and Daum, *Petroleum Industry*, 440–462; Robbins, "Tarbell Papers," 63–91; Miller, *Oil Industry*, 52–54; Leo Marx, *The Machine in the Garden: Technology and Pastoral Ideal in America* (New York: Oxford University Press, 1964); and Alan Trachtenberg, "Mechanization Takes Command," *Incorporation*, 38–69.

23. HDL, *Wealth Against Commonwealth*, 83; Jernigan, *Lloyd*, 67; Williamson and

Daum, *Petroleum Industry*, 712; Robbins, "Tarbell Papers," 277–285; and undated note from CLS, circa 1935, on the Backus testimony, in HDL, mf.

According to Chester M. Destler, some of the documents used to exonerate Rockefeller in the Widow Backus case came from her family after her death, and are therefore questionable. See Destler, *American Radicalism, 1865–1901* (New York: Octagon Books, 1963, 1946), 148–149 and Destler, *Empire of Reform*, 566, footnote 22.

24. HDL, *Wealth Against Commonwealth*, 271; Jernigan, *Lloyd*, 68–69; Tarbell, *Day's Work*, 220–225; and Williamson and Daum, *Petroleum Industry*, 476.

25. Robbins, *American Advocacy*, 119–120 and Gardner, *Legal Argument*, 1.44–1.45.

26. HDL, *Wealth Against Commonwealth*, 301, 352, 367 and Thomas, *Alternative*, 296–298.

27. HDL, *Wealth Against Commonwealth*, 464–465, 533, 535; Sproat, *Best Men*; 158–165; Frederick, *Knights*, 61; 73–75; Thomas, *Lloyd*, 299–300; and Thomas Bender, *Community and Social Change in America* (Baltimore: The Johns Hopkins University Press, 1976).

28. Analyses of *Wealth Against Commonwealth* can be found in John Chamberlain, "Forward," *Wealth Against Commonwealth* (Washington: National Home Library Foundation, 1936), i–ii; Aaron, *Men of Good Hope*, 155; O'Connor, "Henry Demarest Lloyd," 88; Destler, *Empire of Reform*, 295–305; Thomas C. Cochran, "Introduction," *Wealth Against Commonwealth* (Englewood Cliffs, NJ: Prentice-Hall, Inc., 1963); Jernigan, *Lloyd*, 71–77; Frederick, *Knights*, 74–76; Nevins, *John D. Rockefeller: The Heroic Age of American Enterprise*, II (New York: Charles Scribner's Sons, 1940), 331–342; Nevins, *Study in Power: John D. Rockefeller, Industrialist and Philanthropist*, II (New York: Charles Scribner's Sons, 1953), 330–334; Nevins, "Communication," *American Historical Review*, 50(April 1945): 676–689; Chester M. Destler, "A Commentary on the "Communication" from Allan Nevins in the *American Historical Review*, April 1945," unpublished MS, State Historical Society of Wisconsin Collection.

Shorter analyses can be found in Albert H. Carr, *John D. Rockefeller's Secret Weapon* (New York: McGraw-Hill, 1962), 98–99; Abels, *Rockefeller Billions*, 222–226; Williamson and Daum, *Petroleum Industry*, 712–713; Thorelli, *Federal Anti-Trust*, 329–330; Edward Kirkland, *Industry Comes of Age: Business, Labor and Public Policy, 1860–1897* (New York: Holt, Rinehart and Winston, 1961), 306–314; Bruce Bringhurst, *Antitrust and the Oil Monopoly: The Standard Oil Cases, 1890–1911* (Westport, CT: Greenwood Press, 1979), 204–206; Charles and Mary Beard, *The Rise of American Civilization* (New York: The Macmillan Company, 1930), 426–429; Richard Hofstadter, *The Progressive Historians: Turner, Beard, Parrington* (New York: Alfred Knopf, 1968), 185; Paul F. Boller, *American Thought in Transition* (Chicago: Rand McNally and Co., 1969), 107–110; Spiller, *Literary History*, 979–980; Gashman, *America in the Gilded Age*, 62–64; David Freeman Hawke, *John D: The Founding Father of the Rockefellers* (New York: Harper and Row, 1980), 215; and Thomas, *Alternative*, 354–357.

29. Destler, "The Historical Accuracy and Significance of Henry D. Lloyd's *Wealth Against Commonwealth*," paper presented to the Mississippi Valley Historical Society, March 1944, as cited in *Mississippi Valley Historical Review*, 31(September 1944): 233–234; Hidy and Hidy, *Standard Oil Company*, 720; Destler, *Empire of Reform*, 295–305; and Jernigan, *Lloyd*, 71–77.

30. Destler, *Empire of Reform*, 305.

31. HDL to H. Clay Bascom, 1 May 1895; HDL to Rev. B. Fay Mills, 21 May 1896;

and Samuel Bowles to HDL, 7 May 1900; all in HDL, Wisc.

John D. Rockefeller is named only once in *Wealth*, on page 228 in the unabridged first edition.

32. Mason H. Newell, *The Law of Slander and Libel in Civil and Criminal Cases* (Chicago: Callaghan and Co., 1876, 1898), 1–3 and Norman L. Rosenberg, *Protecting the Best Men: An Interpretive History of the Law of Libel* (Chapel Hill, NC: University of North Carolina Press, 1986), 178–197.

33. Sherman to HDL, 30 December 1895, and CLS Journal, both in HDL, Wisc.; Baughman, *Henry R. Luce*, 45–46.

34. Richard T. Ely, "The Nature and Significance of Monopolies and Trusts," *International Journal of Ethics*, 10(April 1900): 273–288; Ely, *Problems of Today: A Discussion of Protective Tariffs, Taxation, and Monopolies* (New York: Thomas Y. Cromwell, 1890); John Bates Clark, *The Control of Trusts: An Argument in Favor of Curbing the Power by a Natural Method* (New York: Macmillan, 1905); and Jeremiah Whipple Jenks, *The Trust Problem* (New York: McClure, Phillips and Co., 1900).

See also Benjamin G. Rader, *The Academic Mind and Reform: The Influence of Richard T. Ely in American Life* (Lexington: University of Kentucky Press, 1966): 90–105; Sproat, *Best Men*, 158–165; Ralph L. Nelson, *Merger Movements in American Industry, 1895-1956* (Princeton, NJ: Princeton University Press, 1959): 1–11; W. Elliot Brownlee, *Dynamics of Ascent: A History of the American Economy* (Chicago: Dorsey Press, 1988), 198–204; and Naomi R. Lamoreaux, *The Great Merger Movement in American Business, 1895-1904* (New York: Cambridge University Press, 1985):1–10.

35. HDL to Ely, 30 March and HDL to Ely, 6 April 1898, both in Ely Papers, Wisc. and HDL, *Wealth Against Commonwealth*, 491.

36. HDL to Charles F. Mosher, 23 September 1895, in HDL, Wisc.; "How Shall the Senate Deal With Powerful Trusts?," *Cleveland Press*, 29 June 1897; *Kansas City Times*, 29 September 1903, clipping in HDL, mf.; Steven L. Piott, *The Anti-Monopoly Persuasion: Popular Resistance to the Rise of Big Business in the Midwest* (Westport, CT: Greenwood Press, 1985), 106–107; Filler, *Progressivism and Muckraking*, 69; Louis Filler, *The Muckrakers: New and Enlarged Edition of Crusaders for American Liberalism* (University Park: The Pennsylvania State University Press, 1976), 25–26; Bringhurst, *Oil Monopoly*, 204–206; Williamson and Daum, *Petroleum Industry*, 712–713; and Jernigan, *Lloyd*, 71–77.

37. HDL, "Wealth Against Commonwealth," *Altruistic Review*, December 1894, MS in HDL, mf.

38. JBL MS Diary, 19 May 1893, CHS.

6

The Legacy of *Wealth*

The research and writing of *Wealth* was an arduous task for Henry Demarest Lloyd. He had his wife and secretary help him in its seven years of preparation, but he could not match the research assistants and financial support that Ida Tarbell received from magazine publisher Samuel S. McClure for her *History of the Standard Oil Company*. Defending and justifying *Wealth* after it was published also took a good deal of Lloyd's time and energy. His obsession with the book and its message was ridiculed by many, especially those who saw him as nothing more than a dreamer. His sister Caro wrote at the time the book first appeared, "Certain types of mind and spirit can not understand self-sacrifice, or the passion for human betterment. They could not . . . interpret Henry Demarest Lloyd and his *Wealth versus Commonwealth* [sic] as written because he was interested in the other side of the market."[1]

The reviews for *Wealth* proved that Lloyd had at least partially touched upon the temper of the early 1890s, especially the public's growing distrust of monopolies, and the book's sales showed that a nonfiction work could sell. Lloyd was most surprised by the Standard Oil Company's failure to rebut his allegations, and the company's silence mystified him for the remainder of his life. It was not until years after Lloyd's death that John D. Rockefeller revealed how much the book had hurt the Standard Oil Company and himself. Throughout the twentieth century, *Wealth* continued to create controversy, from ecstatic endorsements to vindictive attacks. Today, it remains one of only a few American books that continues to inflame passion long after its original purpose has been served, but that has been and will always be the point and nature of true advocacy journalism.

As already indicated, Lloyd sent copies of what he hoped would be his final draft to several publishers in mid-May 1893. The five included one Chicago firm, A. C. McClurg, and four Eastern companies, Appleton, G. P. Putnam's, Harper and Brothers, and Houghton and Mifflin. The Eastern firms were primarily concerned with the nonfictional nature of the book. Appleton promptly turned him down based on its length. Houghton and Mifflin, the tradition-bound Boston-based publisher of the *Atlantic Monthly*, rejected it on its "points of style, which seems . . . more allowable in journalistic writing than in a work which takes the more dignified and permanent form of a book." Putnam declined it because it believed sales of political and economic works were not "remunerative."[2]

The most disillusioning dismissal came from the Chicago-based McClurg's. The company gave the manuscript a serious reading, asking a lawyer with a literary background to critique it. He grudgingly recommended publication, but with an embarrassing number of revisions. Some of his objections were based on Lloyd's trivial misuse of classical imagery:

Occasionally the author, being but human, sacrifices historical or legendary accuracy on the altar of forcible phraseology, as for instance, "Midas would be *snuffed out again* in his own gold." It is questionable if even in legend the mythical Midas of Phrygia was ever "snuffed out." On the contrary, tradition tells us he washed in the since gold laden ripples of Pactolus and, presumably, thence forth was clean.

His other concerns were more significant. One involved Lloyd's ex parte defense. "The fault to my judgment with the author," the reviewer wrote, "is that [he] is biased against monopolies and trusts, so much so that he excludes all evidence for the defense. The fact that the defense calls witnesses may not alter the verdict [but] the feeling that a defense is not allowed may change the whole result." Another problem involved Lloyd's many libels. Assuming that Rockefeller and the Standard would have had an easy time at winning a libel judgment, the reviewer discerned somewhat accurately that Lloyd would "cheerfully reiterate his libels to a crowded and appreciative court." More out of fear of being sued than in disagreement with his words, McClurg's rejected the manuscript.[3]

Fortunately, Lloyd sent the manuscript to Harper and Brothers, one of the leading Gilded Age publishers. In doing so, he took advantage of a friendship that he had formed twelve years earlier during the publication of "Story of a Great Monopoly." William Dean Howells respected Lloyd for his brave article, and the two had remained friends even after Howells had turned to full-time fiction writing. He told Lloyd in late 1893, "There are very few people left in the world, now, whom I care to meet, and I find upon reflection, that you are one of the chief of them." Lloyd asked Howells to read the manuscript and the novelist reported that "the sky seems full of signs" for its publication. When the other firms began rejecting it, Howells took advantage of his leverage with the Harper brothers. They had published several of his popular novels and he suggested that their firm give Lloyd serious consideration. The Harpers were less than enthusiastic about the work at first, noting that it was "so bulky and so full of minute details" that they could not profitably sell it without serious revision. Lloyd protested, telling the firm "I could easily tell the story in one-quarter the space . . . but then the story would be only told; it would not be proved. . . . The condensation into a rapid running narrative is literally, entirely feasible, but it would open the door to the hopeless befuddlement of the public by the outcry ceaselessly reiterated that the facts did not warrant the statements and inferences." With rejection letters pouring in by the end of 1893, however, both the Harpers and Lloyd relented, and they agreed to publish the work if he condensed his thousand-page manuscript into a more manageable reading length.[4]

Lloyd characterized the changes as "cutting himself out" of the book, but the edits were a little more extensive. He rearranged the chapters, omitting some of his more caustic commentary, or lowering the "key of the pitch" as he said. For example, he eliminated lines such as "Colonel Drake's drill broke into another Pandora's box down in the caverns and let loose a wise and wicked host of spirits that have never since ceased going about to serve and trouble and tempt mankind," a reference to the discovery of oil in Western Pennsylvania by Edwin Drake in 1859. Lloyd added data on other monopolies to reduce his seeming vendetta against the Standard. He made stylistic changes, excising thirty-five sections that were wordy, redundant, or poorly written. He trimmed or eliminated lengthy quotations, some filling a page or more of typewritten text. There is no evidence that any of the changes were influenced by the Standard, even though the Harpers' firm could justifiably have been called a big business at the time. The Harpers had the manuscript checked for libel, but let the numerous if oblique references to Rockefeller and the Standard stand as they were.[5]

To sweeten the pot, Lloyd offered to pay for the preparation of the book's printing plates, the same arrangement that he had struck for *Millionaires*. Even though the text was still longer than they wanted, the Harpers, at the prodding of Howells, agreed with his offer on one final condition. They asked Lloyd to come up with a better title than "The Story of a Great Monopoly," his original choice. He sent a list of thirteen alternatives and let them choose the best. "Wealth Against Commonwealth" was fifth among the possibilities that included "The Rule of Gold and the Golden Rule," "Sins of a Trust," "The Next Emancipation," and "Facts for the Epitaph of the Republic." Armed with a new name, Roger Sherman and Adelbert Moot passed a final judgment on the revised manuscript, and Lloyd spent the spring and summer of 1894 correcting the galley proofs. Review copies were mailed in September, marking more than five years from the date that Lloyd had first set to researching and writing the book.[6]

As expected, the most favorable reactions to *Wealth* came from the same cadre of socially-conscious intellectuals that had endorsed his earlier writings. Theologian Edward Everett Hale provided the most quotable review, telling Lloyd that *Wealth* "is as much an epoch-making book as *Uncle Tom's Cabin*." Lloyd was so proud of Hale's remark and its connection to abolitionism that he used it in all of *Wealth*'s promotional literature. William Dean Howells called it a "great book," one that required "nervous strength" to read. "To think that the monstrous iniquity whose story you tell so powerfully," he wrote, "accomplished itself in our time, is so astounding, so infuriating, that I have to stop from chapter to chapter, and take breath." Edwin D. Mead, a Lloyd friend and the editor of *New England Magazine*, wrote, "Mr. Lloyd's book is strong because, facing all the facts, stating them all at their worst, it is not a black and despairing book, like the books of so many of our present social reformers, but a hopeful, brave, and confident book." William T. Harris, the U.S. Commissioner of Education, praised the book as did Tulane University President William Preston Johnston. Feminist reformer Florence Kelley wrote, "I think Mr. Lloyd's campaign is the beginning of the new era in our national life." The former University of Wisconsin president, John Bascom, predicted that the book "ought to mark an era of resistance" to the monopolies. Oil journalist James F. Hudson said, "This impregnable fortification of the facts establishes the work as one of the books of the era." Naturalist John Borroughs told Lloyd, "I have just written to a New York editor who pooh-poohed [*Wealth*] and called you a Populist. etc., [but] if you are a Populist, I am one, and have always been without knowing it; if you are an anarchist, I am too, and glory in it." Social Gospel minister the Reverend Washington Gladden wondered aloud why the book "had not caused more excitement; it surprises me that it does not cause an insurrection." Rockefeller acquaintance and University of Chicago President William Rainey Harper penned a humorous poem in praise of *Wealth*, calling it "Health for the Commonwealth" and "Lloyd's Liverarium."[7]

Although most liberals praised the book, a few were less enthusiastic. Boston attorney and future U.S. Supreme Court Justice Louis D. Brandeis wrote to a friend, "Our people still admire the Captains of the trusts. The facts collected by Lloyd would, if presented to the people, tend to remove this admiration and make Americans conscious of the dangers under which they are living." He continued, "To do this is in the power of Lloyd, and I should say it would be accomplished by stating these facts perhaps under the name of 'The Story of the Standard Oil Monopoly,' telling them in a book perhaps one-third the size of *Wealth Against Commonwealth*, and telling them with the names of the perpetrators appearing where he who runs may read."[8]

More than a hundred newspapers and magazines in the United States and the world reviewed *Wealth*. Some brimmed with praise. The *Boston Advertiser* thought it was an "epoch-making" work. The reform magazine *Outlook* called it "the most powerful book on economics that has appeared in this country since Henry George's *Progress and Poverty*." The *Titusville World*, at the center of the oil industry, called President Grover Cleveland's purchase of the book "one of the most sensible things he has done." Even the staid *Times of London* observed, "Mr. Lloyd's book, in spite of its dull, semi-official external look, is about as racy an attack on unscrupulous trusts and other combinations as we have met with for a long time."[9]

As expected, publications catering to laissez-faire capitalists and Social Darwinists reacted negatively. *Wealth* was panned by the *American Banker*, the Boston *Commercial Bulletin*, and E. L. Godkin's *Nation*. Albert Shaw wrote in the *Review of Reviews* that the book was "too overwhelming in its assault to command" popular influence. The *Boston Journal* complained that *Wealth* overlooked Richard T. Ely's theories on monopolies, noting, "When [Lloyd] comes to his deductions we believe that the field is one in which a wide difference of opinion will prevail even among the unprejudiced students of industrial and economic conditions." *The New York Times*, the *New York Tribune*, and Godkin's *New York Evening Journal* rejected it as well. The *Boston Herald*, which eventually became friendly to Lloyd, initially wrote, "[Lloyd] has undoubtedly been too sweeping in his assertions, and takes too little pains to support them with proof." Another Boston paper attacked the book's factual writing style, complaining, "It is written in a style which we trust is to fall more and more into disuse among us; it must do so if men are reasoning and not merely declamatory animals."[10]

Not surprisingly, the *Chicago Tribune* panned the book too. The *Tribune*, firmly committed to the free-market dogma of Joseph Medill, faulted its stockholder and former employee for a variety of transgressions. Without once mentioning Lloyd's past *Tribune* connections, reviewer Edwin L. Shuman wrote:

This *Wealth Against Commonwealth* is a superstructure of dreams erected on a basis of fact. The facts are valuable. The dreams have been dreamed since the days of Plato and have not upset the world nor revolutionized human nature . . . so the probabilities are Mr. Lloyd's dream will be harmless.

Shuman's criticisms hurt Lloyd more than any other, and he wrote a letter to protest them. Shuman's response revealed something of the antagonism against Lloyd that flourished at the newspaper. "I have not been able to accept the socialistic solution of industrial evils, nor could I have reviewed your book from that standpoint in the *Tribune* if I had desired," Shuman said. "It is rather unusual for the *Tribune* to review a new edition of a book, but I thought you would appreciate my saying something rather than nothing, so I wrote what I did."[11]

Of all of the reactions to *Wealth*, none was more curious than John D. Rockefeller's. Although he claimed never to have read the book himself, Rockefeller was well aware of its major arguments, attacking them in detail in a series of interviews given to a *New York World* reporter, William O. Inglis, between 1917 and 1920 but not made public until the 1970s. "It is the style that an unscrupulous lawyer could use before a lot of ignorant people," Rockefeller said, "throwing a lot of dust in their eyes and absolutely deceiving them as to the facts." Rockefeller denied any involvement in the ill-fated South Improvement Company in 1872, rebutting Lloyd's charge that the Standard had received illegal railroad rebates with the comment that his efforts "led to an advance in all the railroads, and they came to regard us as their best friends and servants because we did 'even' the business for them." Of the Charles B. Matthews Buffalo Lubricating Oil refinery sabotage incident, Rockefeller said, "[Lloyd] makes a great ado over a matter, exploiting all the details for spectacular effect; then comes to a court decision which reaches the conclusion that it is a tempest in a teapot." Of the Widow Backus, Rockefeller cited her brother-in-law, who was one of his employees, with the remark that she had been fairly paid. Rockefeller leveled his most vicious attack against George Rice, a character in another of Lloyd's miniature melodramas, telling his interviewer, "I do not wonder that it was currently reported that this poor man was for a time in an insane asylum in years past. His mind was not well balanced." In the end, *Wealth* hurt its readers more than it damaged Rockefeller because it encouraged them to believe in idealistic and unrealistic solutions to life's problems. The monopolist explained:

How unfortunate that so many young men were fooled by [Lloyd's] book, and were prevented making a fair start in life or acquiring the resultant beneficiary effects of such a start. . . . We have the pride and the satisfaction of knowing that hundreds, thousands, tens of thousands, of practical men following the line of duty with us . . . [and] are today in independent circumstances. . . . Shame to this writer for his false and destructive teachings, and praise to the men who teach men industry and promote them for good service![12]

Unlike Lloyd, Rockefeller attacked his adversary by name in the interview, using epitaphs such as "socialist," "anarchist," "slanderer," "yellow journalist," and sarcastically, "historian." Of Lloyd's personal life, Rockefeller said, "He married a rich wife, and lived uptown in a fashionable neighborhood, and lived on the fat of the land." Rockefeller explained to his interviewer why he never sued Lloyd for libel:

In the first place, a man cannot concentrate his faculties at the same time on two opposite things; and I was concentrated upon extending and developing and perfecting our business, rather than to stop by the wayside and squabble with slanderers. In the second place, we could tell by the nature of the attacks made upon us that [both Lloyd and Ida Tarbell] did not suspect the ways by which we really were making profits in every branch of our business. We saw that not only our enemies but everyone else were up in the air in their guesses as to how we were making money, and we were not going to call them down and point out the sources of our profit. We poor country boys, brought up amid hardships and taught to be self-reliant, knew enough to mind our own business and let the others chatter.

Rockefeller's silence on *Wealth* was the most mysterious aspect of the book, and it confused readers as it confounded Lloyd. More than one wrote to Lloyd with sentiments such as "Mr. Rockefeller ought to sue Lloyd for libel or else in the light of that publication he stands convicted as a commercial pirate even though sailing under his country's flag." But Rockefeller was more interested in the perfection of his business than his public image. Ida Tarbell explained in a 1936 study of late nineteenth-century business, "Rockefeller was a man who gave himself entirely to his business, saw it as a whole, its tiniest detail as well as its largest possible ramification." He could not allow Lloyd or Tarbell to distract him from his larger goals, and he preferred laughing all the way to the bank to defending his reputation.[13]

The Standard never mounted any official rebuttal to *Wealth*, but it did support several unofficial responses. The first appeared as an anonymous *Wealth* review in E. L. Godkin's *Nation* in late 1894. Likely written by W. T. Scheide, a western Pennsylvania journalist and long time Standard supporter, the review held that *Wealth* was "a notable example of the rhetorical blunder of over-statement," calling the book "over 500 octavo pages of the wildest rant." A German political economist who had read *Wealth* during the finishing stages of his own book tried to rebut it in *Trusts or Industrial Combinations and Coalitions in the United States*, which was published in 1895. Ernest Levy von Halle accused Lloyd of several factual errors, but translation problems and an embarrassing number of his own mistakes muted his impact. Although the Standard did not directly support either Scheide or von Halle, it approved of and helped publicize their objections.[14]

A third response turned out more helpful than harmful to Lloyd. George Gunton, a political economist who wrote pro-trust editorials for the *New York Commercial Bulletin* and edited a semi-scholarly journal known as the *Social Economist*, reviewed *Wealth* in July 1895 and labeled it the "latest and worst specimen" of a recent onslaught of "iconoclastic propaganda" against industrial growth. He wrote, "It is indeed typical in its inflammatory style; its violent misrepresentation through garbled statements in quotation marks; and the utter suppression of evidence on the other side. We have taken the pains to go through the public documents referred to in this book, and it may be said that there is scarcely an honest equation in it." In thoughts remarkably similar to those expressed by John D. Rockefeller some twenty-five years later, Gunton called Lloyd a "social insane" and observed that "a form of epidemic delirium comes from reading Lloyd's social slanders, without the opportunity to see those neglected nine-tenths of the story, which, when brought to bear upon the one-tenth that is told, convert it into a lie of atrocious baseness."[15]

If Gunton was not on the Standard's payroll at the time his review was published, he was soon thereafter.   Lloyd elected not to sue him for libel (calling him insane would have been actionable) but he could not allow Gunton's comments about *Wealth* to go unchallenged even though he considered them "an amazingly weak performance." His rebuttal was staged as a speech to Boston's prestigious Twentieth Century Club in October 1895. In his talk, Lloyd took his typical high moral road, refusing to disparage or even name his adversary, instead arguing that Gunton had "failed to discover the only serious error—a typographical one—that was made, so far as we have been able to tell." The use of the Twentieth Century Club as a forum for his reply was a stroke of genius, for it attracted the notice of most of the city's press, which in turn transmitted Lloyd's spin on the controversy to other newspapers around the country. The most favorable story appeared in the *Boston Herald*, which published an interview with Lloyd under the headline, "The Fighter of Trusts: Henry D. Lloyd Scores Gunton's Defense of Standard Oilers." In the interview, Lloyd speculated on why the Standard had failed to rebut his book. "That is the fault of the evidence, not of its presentation," he said. "The fact is, the trusts have never been able to make any valid defense." Gunton accused Lloyd of ignoring the Standard's side of the story, but Lloyd countered that he had used more than two hundred quotes from Rockefeller or his associates. The *Herald* reporter noted that *Wealth* had made the "deepest impression in economics since George's *Progress and Poverty*. Lloyd was so pleased by the *Herald* story that he boasted to a friend, "To get four solid columns given to an unsparing and radical exposition of the methods of the worst monopoly was an advantage, not a detriment, to the cause." [16]

Gunton responded to Lloyd, but in doing so made a faux pas that gave the debate to Lloyd. In a letter to the *Boston Herald* published six weeks after Lloyd's speech, Gunton claimed that he had received a statement from prominent English social scientist John A. Hobson rejecting *Wealth* and embracing the Standard's view on monopolies. Lloyd was an acquaintance of Hobson's, an American correspondent for his Fabian magazine, and immediately demanded an explanation. Hobson replied that he had specifically instructed Gunton to reprint his entire statement and not quote him out of context. Lloyd revealed Gunton's duplicity to *Herald* readers in February 1896 and challenged him to print Hobson's entire letter as he had been instructed to do. When no reply materialized, Lloyd told a friend, "Gunton has placed himself outside of the pale of controversy with gentlemen . . . I should never again condescend to any controversy with him on any subject." [17]

The Standard turned next to the clergy as a tool to discredit Lloyd. John D. Rockefeller considered himself a devoutly religious man, and he was especially hurt when clergymen, many of whom had received free copies of *Wealth* from Lloyd, began openly criticizing him and his company from their pulpits. He invited the Reverend B. Fay Mills, a well-known social gospel minister and an editor of the liberal religious weekly *The Kingdom*, to examine the Standard's financial books at the company's huge New York headquarters in mid-1896. Rockefeller later recalled:

A noted evangelist—B. Fay Mills, I think is the name—who . . . stood up and arraigned the Standard Oil Company, and on being invited to come to the Standard Oil Company's office, where he learned the facts and was proved to be mistake, said: "What can I do? I want to right the wrong!" He was told by [one of Rockefeller's assistants] who had shown him the books and answered every question: "You need do nothing. I think in the future you should be quite sure of what you are speaking about when it affects the character, the good repute of men, in public or in private."

In reality, Mills did more than apologize to Rockefeller. He invited several friends, including theologians Edward Everett Hale, Washington Gladden, Lyman Abbot, George A. Gates, George D. Herron, and Leighton Williams and academics Richard T. Ely, J. W. Jenks, and John R. Commons, to meet with Rockefeller as he had. In return for their attendance, Rockefeller promised to open the Standard's books to them, proving his innocence of Lloyd's charges. Mills also advised Lloyd of his plan and asked for his support. Lloyd assumed that this was the great showdown with the Standard that he had long feared and gave his blessing, noting "The idea of a company of Christian gentlemen coming together to receive the bland assurances of the attorney of the Standard Oil Co. is so transparently absurd that I can hardly believe the written words before my eyes."[18]

Although he publicly approved of the plan, Lloyd had many private reservations. Rockefeller's legendary philanthropy had bought more than one convert before, and he had a reputation for being especially generous to churches and universities. To alleviate his fears, Lloyd complained privately to some of the people that Mills had invited that he should have been invited to New York as well. Several, including Ely, agreed and told Rockefeller they would not attend unless Lloyd was present. Given the prospect of a face-to-face meeting with his adversary, Rockefeller backed down and canceled the entire meeting. At the time, the Standard explained that the clergy did not possess enough business acumen to pass meaningful judgment on the company, meaning their meeting would have been fruitless. Privately, Rockefeller considered the clergy ungrateful for failing to back him in spite of all his generosity. He was especially hurt by the Reverend Washington Gladden, whom he called "an old schoolmate, who pursued me for years viciously, and in after years, when it was shown to him conclusively that he had been wrong, he acknowledged to my friends; he said something about correcting his statements, but did not respond in a manly way as he should do as a convert to the idea that he had wronged me."[19]

Rockefeller's forfeiture deprived Lloyd of the confrontation that he desired, but it strengthened his reputation among the academics and clergymen who knew of the affair. Mills subsequently admitted to Lloyd that he had not been swayed by Rockefeller, only made aware of another point of view. Lloyd absolved him, writing, "I will frankly own up that I was afraid the Philistines had succeeded in deceiving you." To make amends, he invited Mills and his family to stay at the Wayside. The clergy and professors incident did little to increase the sales of *Wealth* because it was not publicized widely, but it did reinforce the impression that Rockefeller could not defend himself to Lloyd.[20]

Even though Lloyd enjoyed his personal victory over Rockefeller, he was discouraged by the failure of *Wealth* to incite a mass public uprising against the Standard and other monopolies. A year after the book's publication, he complained to the *Cincinnati Daily Post*, "The public seems to be utterly stagnant, but their enemy is not." He wrote utopian author and Standard critic F. F. Murray, "One thing which I think accounts for the apathy of the working men, the farmers and the middle class in the cities, is that with the logic which the people seem to possess by instinct they divine that the problem of our times is much more complicated than the various vendors of specific panaceas would have them believe." As time went on, he came to blame public apathy for the totality of Gilded Age corruption:

Think how many times since the Credit Mobilier report [in 1872] and the Erie Essays by C. F. Adams, the alarm has been sounded to the American sheep by faithful shepherds and how placidly the sheep has gone on feeding and being fed upon! Plato says reading destroys memory, I sometimes think it destroys everything. We read to be narcotized.[21]

Still, the first edition of *Wealth* was far from a failure. It sold well, enshrining Lloyd as the leading advocate journalist of his day. A Wisconsin reader wrote, "I am happy to be able to state that the public seems to be about to waken to the prevailing condition of things in this locality." An Iowa farmer chronicled his trials with the railroads and told Lloyd, "I am living in hopes that others are waiting, as I am, for things to ripen; and such courage as yours keeps hopes alive." Jessie noted in her diary, "Reading in my darling's great book." Aaron Lloyd startled his son, writing, "I cannot express in language my admiration of your work for its clear, graphic and masterly exposition of the enormous corruptions and oppressions of the most gigantic monopoly of this country and perhaps the world." The book helped Lloyd get a train ride home one rainy spring evening in 1896. In a letter to "Mr. Benson, Conductor, Chicago City Railroad," Lloyd wrote, "I have asked my publishers to send you a copy of a book of mine which I beg you to accept in acknowledgment of your courtesy in lending me one cent the other night." *Wealth* also angered John D. Rockefeller, probably beyond Lloyd's wildest dreams. Speaking years after Lloyd's death and the forced dissolution of the Standard Oil Company by the U.S. Supreme Court, Rockefeller said, "Be that as it may, the record is made, and Lloyd and Tarbell and all the rest cannot wipe it out. And I, standing alone to make this record after my associates are gone, am proud and happy to record as I do these statements in favor of the organization which was maligned more than any other in the history of this country."[22]

From the start, Lloyd was concerned that the impact of *Wealth* would be muted if it was not made available to the middle and lower classes. On the verge of the mass circulation magazine era of the late 1890s, he had few options beyond newspaper excerpts and a paperback edition. Less than a month after publication, he wrote the Harpers suggesting that extended excerpts be distributed free to newspapers around the country to encourage interest and sales in the book and help spread Lloyd's message. Publication of such excerpts was a common nineteenth-century newspaper practice as Lloyd, a former literary editor of the *Chicago Tribune*, was aware. The Harpers did not like the idea, fearing that excerpts would allow readers to learn Lloyd's gist without buying and reading his entire wordy book. Despite repeated prodding, Lloyd could not coax them to change their minds.

At about the same time, Lloyd was bombarded with complaints from friends that the $2.50 hardcover price was too expensive for many potential readers to afford. To help, Lloyd proposed a softcover *Wealth* edition to the Harpers, priced at twenty-five or fifty cents a copy, without any royalties to him. The firm balked at first, claiming that a paperback edition could not be produced at a profit. More likely, however, a paper edition would have reduced hardcover sales, and that was something major American publishers did not desire to do until the paperback explosion after World War II. In late 1895, Lloyd found another press willing to produce such an edition and since he possessed the copyright, the Harpers reluctantly agreed. Unfortunately, their edition, which appeared in early 1896, sold for one dollar, still more than most low-income people could afford. *Wealth* sold well in paper and hardcover. At the time of Lloyd's death in 1903, some ten thousand copies had been purchased, about half paperback, and it continued to sell until World War I. It was not another *Looking Backward*, but *Wealth* was a popular book by late nineteenth-century standards.[23]

Lloyd finally gave in to custom and briefly entertained the notion of a fictionalized version of *Wealth* in 1898. Realism was still relatively new at the turn of the century and in spite of Lloyd's predictions, many readers preferred fictionalized advocacy works such as *Uncle Tom's Cabin* or *Looking Backward* to Lloyd's nonfictional *Wealth*. Unfortunately, the writer who promised to fictionalize *Wealth* failed to finish his volume before Ida Tarbell's Standard Oil series began in *McClure's Magazine* in 1902, and sales of *Wealth* declined enough to make such a version unprofitable. Still, Tarbell, David Graham Phillips, Ray Stannard Baker, and other muckrakers relied upon embellished scenes and recreated conversations in their muckrake writings and Upton Sinclair's 1906 best-seller, *The Jungle*, was entirely fictional. Muckraker Will Irwin noted in 1911, "Behind every tragedy lies a whole novel, behind every movement for human good a poem."[24]

Sales of *Wealth* were strong enough to warrant the preparation of a revised and updated second edition by the end of the 1890s. The Harpers initially asked Lloyd to undertake the project, but he was too busy with other books so he asked several friends, including journalist James Hudson, if they were interested. None knew enough about the Standard to undertake the effort. In lieu of a complete revision, Lloyd made a few minor changes. The most serious was to drop an accusation from the first edition that the Standard had stolen one particular court file. In researching her book a few years later, Ida Tarbell noticed the discrepancy and asked Lloyd for an explanation. He replied that the missing records had reappeared following the first edition of *Wealth*, probably in an effort to discredit him. The Harpers added several pages of favorable reviews to the second edition to further boost sales but otherwise left the book alone.[25]

The second edition appeared in late 1899, stirring a new round of reviews and reactions. Most were supportive, including this tongue-in-cheek "warning" sent to Lloyd:

Hadn't we better arrest Henry [D. Lloyd] and suppress this book, lest some fool be *inspired* to kill somebody? *Progress and Poverty* has many inflammatory statements; but Henry George is dead and we can't revenge ourselves on him. Let us examine the files of Republican and Democratic papers about election times and we my get some "hot stuff" more inflaming than anything yet found from fool anarchists.

The *Conservator* noted, "Lloyd has proved a true prophet . . . both prophet and historian." Another reader called *Wealth* "a very successful piece of realism—no doubt because it is real" and wrote, "I wish the book might be read everywhere." The *Brooklyn Citizen* noted that "none of the persons inculpated ever attempted to vindicate their characters by proceeding against Mr. Lloyd." Not every review was supportive. *The Independent*, a respected religious journal, staged a three-way debate on the trust question in 1897. It featured Lloyd, George Gunton, and the Standard's chief legal counsel, Samuel C. T. Dodd. Lloyd maintained his high moral road, refusing to name or criticize his detractors, but the two Standard men lamented the public's ingratitude for the Standard and other monopolies, and Lloyd came off as arrogant and self-serving in the magazine. A Standard apologist, John J. McLaurin, attacked *Wealth* in his book on the early history of the oil industry, writing in 1898, "[*Wealth* is] notable for its distortion of facts and suppression of all points in favor of the corporation it assails, caters to the worst elements of socialism. The author views everything through anti-combination glasses and, like the child with the boogie-man, sees the monopoly spook in every successful aggregation of capital." The *Chicago Times-Herald* called the new *Wealth* edition "Yellow Journalism and Economics," and the *New York Evening Post* complained that it was built on "false accusations." Lloyd viewed even bad commentary as beneficial, noting "when these philistines attack me, the Lord almost always puts them in my hands."[26]

The Standard mounted one final, unofficial assault against *Wealth* before turning its attention to Ida Tarbell's "History of the Standard Oil Company" series in *McClure's*. Under mounting public pressure brought about in part by Lloyd, Congress created a special commission to investigate monopolies, trusts, and combinations in 1898. The head of the Federal Labor Bureau, Carroll D. Wright, a Lloyd acquaintance and supporter, was asked to prepare a reading list for the commission's members, and Wright included *Wealth* as one of several important economic books. The appearance of *Wealth* on the list angered the Standard, and the firm sought to discredit Lloyd in its commission testimony. Company vice-president and Rockefeller confidant John D. Archbold said, "I desire to say further with reference to this book of Mr. Lloyd's that if you are disposed to waste your time reading it, you will find it with reference to its statements regarding the business of the Standard Oil Company one of the most untruthful distorted compilations that was ever inflicted upon a suffering public." Before Lloyd was able to learn of Archbold's criticisms, the commission concluded its hearings, but he was allowed to insert a written rebuttal into the commission's final report, and at least one commission member cited Lloyd's response in his final comments.[27]

In a sense, Rockefeller was still trying to discredit Lloyd when he granted Ida Tarbell's request to interview Standard Oil Vice President Henry H. Rogers in the company's New York headquarters in 1901. He naively hoped that Rogers would be able to sway the female Tarbell to get her to discredit *Wealth* in her writings. Only after her first article appeared in 1902 did Rockefeller and others realize her perspective and the true nature of her work, and they quickly called off the Rogers interviews. Though Tarbell replaced Lloyd as the company's main object of wrath, *Wealth* continued to come under occasional fire. A disgruntled Standard supporter attacked it in the *New York Evening Post* in 1905, two years after Lloyd's death, prompting a reply from Lloyd's brother John. A tiny newspaper in the heart of the Pennsylvania oil region, the *Oil City Derrick*, waged a fierce anti-Lloyd campaign for years. In its 1903 obituary of Lloyd, the paper coldheartedly observed:

In his best known work, *Wealth Against Commonwealth*, [Lloyd] made a sensational attack upon the Standard Oil Company. His charges, which have been generally quoted by Miss Tarbell in her alleged history of this great commercial enterprise, were made up entirely from distorted testimony and half truths. . . . It is a pity that a man of such brilliant attainments and vigorous brain power should have spent an entire lifetime in misdirected efforts.

In 1912, as Caro Lloyd was completing a biography of her brother, the *Derrick* lashed out against him in a series called "Standard Oil: A Review of Henry Demarest Lloyd's Misrepresentations Published in *Wealth Against Commonwealth* and an Answer to All Other Imitators and Detractors." Among the charges, it faulted Lloyd for equating "speculative oil enterprises," a reference to the smaller independent producers, to "great industries" such as the Standard. "This method," it noted, "is fairly indicative of the lack of sound reasoning that characterizes every page of *Wealth Against Commonwealth* and is virtually an admission of weakness." When Caro published a response in a competing newspaper, the *Derrick* accused her brother of conspiring with his "attorneys" to level a hostile and unprovoked attack upon the Standard. The *Derrick*'s criticisms were of a distinct sour-grape nature, for the U.S. Supreme Court had dissolved the Standard into thirty-eight separate oil companies the year before.[28]

Even though Lloyd was disappointed at the public's reaction to his book, he succeeded in calling attention to an important public issue, monopolies, in a way that no journalist had been able to do before, and he provided a model for subsequent reformers, including the muckrakers. At the height of Progressivism during the first decade of the twentieth century, he was celebrated as a prophet by a number of individuals. Ida Tarbell wrote upon his death in 1903, "He has left too large a mass of valuable work behind him to be forgotten and the ideas that he has helped to spread are bound to go on." An Ohio minister observed in 1905, "His confidence that students and tyrants would not let the public rest has been amply verified." A South Carolina cleric said the following year, "His book . . . made a lasting impression on my mind and I think the last two chapters of it are among the most profound and illuminating I have ever read." A University of Iowa professor admitted, "It is my opinion that in most instances . . . in which Mr. Lloyd has been accused by opponents of letting his feelings run away with him, he was pretty fully justified by the circumstances of the case. This would apply to some criticisms of his *Wealth Against Commonwealth*." A decade after he labeled *Wealth* another *Uncle Tom's Cabin*, Edward Everett Hale claimed that his opinion had been justified by events and that Lloyd "filled a very important place in our history." Caro Lloyd made her entire 1912 biography of her brother an homage to his prophecies.[29]

As legal efforts were underway to dismantle the Standard, the *Providence News-Democrat* noted in 1907, "Among the pioneers in this great field was [Lloyd] who, when others were worrying over the tariff, saw that it was not a reduced tariff that really hurt us, but the bold violators of the law whom he denounced without any fear that in so doing he would injure honest business." That same year, the Harper brothers reported that *Wealth* continued to hold a distinguished place in their catalogue, telling his sister, "We feel it an honor to be the publishers of so important a book." Humanitarian Helen Keller wrote, "The time we are in has been eloquently described by Henry Demarest Lloyd." Wisconsin Governor Carl D. Thompson said, "I have prized *Wealth Against Commonwealth* because of its terrific arraignment and the unanswerable evidence which he introduced in the course of its discussion." U.S. Senator Robert "Fighting Bob" LaFollette, the 1924 Progressive Party presidential candidate, told Lloyd's oldest son Will, "I just worshipped your father." The *St. Paul*

Pioneer Press wrote in 1913:

It is twenty-five years now since *Wealth Against Commonwealth* appeared and started men thinking in a new way. That book, it is generally conceded, did more than any other one thing to initiate the progressive movement that has flowered in this day into the political reform typified by Roosevelt, LaFollette and Wilson."[30]

For a few, the grudge against Lloyd lingered for a long time. In 1907, the *Chicago Tribune* published a special edition honoring its sixtieth anniversary, celebrating the many accomplishments of its present and former employees. Lloyd was not included or even mentioned, a startling omission in the era of trust-busting. A 1913 *Tribune* review of Caro Lloyd's biography of her brother failed to mention any Lloyd-*Tribune* connection even though there was much about the subject in the book. The snubs continued under the reign of the ultra-conservative Robert R. McCormick, *Tribune* publisher from 1914 to 1955 and the grandson of Joseph Medill. The *Pictured Encyclopedia of the World's Greatest Newspaper*, produced by the *Tribune* in 1928, jumped from "lithography" to "local advertising," overlooking its former employee and stockholder. According to McCormick's biographer, "in McCormick's memoirs there is nothing to indicate the *Tribune* had ever harbored such a person [as Henry Demarest Lloyd]." Not until 1993, long after McCormick's death and the dissolution of the Medill-McCormick trust fund that had controlled the newspaper into the 1980s, was there more than passing reference to Lloyd in the *Chicago Tribune*, and then only as part of an article on Winnetka real estate. Ironically, one of Lloyd's granddaughters, who remained a stockholder of the company, gave $10,000 in the support of printers striking against the firm in 1986.[31]

World War One and the demise of Progressivism pushed *Wealth* out of the public consciousness, but the academic debate over the book was just beginning. Predictably, detractors of laissez-faire capitalism have found little fault with *Wealth* over the years as Rockefeller historians have continued to criticize it. John Chamberlain introduced an abridged version of *Wealth* during the Great Depression with the observation, "It is sad to realize that Lloyd wrote so long ago and that so little has been done since he wrote." Historian Daniel Aaron noted in his 1951 *Men of Good Hope* that *Wealth* "must be read as a prophet's cry to a sinful people." Radical activist and Lloyd grandson-in-law Harvey O'Connor wrote in 1957 that Lloyd was "more than a historian, he was a prophet in his time." Historian Thomas C. Cochran wrote in his 1963 *Wealth* abridgement, "Lloyd skillfully contrasts his examples with the American cultural traditions of equality of opportunity, protection of individual rights, and verbal honesty." Biographer Chester M. Destler called Lloyd "the first great publicist of a new liberal, progressive policy" in 1963 while E. Jay Jernigan observed in 1976, "[Lloyd] posed with precision the still moot question—in spite of subsequent Square Deal, New Deal, Fair Deal, and post-Watergate legislation—of how the people can best control big business." Peter J. Frederick maintained the same year in his book on Gilded Age social reformers, "One of [Lloyd's] relative successes as a reformer has been the great number of twentieth-century fulfillments of his turn-of-the-century proposals."[32]

The leading Lloyd critic of the twentieth century was historian and John D. Rockefeller biographer Allan Nevins. Oddly, Nevins recommended *Wealth* at first, calling it a "searching exposure amply buttressed by detail" in his 1933 biography of Grover Cleveland. In the wake of the industrialist's death in 1937, Nevins changed his mind, denigrating *Wealth* as a "a piece of industrial history . . . almost utterly worthless . . . ludicrous . . . at best misleading, at worst maliciously false." For years, Nevins and Lloyd biographer Chester M. Destler debated *Wealth* in academic journals and conferences, settling little other than to prove how inflammatory the book could be. Still, Nevins influenced subsequent Rockefeller historians. Jules Abels labeled *Wealth* "a sensational indictment of the Trust's operations." Albert Carr complained that Lloyd "fused truth and allegations into the stereotype of villainy." David Freeman Hawke noted in 1980 that Lloyd, "seemed to be grinding an ax, playing the role of prosecutor rather than that of historian." John Ensor Harr and Peter J. Johnson wrote of "William [sic]" Demarest Lloyd, "[although] criticized by responsible journals at the time and discredited later by historians, Lloyd's book nevertheless had its impact on the public."[33]

Another group of historians has praised *Wealth* for less ideological reasons. Charles and Mary Beard rescued it from the refuse of Progressivism in their 1930 *American Civilization*, noting that it had "enough truth in [the] sweeping indictment to spread among the mighty much trepidation over the safety of their institutions." Richard Hofstadter called it a "reality . . . one did not find in the standard textbooks on constitutional law, political science, ethics, economics or history." Paul F. Boller determined that *Wealth* had a significant impact on the development of American social welfare. Robert E. Spiller gave it "a distinguished place in the literature of ideas of the last quarter of the nineteenth century." Sean Gashman called it "a seminal work with all its salient facts carefully documented." John L. Thomas observed that *Wealth* can still be found on "publishers' lists of the Ten Greatest American Books." One hundred years after its publication, *Wealth* remains one of the seminal efforts in the history of American advocacy journalism.[34]

Lloyd's writing career declined following the appearance of *Wealth* in 1894. He could not find another topic as controversial or noteworthy as monopolies for his advocacy journalism. Personal problems, especially money, deterred him as well. He turned to another venue for his messages, the podium. Public speaking was less permanent and does not receive as much credence as print in the twentieth century, but Lloyd garnered as much popularity and more profits from his late nineteenth-and early twentieth-century speeches than all of his books combined. With his contributions to Populism, Lloyd's speech making career made him one of the best-known reform figures in the United States.

NOTES

1. CLS Journal, HDL Wisc.

2. Ripley Hitchcock to HDL, 13 December 1893, 11, 30 January, 15 February 1894; G. P. Putnam's Sons to HDL, 9 March 1894; and Francis J. Garrison to HDL, December 22, 1893; all in HDL, Wisc.

3. Stuart Charles Wade to A.C. McClurg, 5 January 1894, in HDL, Wisc.

4. HDL to William Dean Howells, 20 May 1893, 4 January 1894; Harper Brothers to HDL, 9, 16 June, 13 July, 24 October 1893; HDL to Harper Brothers, 20 May, 17 July 1893; all in HDL, Wisc.; Eugene Exman, *The House of Harper* (New York: Harper and Row, 1967), 153–156, 179; Chambers, "Magazine," 16; and Hough, *The Quiet Rebel*, 112.

5. MS memorandum from HDL to Harper and Brothers, n.d., circa early 1894 and "Revisions to *Wealth Against Commonwealth*," both in HDL, mf.

6. Harper Brothers to HDL, 12 December 1893, 13, 23 March 1894; HDL to J. Henry Harper, 19 February, 7, 31 March 1894; William Dean Howells to HDL, 4 January 1894; Roger Sherman to HDL, 12 September 1893, 2, 8 June 1894; and Adelbert Moot to HDL, 22 May 1894; in HDL, Wisc; Destler, *Sherman*, 223–227; William Dean Howells, *Life in Letters of William Dean Howells*, ed. Mildred Howells (Garden City, NY: Doubleday, Doran and Co., 1928), 46; and CLS, *Lloyd* I, 189–191.

7. Edward E. Hale to Edwin D. Mead, 17 November 1894; Roger Sherman to HDL, 26 February 1895; Washington Gladden to HDL, 24 April 1900; CLS, "Talk with Edward Everett Hale," n.d., MS; and John Burroughs to HDL, 18 September 1896; all in HDL, Wisc.; undated autobiography, circa 1895 and MS of CLS conversation with Hale, n.d., circa 1905, both in HDL, mf.; anonymous, but attributed to William Rainey Harper, "Health for the Commonwealth," n.d., circa 1896, in JBL, CHS; Howells to HDL, 2 November 1894, in Howells, *Letters*, 54; Edwin D. Mead, "Church, State, School and Money," republished from *New England Magazine*, (November 1895) in State Historical Society of Wisconsin; Florence Kelley to JBL, 31 October 1894 as quoted in Dorothy Rose Blumberg, *Florence Kelley: The Making of a Social Pioneer* (New York: A. M. Kelley, 1966), 155; and "Notices by the Press," in *Wealth Against Commonwealth*, 1899 edition.

8. Louis D. Brandeis to Edwin D. Mead, 9 November 1895; George Rice to HDL, 12 October 1894; J. H. Steffe to HDL, 5 January 1896; and William Clarke to HDL, December 1896; all in HDL, Wisc.

9. "Wealth Against Commonwealth-Reviews and Notices," typed MS listing in HDL, mf., and brochure advertising the paper edition of *Wealth Against Commonwealth*, circa 1896, in HDL, Wisc.

10. "Wealth Against Commonwealth-Reviews and Notices," ibid.; Albert Shaw, "Recent American Publications," *Review of Reviews*, 10(November 1894): 571; *Boston Journal*, 4 November 1894; *Boston Herald*, 18 November 1894; and *The Literary World*, 13 November 1894; all clippings in HDL, mf.

11. *C.T.*, 27 October 1894; HDL to Edwin L. Shuman, 16, 28 May and Shuman to HDL, 23 May 1896, all in HDL, Wisc.

12. *JDR Interview*, 15–19, 67, 990–995, 1087–1094.

13. Reverend Frank G. Tyrell to HDL, 18 September 1897, in HDL, Wisc.; *JDR Interview*, 115–116, 1291, 1286–1287; Ida M. Tarbell, *The Nationalizing of Business, 1878–1898* (New York: Macmillan, 1936), 74; and Kathleen Brady, *Ida Tarbell: Portrait of a Muckraker* (New York: Seaview/Putnam, 1984), 231–234.

14. "Review of *Wealth Against Commonwealth*," *Nation*, 59(8 November 1894), 348 and Ernest Levy von Halle, *Trusts or Industrial Combinations and Coalitions in the United States* (New York: Macmillan, 1895) as quoted in Destler, *Empire of Reform*, 316.

The *Nation* did not identify its reviewer but Roger Sherman, who knew Scheide personally, named him in a letter to Lloyd, 11 January 1895, in HDL, Wisc. Rockefeller historian Jules Abels attributed the review to Wendell Phillips Garrison, Jr., who was also a vocal supporter of the Standard. See Abels, *Rockefeller*, 225.

15. George Gunton, "Integrity of Economic Literature," *Social Economist: A Journal of Statesmanship, Economics and Finance*, 9 (July 1895), 11–25; George Rice to HDL, September 1895 and Charles B. Spahr to HDL, 22 July 1895, both in HDL, Wisc.; Robbins, "Tarbell Papers," 165–169; CLS, *Lloyd* I, 211; and Thorelli, *Anti-Trust*, 330.

16. HDL to Charles B. Spahr, 22 July 1895; HDL to Walter M. Raymond, 6 November 1895; and HDL to James C. Moffet, 1 April 1896,; all in HDL, Wisc.; "The Fighter of Trusts: Henry D. Lloyd Scores Gunton's Defense of Standard Oilers," *Boston Herald*, 23 October 1895, and *Boston Daily Advertiser*, 25 November 1895, both clippings in HDL, mf.; and Mann, *Yankee Reformers*, 172.

17. John A. Hobson to HDL, 8 January 1896 and HDL to James C. Moffet, 1 April 1896, both in HDL, Wisc.; Gunton, *Boston Herald*, 16 December 1895 and HDL, *Boston Herald*, 1 February 1896, both in HDL, mf.; and CLS, *Lloyd* I, 206–211.

18. The Reverend B. Fay Mills to the Reverend Edward Everett Hale, 21 April; Charles B. Spahr to HDL, 24 April; the Reverend Thomas C. Hall to Mills, 24 April; the Reverend George D. Herron to Mills, 25 April; HDL to various religious figures, 28 April; HDL to the Reverend Washington Gladden, 28 April; HDL to Mills, 28 April; Edwin D. Mead to HDL, 30 April; Spahr to HDL, 2 May; Roger Sherman to HDL, 4 May; HDL to Dr. Lyman Abbot, 7 May; Mills to HDL, 7 May; Josiah Strong to HDL, 11 May; HDL to Mills, 12 May; Mills to HDL, 16 May; HDL to Mills, 21 May; all 1896 and in HDL, Wisc.

19. Ely to HDL, 1 May 1896, in HDL, Wisc.; CLS, *Lloyd* I, 212–223; and *JDR Interview*, 1099.

20. George D. Herron to HDL, 15 May; John R. Commons to HDL, 18 May; Henry E. Harris to HDL, 22 May; J. W. Jenks to HDL, 22 May; Mills to HDL, 1 June; HDL to Mills, 3 June; George A. Gates to HDL, 3 June; Mills to HDL, 2 July, 2 October; all 1896 and in HDL, Wisc.; Tarbell, *Day's Work*, 240.

21. HDL to Charles F. Mosher, 23 September 1895; HDL to F. F. Murray, 9 January 1896; HDL to Alex F. Irvine, 23 November 1896; and HDL to William J. Skillman, 7 October 1895, all in HDL, Wisc.

22. JBL diary, 13 October 1894, CHS; Paul Findlay to HDL, 12 March 1895; Aaron Lloyd to HDL, 12 November 1894; Eugene G. Updike to HDL, 5 April 1895; L. A. Veland to HDL, 20 February 1896; H. D. Dupee to HDL, 25 April 1896; HDL to Mr. Benson, 29 April 1896; CLS to HDL, 1 November 1896; CLS to HDL, 8 November 1896; John J. Hamilton to HDL, 17 July 1897; HDL to F. Southworth, 30 March 1898;

James F. Hudson to HDL, 14 August 1898; all in HDL, Wisc.; *Wisconsin State Journal*, 23 March 1895, in HDL, mf.; *JDR Interview*, 1045; and Frederick A. Sorge, *Labor Movement in the United States: A History of the American Working Class from 1890 to 1896* (Westport, CT: Greenwood Press, 1987, 1897), 125.

23. Harper Brothers to HDL, 19 October 1894; Harpers to HDL, 13 February, 16, 18 April, 15 May 1895; J. B. Dickinson to HDL, 13 September 1895; J. A. Wayland to HDL, 13 September 1895; Harpers to HDL, 15 January 1896; Davidson to HDL, 20 January 1896; Davidson to Harpers, 20 January 1896; Harpers to HDL, 31 January 1896, 13 April 1903; all in HDL, Wisc.; *Wealth Against Commonwealth* sales listing, circa 1903 and CLS MS note on second edition, 1936, both in HDL, mf.; and CLS, *Lloyd* I, 195–196.

24. HDL to Lee Meriwether, 26 November 1898, in HDL, Wisc. and Miraldi, *Muckraking and Objectivity*, 23–56.

25. Harper Brothers to HDL, 11 July 1899, in HDL, Wisc.; "Affidavits Miss Tarbell has in the Scofield case," undated note in HDL *Wealth Against Commonwealth* notebook, circa 1902, in HDL, mf.; CLS, *Lloyd* I, 230–231; Tarbell, *Day's Work*, 209–210; HDL, *Wealth Against Commonwealth*, 2d ed. (New York: Harper and Brothers, 1899), i–x.

26. Anonymous handwritten note, n.d., in HDL, scrapbook; *The Independent*, 49(4 March 1897): 266–268, 278–279; *Social Economist*, 15(November 1898): 322; "Yellow Journalism and Economics," *Chicago Times-Herald*, 22 November 1898; "Henry D. Lloyd's Protest," *Chicago Times-Herald*, 5 December 1898; Horace L. Traubel, *The Conservator*, 11(April 1900); *New York Evening Post*, 18, 26 September 1899; *Brooklyn Citizen*, 20 September 1899; and *Nation*, 49(21 September 1899): 218–219; all in HDL, mf.; C. B. Matthews to HDL, 18 March 1897; HDL to H. H. Kohlsaat, 2 December 1898; HDL to Willis J. Abbot, December 3, 1898; the Reverend A. C. Grier to HDL, 16 April 1897; HDL to Eltweed Pomeroy, 3 January 1900; L. D. DeWitt to HDL, n.d., circa 27 February 1900; Frederick W. Gookin to HDL, 6 March 1900; HDL to Gookin, 9 March 1900; and J. H. Burnell to HDL, 3 January 1901; HDL to *New York Evening Post*, 26 September 1899; HDL to Samuel Bowles, 5 October, 11 November 1899; George Iles to HDL, 6 October 1899; Wendell L. Garrison to HDL, 6 October 1899; Josiah Strong to HDL, 10 October 1899; the Reverend Washington Gladden to HDL, 12 October 1899; Horace White to HDL, 10, 12 October 1899; the Reverend R. Heber Newton to HDL, 24 February, 13 March, 1900; HDL to Newton, 6 March 1900; all in HDL, Wisc.; John J. McLaurin, *Sketches in Crude Oil: Some Accidents and Incidents of the Petroleum Development in All Parts of the Globe* (Harrisburg, PA: Published by the Author, 1898), 414–417; and Williamson and Daum, *Petroleum Industry*, 713–714.

27. HDL to Carroll D. Wright, 5 January 1898; HDL to Jeremiah Jenks, 1 March 1900; HDL to the Reverend Washington Gladden, 24 April 1900; Willis J. Abbot to HDL, 27 April 1900; HDL to Edward Bemis, 1 May 1900; Horace C. White to HDL, 26 May 1900; S. S. Mehard to HDL, 28 June 1900; all in HDL, Wisc.; "From the testimony of Mr. J. B. Archbold before the Industrial Commission, p. 559," MS; "Standard Oil Combinations: Affidavit of Henry Demarest Lloyd," MS; M. L. Lockwood, "Standard Oil Methods Exposed," *The Anti-Trust Bulletin*, 1 (August 1898): 1–8; all in HDL, mf.; CLS, *Lloyd* I, 225–227; McLaurin, *Crude*, 420; Nevins, *John D. Rockefeller* II, 500; and John R. Commons, *Myself* (New York: Macmillan, 1934), 71–79.

28. *New York Evening Post* clipping, 17 June 1905 and MS note, both in HDL,

Wisc.; *Oil City* (Pennsylvania) *Derrick*, n.d., circa October 1903; Charles Everet Kern, "Standard Oil: A Review of Henry Demarest Lloyd's Misrepresentations Published in *Wealth Against Commonwealth* and an Answer to All Other Imitators and Detractors," *Oil City Derrick*, various dates, 1911; CLS, "Letter to the Editor, *Petroleum Gazette*, 6 June 1912; and Kern response, n.d., circa June 1912, *Oil City Derrick*; all in HDL, mf.; Brady, *Tarbell*, 157–159; Tarbell, *Day's Work*, 240–241; and Mary E. Tomkins, *Ida Tarbell* (Boston: Twayne, 1974), 66–67.

29. Ida M. Tarbell to JBL, 9 November 1903; J. W. Magruder to CLS, 26 January 1905; John Mershau to CLS, 2 July 1906; Professor David Kinley to CLS, 9 November 1906; all in HDL, Wisc.; CLS, "Talk with Edward Everett Hale," MS, n.d., circa 1906, HDL, mf.

30. William Bross Lloyd to CLS, 29 April 1905; Harper & Brothers to CLS, 4 March 1907; Carl D. Thompson to CLS, 1 April 1907; *Providence News-Democrat*, 7 August 1907 in Caroline Stallbohm to CLS, 19 November 1907; Helen Keller in undated *Metropolitan* clipping; all in HDL, Wisc.; Graham Taylor, "The Social Vision of a Chicago Seer," *Chicago Daily News*, 29 September 1906; *St. Paul Pioneer Press*, 6, 18 April 1913, all clippings in HDL, mf.; and Merle E. Curti, *The University of Wisconsin: A History, 1848–1925* (Madison: University of Wisconsin Press, 1949), 288–289.

31. CLS, MS note on *Chicago Tribune*, n.d., circa 1907, HDL, Wisc.; *C.T.*, 10 June 1907 and Herbert Caxton, "Review of *Henry Demarest Lloyd*," *C.T.*, 28 June 1913, both in HDL, mf.; Frank C. Waldrup, *McCormick of Chicago* (Englewood Cliffs, NJ: Prentice-Hall, 1966), 28; and Casey Bukro, "Old-line Opulence: Determined Individualists Give Village its Flavor," *Chicago Tribune Home Guide*, 1 May 1993.

Known prior *Tribune* articles on Lloyd include Jessica Seigel, "Winnetka's 90-year-old Electric Plant Bowing Out Gracefully," 12 December 1990; John McCarron, "Best, Brightest Take on the 21st Century," 26 March 1989; Ron Grossman, "North Shore Lore," 28 June 1988; "Tribune Stockholder Aids Striking Workers," 6 May 1986; and HDL clipping, 25 February 1981, *Chicago Tribune* archives.

32. Chamberlain, "Forward," *Wealth Against Commonwealth*, i–ii; Aaron, *Men of Good Hope*, 155; Harvey O'Connor, "Henry Demarest Lloyd: The Prophetic Tradition," in Goldberg, *American Radicals*, 88; Destler, *Empire of Reform*, 9; Cochran, "Introduction," *Wealth Against Commonwealth*, 4; Jernigan, *Lloyd*, 75; and Frederick, *Knights*, 74.

33. Allan Nevins, *Grover Cleveland: A Study in Courage* (New York: Dodd, Mead & Company, 1933), 607; Nevins, *John D. Rockefeller* II, 334; Nevins, *Study in Power* II, 330; Nevins, "Communication," *American Historical Review*, 676–689; Chester M. Destler, "A Commentary on the "Communication" from Allan Nevins," in State Historical Society of Wisconsin Collection, Madison, WI; Nicholas Kelley Oral History, Columbia University, 3; Carr, *John D. Rockefeller's Secret Weapon*, 98–99; Abels, *Rockefeller's Billions*, 222–226; Hawke, *John D*, 215; and John Ensor Harr and Peter J. Johnson, *The Rockefeller Century* (New York: Charles Scribner's Sons, 1988):58.

For a revealing perspective on Allan Nevins thoughts toward historical revisionism, see "Should American History Be Rewritten," *Saturday Review*, 37(6 February 1954), 7–9, 47–49.

34. Beard, *American Civilization*, 426–429; Hofstadter, *Progressive Historians*, 184–185; Boller, *American Thought*, 109; Spiller, *Literary History*, 979–980; Gashman, *America in the Gilded Age*, 62–64; and Thomas, *Alternative*, 354–357.

7

The Rhetoric of Populism

Wealth never was the best-seller that *Looking Backward* had been, but Lloyd did enjoy a revival of the fame he had experienced after "Story of a Great Monopoly" and his first magazine articles. Readers across the country scrambled to find scarce copies of *Millionaires*, "Story," "New Conscience," and his other works, and those who could not find them begged Lloyd to help them in their search. The Wayside became a center of late nineteenth-century genteel radicalism, and a host of elite reformers streamed in and out of Winnetka to meet and talk with the nation's best-known reform advocate. Jessie Lloyd staged elaborate Sunday dinners, with Lloyd presiding over a "Round Table" of distinguished guests each week. There were other, less appreciated demonstrations of the popularity of *Wealth*, too. Lloyd was the unexpected recipient of a forty-two gallon barrel of pure Pennsylvania crude oil, delivered to his Winnetka doorstep by an appreciative independent refiner following the book's publication. Gratefully acknowledging the sentiment, Lloyd politely requested that the gift be taken away.[1]

Mystified by the lack of a popular uprising against the Standard in response to *Wealth*, Lloyd remained concerned that the monopolies were still controlling the magazine and book industries. The podium represented an alternative forum for his writings. He was a popular public speaker, from his first efforts for labor in the wake of the Haymarket bombing in 1886 to cross-country tours on economic reform between 1894 and 1903. He addressed audiences on a variety of subjects, including the eight-hour workday, monopolies, "The New Conscience," and Populism. The public address was a distinguished and popular means of reaching the public, especially in the late nineteenth century, and Lloyd considered the "circuit" an unparalleled opportunity to reach, listen to, and thank his readers and supporters, even as it kept him from his wife and family for long periods of time. Although not advocacy journalism in the strictest sense of the term, Lloyd's speeches were in support of various causes and constituencies and were presented to the largest audiences he could find in the era before broadcasting.[2]

Rhetoric has always been an important outlet for public dissatisfaction in American life. In the nineteenth century, literate people knew they had to pay for newspapers and books but conversations about ideas were free and therefore were viewed as more democratic and meaningful. The demise of classical rhetoric and the advent of mass circulation magazines, movies, radio, television, and cable have reduced the demand for the speaker's art in the late twentieth century, but Lloyd's generation thrilled to the substance and style of a good speech. Humorist Garrison Keillor satirized this infatuation, and how broadcasting changed the publicly-spoken word, in *WLT: A Radio Romance*, writing of a William Jennings Bryan speech in 1896:

Bryan's voice—so strong, so vibrant, so *beautiful*, and he spoke for more than an hour, and the crowd was so still, you could hear the banners flapping when a breeze came up. Bryan was too far away for him to hear, except for a word now and then, and yet it was so moving and memorable. The address was printed the next week in the newspaper. People bought it and read it and placed it neatly in a trunk, or a box, or in a Bible, pressed like it was a leaf, and though seldom read, it was cherished.

As Keillor explained, an hour-long public speech could take a week to write and was valued as such, but an hour's time on radio came to mean less and less as all the hours in a broadcast day had to be filled. Spoken words have never been quite the same.[3]

Like most classically-educated men of his generation, Lloyd revered the art of public speaking. He gave a commencement address at his Columbia College graduation in 1867, arguing in support of the modernizing influence of science, and honed his skills in front of audiences at the Winnetka Improvement Association, the Winnetka school board, and the Winnetka village council during the early 1880s. Most of his early magazine articles, including "Story of a Great Monopoly," began as public speeches. His brother David wrote in 1888, "Three or four articles like ["Lords of Industry"], delivered as speeches in Congress, would give you a national, and even international reputation." He was suited to the podium. His finely-carved face, walrus mustache, and lion-like pompadour of gray hair fated him with the look of an important man. Both family and friends teased him about a career in politics, mostly for his appearance. William Dean Howells recalled that his first impression of Lloyd was "what a fine man for president that would be. He was made to stand in the high places, and be a guide to many." Lloyd's old-line ancestry and classical education gave him a style that attracted public attention as well, and he went out of his way to conduct himself in a distinguished way so as not to detract from his radical views. When he appeared before audiences, his bearing focused attention on his words, added credibility to his message, and made him a memorable personage.[4]

In spite of his physical attributes, Lloyd's delivery was often characterized as stiff and ineffective. He was too nervous to speak extemporaneously, so he usually wrote out and memorized his speeches ahead of time, speaking from only a few notes. His memorized speeches often lacked the spontaneity and freshness that a less rehearsed presentation would have provided. Once, rather than ad-lib when his memory failed him on the platform, he looked to Jessie who mouthed the missing words for him from the audience. Lloyd also lacked a distinctive enunciation and took periodic lessons from a speech teacher. To practice, he spoke to the waves of Lake Michigan across Sheridan Road from the Wayside, Jessie encouraging him with taunts such as "Come on, Demosthenes." With practice Lloyd became adroit enough to leave audiences applauding long after he had left the podium. One newspaper engraving during the 1896 Populist campaign even showed Lloyd mesmerizing a Milwaukee crowd during a drenching summer thunderstorm.[5]

The first Lloyd speech to attract serious public attention was his "The New Conscience, or the Religion of Labor" address, delivered to the Chicago Ethical Society in February 1888, two days after the Haymarket execution. As previously indicated, the speech unveiled Lloyd's new civic religion, but it was done with particularly forceful rhetoric that was fueled by the bitterness Lloyd had bottled up inside himself during and after the Haymarket trial, executions, and his own social ostracism. "The ancients bought and sold men; we buy and sell the heart-beats only," he said. "If you shall not buy the whole man, you shall not buy or sell part of a man. You shall not count into your purses the ruddy drops, from morn till noon, from noon to dewy eve, and then say, 'I know not whence they came or how.'" Lloyd attacked his onetime friend Henry Ward Beecher and other complacent laissez-faire churches and ministers for sanctioning the Haymarket executions and rationalizing the inhumanity of industrialization. "We have struck the shackles from the slave, and made him free and a citizen," Beecher had said, "Now he must take care of himself, and work out his own social and industrial salvation." Lloyd replied, "When you work with him, will the God of Plymouth Church considerately turn his back, so as not to see whether you love your neighbor as yourself? . . . It is not by free will that the workingmen of today work ten, twelve, or fourteen hours, take competitive wages, live in poor tenements at high rents, spend their days as the mere servants or grooms of machinery, and sending out their little boys and girls, and their pregnant wives to work, sacrifice almost everything that makes family life for you and me so sweet." The speech, which was published in the *North American Review* the following year, became one of the anthems of the

Social Gospel movement.⁶

Lloyd talked about the eight-hour question to labor audiences in the wake of Haymarket as well. Reduced workdays had been an issue among labor activists since before the Civil War, but the labor unions launched a coordinated national eight-hour campaign on May 1, 1886. Three days later, the Haymarket bombing derailed that effort. Labor leaders such as the American Federation of Labor President Samuel P. Gompers were only too pleased to have the patrician Lloyd help them revive their cause. Lloyd argued that an eight-hour workday was more than a rallying cry for organized labor, it was the essence of the debate over the industrial revolution. Instead of the then common, dehumanizing workdays for pitiful wages, Lloyd advocated a wage system based upon medieval guilds in which employers paid workers what they were worth for work well done. He disagreed with political economists and Social Darwinists who argued that employers could not afford to pay the same wages for fewer hours of work, the ultimate economic impact of a lessened workday. To the delight of working-class audiences, Lloyd likened eight-hour workday opponents to the colonial British, telling a Chicago Labor Day rally in 1889, "The labor movement is not a fanaticism. It is an effort to curb a fanaticism, the fanaticism of moneymaking, the mania of the markets. . . . Seventeen hundred and seventy-six broke away from colonial dependence.   Eighteen hundred and eighty-nine declares against industrial dependence." To another audience he called the eight-hour workday the "the moral paradox of our times":

What we call the labor movement is but the appearance in a wider field of the expanding manhood of the world. No paternalism can solve any social problem. The good king, the chivalrous Baron, the Christian slaveholder, the merciful master, the philanthropic monopolist . . . have been charming, but they cost too much. They march in a vanishing procession. Only the brother stays.

In spite of such rhetoric, the stigma of Haymarket lingered long after the bomb's damage had been repaired, and conservative labor organizations such as the A.F.L. and Lloyd were forced to abandon the eight-hour workday as an issue by the early 1890s.⁷

Lloyd combined the subjects of character and industrialization into a speech he called "What Washington Would do Today," delivered at the Chicago Central Music Hall on Washington's birthday in 1890. He used Washington as an example of a man of character, so lacking, he said, in late nineteenth-century America. He could not avoid drawing a parallel again between the British colonialists of 1776 and modern-day monopolists. "Cheapness is the defense made by our King Georges of the markets," Lloyd said. "Washington's healthy conscience and common sense told him that if a thing was wrong it could not be cheap." Labeling industrialists "millionaire microbes, pestilence germs of plutocracy, the worst kind of grip," Lloyd concluded by harkening back to Haymarket:

A country in which the right of free speech and free assembly are regulated by the private temper of the policeman instead of public policy of centuries of constitutional freedom is not the Republic of Washington. A country where people submit to industrial piracy, because the pirates sell their stolen goods cheap, is not the Republic of Washington. What the people of America believe in, what the people of Europe came here for, is the Republic of Washington. And they mean to get it back from the plutocrats who are stealing it away like thieves in the night.[8]

The World's Columbian Exposition, which opened on Lloyd's birthday in 1893, marked a turning point in Lloyd's public speaking career. The World's Fair was a magical experience for Chicagoans, a celebration of the city's Phoenix-like rebirth from the ashes of the 1871 fire to a world-class metropolis. Situated on the Lake Michigan shoreline south of downtown Chicago in what is now known as Jackson Park, the fair was constructed as a miniature city of all-white buildings. Lloyd characterized it as an event five hundred years ahead of its time, telling architect John Burnham:

The World's Fair revealed to the people possibilities of social beauty, utility, and harmony of which they had not been able even to dream. No such vision could otherwise have entered into the prosaic drudgery of their lives, and it will be felt in their development unto the third and fourth generation. Hope and inspiration for the future were printed on the minds of many millions in that picture.[9]

Lloyd was asked to organize a series of meetings honoring the achievements of labor as part of the fair's Congress of World Thinkers. The Congress brought together the best in practically every human endeavor—from government, religion, and education to feminism, units of measurement, and world peace. Lloyd eagerly embraced the labor meetings even as he was struggling to finish his final *Wealth* manuscript. With the advice of Ethelbert Stewart, Richard T. Ely, and others, he invited as many of the world's leading labor advocates as he could locate. His list covered the spectrum of labor, from monarchists and laissez-faire political economists to Single Taxers, Fabians, Marxists, Christian Socialists, and other radical ideologues. His goal was to expose fair-goers to the spectrum of late nineteenth-century labor issues in the hope that the eight-hour workday and other American labor proposals would seem less radical.[10]

The Labor Congress, which convened on August 28, 1893, was especially timely given contemporary economic conditions. Chicago, like the rest of the United States, had plunged into a major depression during the summer of 1893. With unemployment growing, interest was so high in labor that Lloyd's meetings had to be held outdoors to accommodate the crowds. The discussions ranged from slums and childhood labor to new social legislation and binding arbitration. Most influential labor leaders were present, but the best received was A.F.L. President Samuel Gompers, who spoke at an August 30 keynote session. More than twenty-five thousand people heard Gompers, the largest turnout for any

Congress of World Thinkers. Gompers repaid Lloyd's invitation by asking Lloyd to speak at the A.F.L.'s 1893 annual convention and the two remained friends for several years. The exposition itself closed to rave reviews in October. By then, many of Chicago's unemployed had been hired as maintenance workers at the fair and allowed to sleep there at night to keep them out of the view of tourists. The fair's closing put them back on the streets, where it became increasingly more difficult for well-to-do Chicagoans to ignore their plight.[11]

The unemployment problem turned Lloyd from speaking to action. He had always been, as he had once confided to prohibitionist Frances E. Willard, "a man without a party," especially after the bitter defeat of the Liberal Republicans in 1872, but the suffering brought on by the Depression of 1893 and the continuing corruption of late nineteenth-century government rekindled his sense of noblesse oblige. He wrote in his 1888 notebook:

A prostituted Congress, prostituted to the service of the class, the interest, the organization, the Power that for the time holds society and its machinery in hand, [is] not the source to which to look for the prophetic secrets of the times. The unattached, who have not where to lay their heads, most frequently in every age catch up and spread the truth feared or despised by the great.

Lloyd's attachment was the ill-fated political movement known as Populism.[12]

At first glance, Lloyd's urban-oriented, pro-labor social philosophy was at odds with the agrarian-based reforms of Populism, but they shared some common ground—especially the traditions of individualism and optimism for the future. Lloyd wrote in his 1892 notebook, "The common people are the hope of the world and the leaders of reform, because by their numbers and position they are incorruptible." Such thinking, which was at the core of Lloyd's "New Conscience," was popular in small-town America, where Populism was centered. Lloyd and the Populists shared a disdainful view of the industrial revolution as well. Instead of perpetual economic growth, which Lloyd associated with the "cheaper goods" philosophy of the plutocrats, Lloyd preferred the nineteenth-century agrarian myth, the sentimental attachment to a rural past attributed to Thomas Jefferson. Lloyd had little interest in returning to his own impoverished agrarian past, especially the years he spent hand-raising corn on the Illinois prairie, but he was certain that recapturing disappearing agrarian-style values such as character and altruism would save America from impending class revolution. He pined for a simpler, less industrialized past in most of his speeches and advocacy writings, including *Wealth* and "The Political Economy of Seventy-three Million Dollars."[13]

Even so, Lloyd was oblivious to the first bloomings of Populism. Symptoms of organized discontent erupted on farms in the South and Midwest as early as the 1870s, but it was the vocal protestations of the Texas Farmers' Alliances in the 1880s that gave prominence to the Populist movement. Lloyd wrote about the influx of bankrupt farmers pouring into Chicago in 1889, "I want to reverse the current; no one wants it reversed more, but it seems a hopeless work to 'colonize' the wreckage of this civilization." The early Populist protest climaxed in 1892 when an eclectic collection of reformers met in Omaha, Nebraska, and formed the National People's Party. Prohibitionist Frances E. Willard invited Lloyd to join her at the convention, but Lloyd politely refused, confiding to Samuel Gompers after the gathering that he could find nothing of personal interest in the new party's platform.[14]

With the deepening of the depression, Lloyd attended several Illinois Populist meetings in early 1894. He was invited to address the state convention in Springfield in July 1894 because of his fame as an advocate journalist and reformer. His speech stressed the benefits of cooperation between urban and rural reform interests. "I would not enter it, did I not see in it the promise of the ultimate supremacy of labor," he said. "We stand on the brink of a great step forward. . . . The people are about to take possession of the property of the people. We are almost to enter a new paradise." Beyond his speaking skills, Lloyd won acclaim at the state convention for mediating a compromise between factions warring over a controversial labor proposal advocating "collective ownership by the people of all means of production and distribution." Lloyd sensed room for compromise on the issue, even though its socialist premise was opposed by many rural delegates, and in a one-hour speech, he urged accommodation. The *Chicago Tribune* reported that he was "the only man . . . whose remarks were received with marked courtesy and without interruption." His proposal recognized the principle of collective ownership, making labor supporters happy, but it called for an appropriate public referendum before any definitive action could be taken, a move which appeased farmers. Even with such delicate phrasing, the proposal passed by a one-vote margin, but it helped create the first urban-rural Illinois reform party in twenty-four years. With Lloyd's assistance, the convention adjourned on a harmonious note, and Lloyd returned to the Wayside with accolades as the new party's chief theorist.[15]

The Springfield gathering was distracted by a more significant event during the sultry July of 1894. Members of Eugene V. Deb's American Railway Union had joined a strike against George Pullman's Railroad Car Company in Chicago the previous month and had succeeded in shutting down most of the railroad traffic in and out of Illinois. Leery of the state's reform-minded Governor John P. Altgeld, the railroads had asked Democratic President Grover Cleveland to send federal troops to Chicago to break up the strike under the pretext of protecting the U.S. Mail. Pitched battles broke out between the soldiers and strikers in early July, coinciding with the Springfield convention. The strike was ultimately broken, and Debs was arrested and sentenced to a prison not far from Lloyd's Winnetka home. Following the adjournment of the People's Party convention, Lloyd met with some of the strikers in their makeshift camps in Chicago and gave Debs a copy of *Wealth* to read in his prison cell. He also organized and spoke at a welcoming party for Debs upon his release the following year. The image of the Pullman strikers, desperate because they could not live on their wages, remained with Lloyd for the rest of his life.[16]

Lloyd called on Governor Altgeld the night that President Cleveland issued his troop mobilization order in July 1894. The railroads contended that Altgeld could not be counted on to order his Illinois national guardsmen to confront the strikers because he had pardoned the Haymarket anarchists the previous year. Lloyd remembered seeing a piece of paper on Altgeld's desk that night, complete except for his signature, committing the state militia to the strike. All that was needed was sufficient cause. In the end, Altgeld was so incensed by President Cleveland's intrusion into what many considered a state matter that he telegraphed a vigorous protest to the White House and broke with Cleveland politically, as did many other Democrats. His contention was that the Illinois troops would have been more indulging of the strikers. Nearly thirty strikers or their supporters were killed by the federal troops, many at point-blank range, a carnage that Lloyd, Altgeld, and many others believed could have been avoided if state troops had been used.[17]

Lloyd tried to hold together the delicate labor-farmer coalition in absentia as he vacationed in Rhode Island over the summer of 1894. He suggested to Samuel Gompers that another state convention be called for no later than September of that year to allow "all the reform elements to give immediate direction and concentration to the acts of the people in the coming election." He was fearful that a Populist defeat in the upcoming election would encourage further Pullman-style violence, writing, "If the people will not, out of their bovine peaceableness, do the acts of violence that would afford the pretext for the 'saviors of society' to keep possession, these latter will themselves commit the violence, and charge it upon the people. They did this in Chicago [in the Pullman Strike], I verily believe." Lloyd respected Gompers's leadership role in the new party, telling him, "No man in history has had a greater opportunity for usefulness and glory than now begs you to embrace it." Gompers had a less optimistic view of Populism, however, especially Lloyd's urban-rural coalition, and ignored Lloyd's entreaties until the fall campaign.[18]

The publication of *Wealth* in September 1894, combined with Lloyd's popularity at the Springfield convention, made him the hottest Populist speaker of the fall campaign. To cash in on his fame, the Populists listed Lloyd as a token congressional candidate in his heavily Republican Winnetka district, giving them an excuse to feature Lloyd at Populist gatherings. Lloyd resisted the idea at first, having lost a similar mock bid at the behest of a short-lived labor party in 1888, but the Populists convinced him that even a non-candidacy would aid the party and he finally agreed. For three months, he was a tireless campaigner, addressing an unknown number of audiences in Illinois, Minnesota, and Iowa. The Illinois People's Party officially kicked off its campaign in early October with a massive rally at Chicago's Central Music Hall. Joining Lloyd on the podium were Clarence S. Darrow and former Illinois Senator and Independent Republican Lyman Trumbull. In his address, Lloyd linked the legacy of abolitionism to the spirit of Populism:

It is a fact of political history that no new party was ever false to the cause for which it was formed. If the People's Party as organized in Cook County is supported by the country, and the people get the control of their industries as of the government, the abolition of monopoly will as surely follow as the abolition of slavery followed the entrance of Abraham Lincoln into the White House in 1861.

Lloyd was so popular as a campaign speaker that the *Chicago Tribune* observed that he was being advertised at more rallies than he could possibly have attended. He did his best, for Jessie noted in her diary on September 27, 1894, "My birthday, full of kindliness and yet . . . full of loneliness." Lloyd's most popular theme was to refute the notion that the Populists were a one-issue party. As he told audiences, "The People's Party is not a passing cloud in the political sky. . . . It is an uprising of principle and the millions who have espoused these principles will not stop until they have become incorporated into the constitution of the government and the framework of society." The night before the final November election, the Populists staged a torchlight parade through the streets of downtown Chicago, in front of a crowd estimated at between twelve and fifteen thousand people. Lloyd told them, "The People's Party represents the mightiest hope that ever stirred the masses. . . . The hope of realizing and incarnating in the lives of the common people the fullness of the divinity of humanity."[19]

The election was a success for the Populists and a pleasant surprise for Lloyd. He lost his district to the Republican incumbent but gathered 16 percent of the ballots, finishing only four thousand votes behind his Democratic contender. In Chicago, the Populists received about one-third of the labor vote, attracting a sizable showing among disenchanted Socialists. Statewide, the People's Party improved on its 1892 performance by seventy-five thousand votes, and nationally, the party elected six senators and seven congressmen. In a press release, the Chicago Populists called the 1894 election "something wonderful" and predicted that their party would be a "considerable force" in the presidential year of 1896.[20]

Unfortunately, Lloyd's success both as a public speaker and candidate masked his lack of a deeper commitment to the Populist cause. In part, his indifference to agrarian reform hurt his credibility among rural supporters. He sidestepped the issue in most of his speeches, concentrating his rhetoric on unity, but his private disgust toward the boredom of unmechanized late nineteenth-century farming was unmistakable. Fellow Populist Ethelbert Stewart admonished him at one point during the 1894 campaign for an unrecorded comment:

I was surprised and pained at what you said about the farmers last night. I cannot imagine how you could say such things in view of Kansas, Colorado, Nebraska, Minnesota and every state in which the People's Party has a ghost of a show of carrying the state. . . . No man in Illinois is better known or loved by the farmers of this state than yourself, and if they get hold of what you said . . . it will hurt their feelings, wound them to the quick, for it is not fair.

Lloyd's uninterest in practicing his advocacy journalism for the Populists hurt their cause as well. As popular a platform speaker as he was, his written words were always more powerful and would have reached far more potential converts than his talks, yet he wrote no major articles or books on Populism, relying entirely on reprints of his speeches to spread his words beyond the podium. He even rejected a bid by a group of prominent Populists including Clarence S. Darrow, journalists Willis J. Abbott and Benjamin O. Flower, and writer Hamlin Garland, to edit a Chicago-based Populist newspaper during the fall of 1894. Lloyd knew the party lacked a big-city newspaper voice for its views and that his name, talents, and financial support would have greatly aided such a venture. His conservative instinct toward business led him to refuse, however, and his reluctance effectively killed the project. Illinois Populists were forced to depend upon the indifferent generosity of other newspapers to publicize their views in contrast to the newspaper voices of the Democrats and Republicans.[21]

As Lloyd watched the sales of *Wealth* climb, he also failed to deal with another book that would have a much more direct impact on Populism. Small in size, William H. Harvey's *Coin's Financial School* offered what Lloyd and other students of the social question had always been unwilling or unable to do, an easily-understood panacea to the nation's economic ills. In the guise of a fictional Professor Coin, Harvey phrased his solution in the simple, "common sense" language of farmers:

You increase the value of all property by adding to the number of money units [dollars] in the land. You make it possible for the debtor to pay his debts; business to start anew, and revivify all the industries of the country, which must remain paralyzed so long as silver as well as all other property is measured by a gold standard.

Lloyd knew that Harvey's solution, to increase inflation through the reintroduction of silver as a form of currency, would fail to revive the flagging economy, but he failed to effectively counteract Harvey's arguments by providing a counter solution. For all of Lloyd's concern for the working class, it was Harvey's book, not Lloyd's, that became the bible of the Populism.[22]

Professor Coin's quick cure was especially bad medicine for Lloyd because Lloyd remembered Jay Gould's disastrous 1873 gold corner that had led to a bank panic and depression. He feared that dishonest investors like Gould would again seek to control silver if it was reintroduced as a legal tender. As such, he found himself in the uncomfortable position of defending more orthodox economics and opposing free silver to his Populist friends. He wrote as early as August 1894, "I am no '16 to 1' man. In fact, I think the agitation along those lines serves the purpose of the plutocrats and the imperialists admirably because it keeps attention from settling down upon the real issues." Lloyd especially wanted to avoid the one-issue trap that had destroyed previous reform parties such as the Greenbackers, and he was afraid that silver would be that issue. He told another free-silver friend:

It is easy to see upon analysis that the currency issue and the demand for government ownership of railroads and telegraphs and the control or ownership of monopolies are not separate issues but merely the same issue turning a different face to the different interests and sections of our country. . . . While the issue you lay most stress upon was all-important to you, yet it had its counterpart in issues equally vital to us.[23]

In spite of his lack of commitment, Lloyd remained supportive of Populism into 1896. Temperance advocate Frances E. Willard paid tribute to him in 1895, writing, "I feel that you have this whole [reform] question at heart more than almost anybody that I have seen. . . . It comes to me that you ought to be the candidate of the people for President of the United States in 1896." Lloyd joined with Clarence S. Darrow and other Chicago Populists to organize and support a candidate for mayor in 1895. Advocating public-utility ownership, a city-owned elevated rail system, fairer property tax assessments, and a civil service system, the party gathered 6 percent of the popular vote. Lloyd also attended the national Populist conference in late 1895, opposing efforts to revise the 1892 Omaha platform that he had once scorned.[24]

Free silver grew as the major issue among both Illinois and national Populists by 1896, in spite of Lloyd's misgivings. The momentum in favor of silver was so strong that Lloyd complained to the state party chairman in July of that year, "One trouble with the People's Party is that so many of its members think that political problems which are being manufactured by steam engine and dynamo methods can be cured by spinning wheel and ox team political remedies." The beginning of the end for the People's Party came in mid-1896 when the Democratic party convinced the Populists to delay their 1896 national convention so that the party of Jefferson and Jackson could have a first crack at the silver issue. The 1896 Democratic National Convention, held in Chicago, was far from harmonious. Grover Cleveland's use of federal troops to quell Chicago's 1894 Pullman strike had split the party, and only onetime journalist William Jennings Bryan was able to unite the party through the rhetoric of his famous "Cross of Gold" speech, which advocated free silver. With the Democrats on the free-silver wagon, Lloyd realized that the Populists faced what he called a "Hobson's choice." Either they could fuse with the Democrats on free silver, forever losing their identity as a political party, or keep their distance and watch the Democrats steal their most popular issue. Either option handed the election to William McKinley and the Republicans, and spelled the end of Populists as a viable political entity.[25]

Lloyd retreated to his Rhode Island summer house to watch the events of 1896 unfold. He resolved to stay away from the Populists' national convention, scheduled for late July in St. Louis, but as the date drew nearer, friends coaxed him to attend. Feminist reformer Florence Kelley argued that the demise of Populism could be the birth of a new Fabian-style party of "socialists of American nationality and traditions," and that was a prospect that Lloyd found intriguing enough to make the long journey to St. Louis tolerable. He told the *Chicago Tribune*:

One of the immediate results of this merger at St. Louis will be a large percentage of the party will go into one or another of the Socialistic parties or organizations. . . . A large proportion of the survivors will become socialistic. Perhaps in 1900, perhaps not until 1904, the ideas and the men who went down here before the silver cyclone will reappear. The politicians in the party who have been having all the fun of a witch-burning heresy will find that they have not even scorched the snake.[26]

Lloyd arrived in St. Louis prepared to support either American Railway Union president Eugene V. Debs or former General Jacob S. Coxey, leader of the so-called "Coxey's Army," as the Populists' presidential nominee. Debs stood the best chance of winning, but he had been converted to Socialism during his prison stay and forbade Lloyd or anyone else to nominate him. As support for fusion with the Democrats built, a group of delegates proposed Lloyd as a last-minute presidential candidate. Their effort was too late and William Jennings Bryan won overwhelming endorsement. Remembering the Liberal Republicans debacle in 1872, Lloyd left St. Louis depressed and frustrated, complaining, "The party was buried, hopelessly sold out." In spite of the Populists' endorsement and prodding from his father, Lloyd refused to cast his ballot for Bryan in November, voting Socialist instead. Richard T. Ely later observed that the defeat of Populism proved once again that Lloyd could not function within the constraints of any single political party or ideology, be it Populism or Socialism.[27]

The St. Louis disaster inspired Lloyd to return to his public speaking and journalism. He explained to a friend that "[The Populists] had only to keep to the middle of the road to fulfill their destiny." To Ely, he wrote, "St. Louis was a nightmare. . . . What are we to think of the wits of people who allow themselves to be hypnotised by gifts of a few millions by men who at the same moment are stealing ten times as many millions, and all the people's liberties?" Lloyd told another correspondent, "It is preposterous for an intelligent people to hold themselves dependent on the freaks of the bonanzas and placers for their means of exchange." As Bryan's impending defeat drew nearer, Lloyd likened the silver issue to a bird that steals the nests of other birds in an article for the

Boston Times and Advertiser:

The Free Silver movement is a fake. Free Silver is the cowbird of the Reform movement. It waited until the nest had been built by the sacrifices and labor of others, and then it laid its eggs in it, pushing out the others which lie smashed on the ground. It is now flying around while we are expected to do the incubating. I for one decline to sit on the nest to help any such game.[28]

British reform journalist William T. Stead asked Lloyd to explain the St. Louis convention for his *Review of Reviews* magazine. The article revealed Lloyd's intense frustrations at the Populists and a surprisingly intimate knowledge of the behind-the-scenes mechanics of the Bryan endorsement. Lloyd noted that many of the Populist leaders privately admitted that they had been had by the Bryan forces, but that the lure of success and a fear of disunity had overcome their better judgment. He wrote, "A party which hates [the Democratic party] accepted the Democratic nominee and a party which has no faith in silver as a panacea accepted silver practically as the sole issue of the campaign." He was also bitter toward the tiny group of Populists who had managed the Bryan nomination, "who for years had been planning to get by fusion . . . the substance if not the name of victory."[29]

Lloyd's obituary for Populism was interesting but as misdirected as was his notice for the Liberal Republican movement in 1872. The potential of a Populist-Democrat fusion had existed for years, the *Chicago Tribune* predicting it as early as 1888. Farmers' parties, including the Populists, had tended historically to concentrate their power in too few hands, making nominations such as Bryan's easy to accomplish. Lloyd did not understand fully that the Populists had ceased to be a party by 1896 and had been taken over by a small group of free-silver ideologues. Under better circumstances, rank and file delegates could have mustered enough opposition to free silver and fusion on the convention floor with the proper encouragement, but Lloyd and other free-silver detractors allowed themselves to be defeated prematurely by their own gloom-and-doom predictions.[30]

Lloyd continued to be optimistic about reform even as he wept over the ashes of Populism. He told a Seattle newspaper the day after Christmas in 1896, "Noah was a calamity howler and the bones of the men who laughed at him have helped to make the phosphate beds out of which fertilizers are now dug for the market." It was the events of his own life that began to divert more of his energy and attention in his final years. In particular, he was put in the awkward position of having to ask payment for some of his speeches after 1896. Money, along with other personal problems, cast an ever-growing cloud of adversity over his life and career, and eventually brought on a relapse of the nervous prostration condition that had plagued him in his earlier years.[31]

To outsiders, the Lloyd family was growing up strong, healthy, and privileged by the 1890s. All four of Lloyd's sons were either attending or preparing for Harvard University, and his oldest, William Bross Lloyd, graduated from Harvard Law School in 1902. There was revolt lurking behind the public image, however, just as Lloyd had once challenged his own father. Lloyd was particularly disturbed that none of his sons seemed to share his passion for journalism, reform, or even for the working man. The *Saturday Evening Post* ridiculed his dilemma in a 1900 editorial, "A Decision for the 'Octopus'." According to the magazine, William Bross Lloyd had decided to "become the attorney for a big corporation" rather than a reformer, a fact, the magazine gloated, that was "unquestionably the hardest hit that Mr. Lloyd [had] ever received." Will, as Lloyd's oldest was called, was a trial to his father in other ways as well. He was characterized by friends and family as "a wild boy with the girls" and a "cruel and unreasonable man . . . [who] had never really grown up." Will once told his aunt, "Daddy whipped me once and told me not to cry but I had hard work to keep from laughing." He was selfish, spoiled, and rich, in marked contrast to his quiet, reserved, and kindhearted father. Even though they stood to inherit sizable legacies from their grandfather's estate as well, the prospects for Lloyd's three other sons were equally discouraging. His second and namesake was characterized as "one of the most devilish kids ever born" and became a doctor. The third, David Demarest, named after Lloyd's playwright brother, was the only Lloyd boy to share his father's interest in journalism. As an adult, Demarest worked for the conservative *Christian Science Monitor* and was a vocal critic of Franklin Roosevelt's New Deal. He had no qualms over displaying his wealth, creating an oddity among his less affluent colleagues by covering assignments in a chauffeur-driven Rolls-Royce. He also served on the *Chicago Tribune*'s board of directors from 1926 to 1931. The youngest, nicknamed Jack after Lloyd's grandfather John, suffered from a mental disorder that required constant surveillance by family and friends. One of Lloyd's stenographers, who lived with the family, recalled, "I have sometimes said that while Mr. Lloyd was the simplest and the most democratic of men, on the other hand it seemed to me that his boys were entirely the opposite—in fact, I am afraid I used the word 'snobbish' in the characterization."[32]

Jessie Bross Lloyd experienced a steady decline in her health after the birth of her last child in 1886, leaving her a virtual invalid and an increasing burden on Lloyd. She suffered from rheumatoid arthritis and took electric shock therapies to mitigate the condition. She was diagnosed as a diabetic in 1897 and forced to endure bizarre skim milk and water diets to control the then often fatal disease. Lloyd was so concerned about her declining health that he purchased a cemetery plot for her in 1898. Jessie blamed her physical disabilities on the demands of motherhood, telling a friend in 1900, "A mother's first duty is to take care of herself, I grow more and more sure of that. It does not seem as if it did any harm to go to bed night after night tired to death, but you have to pay these bills sometimes, and it isn't agreeable business as I find every day." She blamed her depressed mental condition on the strict Victorian separation of the sexes and the denial to her of opportunities outside the home. As she told the Chicago Woman's Club in a speech delivered during the 1890s, "It seems strange that in a country whose noble flag of stars and stripes was designed by a woman . . . there should be such a fierce belief in the doctrine that women and idiots have a divine right to the same seclusion and protection." Lloyd remained deeply in love with his wife nevertheless, writing her on her birthday in 1891, "I never felt that I needed you . . . never looked forward to the daily walk and conversation on the future or back to the lovely memories of the past with a fuller heart than now." She reciprocated with a note left upon the icebox: "Dearest, how I have missed you. . . . there is plain fresh cake, rye bread, and milk on the ice and a welcome upstairs for you."[33]

Lloyd's health was deteriorating as well. He had always been troubled by insomnia, but the condition worsened in his final years. At times, his only relief was to have Jessie or his secretary read him to sleep each night. He avoided coffee, which he believed was a deleterious drug, and friends lampooned him as saying to waitresses, "Bring me a cup of hot water, very weak please." He learned of a new book on sleep in 1896 and wrote the author acknowledging the "indebtedness to you . . . which I know I shall owe you after I have read your book," but the problem persisted. A guest to the Wayside left a humorous note in his room, "In case of fire, come down softly, and do not wake Mr. Lloyd." Combined with his nervous prostration condition, Lloyd was left virtually disabled for varying periods of time. He told a friend in 1899, "I have not been very well this winter and such a rest as I know I would get with you would do a great deal to build me up."[34]

The social ostracism that Lloyd had experienced as a result of his Haymarket Square activities was another burden on him as the years went by, and he found Chicago an increasingly less appealing place to be. He told a friend in 1895, "Chicago grows more and more repulsive but the more I suppose it is my duty to stay there." An average of thirty friends and guests filled the Lloyd's Rhode Island summer house each day, and Lloyd was frequently forced to pound the dinner table for quiet to allow his minister father to pronounce a simple grace before meals. It was with growing reluctance that he left Rhode Island to return to the reproachments of Chicago each fall. He finally acted upon his disenchantment in 1899, renting a winter house on Beacon Street in Boston so that Jessie could be close to her sons at Harvard. The couple assimilated quickly into Boston's liberal, intellectual society, in contrast to their Chicago isolation. Lloyd returned to the Wayside in subsequent winters, staying there for varying periods of time, but Chicago was never the center of his life that it had been during the 1870s and 1880s.[35]

Lloyd might have been able to weather such distractions and continue with his advocacy journalism had it not been for money. When he retired from the *Chicago Tribune* in 1885, William Bross failed to guarantee Lloyd that he would never have to work again, and the Depression of 1893 and its aftermath reminded Lloyd about that lack of guarantee. Lloyd's parents, younger brother, and both younger sisters all suffered as a result of the 1893 depression, and Lloyd felt a relational obligation to help them financially. His father, who never returned to the ministry after he moved back to New York in 1861, invested heavily in real estate during the 1870s and 1880s, but was hard-pressed by declining land values during the 1890s. Aaron Lloyd became so destitute that he and Lloyd's mother Maria lived much of the year at Lloyd's Rhode Island summer home as an economy measure after the depression. Lloyd's only surviving brother John lost his job in 1894 and was forced to depend upon Lloyd's and others' charity for several years until he found work. Both of Lloyd's sisters had financial and family problems of their own. Added to such demands was a disruption in Lloyd's yearly *Chicago Tribune* dividends. Normally his 1/20th share of the newspaper paid handsome profits, but the newspaper's board of directors decided to build a new office building in 1895 and diverted most of their profits toward the project. Lloyd was denied an opportunity to serve as a director by his detractors on the newspaper and had no choice in the matter other than to sell his stock, something he didn't want to do. His and Jessie's real estate holdings also declined in value at the time, leaving the Lloyds wealthy on paper but cash poor.[36]

The result was that Lloyd found himself depending more and more upon the legacies left to Jessie and their sons by her father William Bross and the money he earned from his speeches. In other words, the reputed millionaire-socialist Henry Demarest Lloyd (one newspaper said he was worth ten million dollars) had to work to maintain his lifestyle after 1895. Lloyd did not sacrifice all of the trappings of his upper-class existence, especially his secretaries, stenographers, servants, and summer and winter houses, but he and Jessie cut other expenses whenever they could. Lloyd hired an agent to arrange his speaking dates and fees and what had started out as a diversion became a job, and a tiring one at that. One newspaper reported, "Mr. Lloyd's lecture was mostly taken up with quotations from other authors. . . . There would have been much more life in his remarks had he not read them from type-written sheets. He spoke, or read, for about three-quarters of an hour." Lloyd used his status as a former journalist to obtain free publicity for his talks and even sleeping accommodations in towns where hotel space was scarce of lacking. He wrote Richard T. Ely in 1901, "I have had a successful [speaking] trip because I am a newspaper man and have had the generous cooperation of the fraternity. But such experiences would break your heart." Still, with his economies, speechmaking provided Lloyd with enough money to remain solvent, retain much of the upper-class lifestyle that he had come to enjoy, and continue his other reform activities.[37]

By necessity, the topics of Lloyd's speeches in his final years were more marketable, but he never quite lost his radicalism or the penchant for reproaching the upper class that he developed after Haymarket. In "Is Personal Development the Best Social Policy," a speech he delivered to Boston's Browning Society in 1902, Lloyd claimed that social and cultural interbreeding was weakening late nineteenth-century American society. "They who feed wholly on white bread and the tenderloin . . . soon get rickets. The man I heard say he liked to eat with the common people once in while; the woman you heard say that she thought it was her duty to associate with the middle class, confess the approach of extinction." In the "National Ownership of Anthracite Coal Mines," a speech Lloyd presented to a federal committee in 1903, Lloyd said, "Only by instant action can the country be saved from the catastrophe towards which its rights, prosperity, and liberties are being hurried by the greed and lust of a small body of the richest and most disloyal men popular government has ever been threatened by." Lloyd told the Massachusetts Reform Club two months later, "Wall Street robs us, waters and capitalizes the plunder, and sells back to us at high prices what it took from us for nothing, and then we fondle the quotations as evidence of our wonderful prosperity. The standard of value of . . . securities and the measure of . . . prosperity is the length of the public ears and the limit of its submission."[38]

Journalist William Allen White once wrote, "The history of reform is a history of disappointment. The reform works, of course. But in working it does only the one little trick it is intended to do, and the long chain of incidental blessings which should follow, which the reformers feel must inevitably follow, wait for other reformers to bring them into being." Lloyd's final days were filled with despair, for the reason that William Allen White explained, and more. It was the birth of a new movement, Progressivism, that gave him hope for the future. Although he failed to live to see the flowering of Progressivism, his efforts to help other writers, most notably Ida M. Tarbell, became his final and most lasting contribution to reform.[39]

NOTES

1. Various photographs; C. S. Jackson to HDL, 25 September 1888; HDL to Richard T. Ely, 12 January 1894; Maria Lloyd to HDL, 29 April 1895; and HDL to F. F. Murray, 9 January 1896; all in HDL, Wisc. and Roger Sherman to HDL, 21 December 1894, in Sherman papers, Yale.

2. Lloyd learned about Guglielmo Marconi's development of radio during an Italian tour in 1902 and envisioned a publicly-owned network of powerful, clear-channel radio stations that would have broadcast his and other people's ideas for free. See "The Socialist Regime," *The Independent* and *New York Tribune* clipping, both 1 May 1902 and in HDL, Wisc.

3. DeWitte Holland, *America in Controversy: History of American Public Address* (Dubuque, IA: William C. Brown Co., 1973), vii-xix; Ronald H. Carpenter, *The Eloquence of Frederick Jackson Turner* (San Marino, CA: Huntington Library, 1983);

and Garrison Keillor, *WLT: A Radio Romance* (New York: Viking Press, 1991), 153.

4. Various photographs and CLS Journal, both HDL, Wisc.

5. Various newspaper clippings and speech notes, 1886–1896, HDL, mf.; CLS, *Lloyd*, I, 83–99, 112–114, 143–146; CLS Journal, HDL, Wisc.; Thomas, *Alternative*, 280; and "Boycott Still in Force," *Chicago Chronicle*, 14 June 1896.

6. HDL, "The New Conscience," *North American Review*, (September 1888): 325–339; Josephine E. Hall, 27 March 1892, in HDL, Wisc.; CLS, *Lloyd* I, 108–116; Paul H. Boase, "The Social Gospel," in *America in Controversy*, 185–203; and Susan Curtis, *A Consuming Faith: The Social Gospel and Modern American Culture* (Baltimore: The Johns Hopkins University Press, 1991).

7. HDL, "Eight-hour Movement," as published in the *Trade Assembly Record*, 2 September 1889; *Chicago Herald*, 5 March 1890; *Grand Rapids Telegram*, 31 March 1890; *Chicago Sun*, 22 February 1891; and *C.T.*, 28 December 1891; and HDL, "Free Speech and Assemblage" and "Money Power," n.d., circa late 1880s; all in HDL, mf.; Warren W. Bailey to HDL, January 18, 1890; Horace E. Deming to HDL, September 20, 1893; George Iles to HDL, 7 October 1893; Charles N. Gregory to HDL, 10 October 1893; and HDL, notebook 11, circa 1889, 272–274; all in HDL, Wisc.; Jonathan Lurie, "H. D. Lloyd: A Note," *Agricultural History*, 47(January 1973): 76–79; Samuel Gompers, *Seventy Years of Life and Labour* (New York: Augustus M. Kelley, 1967, 1925): 96–99; and David R. Roediger and Philip S. Foner, *Our Own Time: A History of American Labor and the Working Day* (Westport, CT: Greenwood Press, 1987), 115–144, 155–162.

8. HDL, "What Washington Would Do Today," as reprinted in HDL, *Lords of Industry* (New York: G.P. Putnam's Sons, 1910), 159–176.

9. HDL to John Burnham, 26 March 1895 and William T. Baker to HDL, 28 October 1891, both in HDL, Wisc.; John F. Kasson, *Civilizing the Machine: Technology and Republican Values in America, 1776–1900* (New York: Penguin Books, 1976), 183–234; Frank A. Cassell, "Welcoming the World: Illinois' Role in the World Columbian Exposition," *Illinois Historical Journal*, 79(Winter 1986): 230–244; and Pierce, *History of Chicago* III, 501–512.

10. *Programme of the Labor Congress, August 29–September 4, 1894*, CHS; *C.T.* and *Chicago Times*, various dates in August and September 1894; HDL to Carroll D. Wright, 6 March; HDL to Samuel Bowles, 15 March; HDL to Eltweed Pomeroy, 26 May; Pomeroy to HDL, 31 May; Booker T. Washington to HDL, 24, 25, 26 August, all 1893; and William Dean Howells to HDL, 4 January 1894; all in HDL, Wisc.; HDL to E.R.A. Ross, 4 February, 20 July 1893, in E.R.A. Ross papers, State Historical Society of Wisconsin; Thomas, *Alternative*, 283–284; Kinsley, *Tribune* III, 210–216; Chamberlain, *Reform*, 21; Trachtenberg, *Incorporation*, 208–234; and Pierce, *History of Chicago*, 508–509.

Also see David F. Burg, *Chicago's White City of 1893* (Lexington: University of Kentucky Press, 1976); R. Reid Badger, *The Great American Fair: The World's Columbian Exposition and American Culture* (Chicago: N. Hall, 1979); and Robert W. Rydell, *All the World's A Fair: Visions of Empire at American International Expositions* (Chicago: University of Chicago Press, 1984).

11. HDL to Ignatius Donnelly, 28 May 1891; Donnelly to HDL, 30 May 1893; and HDL to Frances E. Willard, 1 February 1892; all in HDL, Wisc.; "Summary of Facts submitted by Henry D. Lloyd before the Anti-Monopoly Convention recently held in

Chicago," 1893, HDL, mf.; John D. Hicks, *The Populist Revolt* (Minneapolis: University of Minnesota Press, 1931), 443–444; and Samuel Gompers, "Organized Labor in the Campaign," *North American Review*, 155(July 1892): 92–95.

12. HDL notebook 4, circa 1887–1888, 74 and HDL to Frances E. Willard, 28 January 1892, both in HDL Wisc.; Ruth Bordin, *Frances Willard: A Biography* (Chapel Hill: University of North Carolina Press, 1986); and Rader, *Academic Mind*, 132.

13. Paul Wachtel, *The Poverty of Affluence: A Psychological Portrait of the American Way of Life* (New York: Free Press, 1983); HDL, notebook 23 dated 1892, 560 and HDL to Samuel Gompers, 15 July 1892, both in HDL, mf.; Altschull, *Milton to McLuhan*, 213–217; Gene Claton, *Populism: The Humane Preference in America* (Boston: Twayne, 1991); William A. Peffer, *Populism, Its Rise and Fall* (Lawrence: University Press of Kansas, 1992); Theodore Saloutos, "Radicalism and the Agrarian Tradition," in *Failure of a Dream: Essays in the History of American Socialism* ed. John H. M. Laslett and Seymour Martin Lipset (Berkeley: University of California Press, 1984), 52–81; HDL, "Political Economy of Seventy-Three Millions," 75; Richard Hofstadter, *The Age of Reform: From Bryan to F.D.R.* (New York: Alfred A. Knopf, 1956), 23–93; Henry Nash Smith, *Virgin Land* (Cambridge: Harvard University Press, 1950); Marx, *Machine in the Garden*; Sproat, *Best Men*, 143–158; Trachtenberg, *Incorporation*, 38–69; and Strauss, *Generations*, 224–225.

14. HDL to William M. Salter, 18 October 1889; Frances E. Willard to HDL, 29 October 1891 and 1 February 1892; HDL to Willard, 28 January 1892; HDL to Samuel Gompers, 10 July 1892; all in HDL, Wisc. and Ruegamer, "Women," 129–132.

15. Thomas J. Morgan to CLS, 31 July 1905; Robert H. Howe to CLS, 22 August 1906; HDL to George A. Gates, 23 May 1895; Ignatius Donnelly to HDL, 30 May 1893; Mrs. A. P. Stevens to HDL, 7 June 1893; M. M. Madden to HDL, 27 June 1894; and HDL to Gompers, 5 April, 30 July 1894, all in HDL, Wisc.; "Populist Platform," May 1894; draft preamble and platform for "The People's Party Convention at Springfield, Illinois, July 4, 1894,"; and HDL, "The Natural History of a Social Reformer," written for Henry Latchford, n.d., circa summer 1894; *C.T.*, 6 July 1894 and undated *Chicago Times* clipping, circa June 1894; all in HDL, mf.; Samuel F. Gompers to HDL, 9 June 1893, Samuel Gompers's Letterbook, American Federation of Labor microfilm, 1966 (hereafter Gompers's Letterbook); CLS, *Lloyd* I, 241–245; Destler, "Consummation of a Labor-Populist Alliance in Illinois, 1894," *Mississippi Valley Historical Review*, 27(March 1941): 589–602; Destler, "The People's Party in Illinois: 1888–1896: A Phase of the Populist Revolt," (Ph.D. diss., University of Chicago, 1932), 109–126; CLS, *Lloyd* I, 241–245; Thomas, *Alternative*, 317–320; and Foner, *Labor*, 287–288.

16. Selig Perlman and Philip Taft, *History of Labor in the United States, 1896–1932*, IV (New York: The Macmillan Co., 1935), 221–227; Ray Ginger, *Eugene V. Debs: The Making of an American Radical* (New York: Collier Books, 1949), 123–171; Howard Wayne Morgan, *Eugene V. Debs: Socialist for President* (Syracuse, NY: Syracuse University Press, 1962); Hofstadter, *Reform*, 236–244; and Johnpoll and Klehr, *Biographical Dictionary*, 90–99.

Also see William Carwardine, *The Pullman Strike* (Chicago: C. H. Kerr, 1973) and Almont Lindsey, *The Pullman Strike, the Story of a Unique Experiment and of a Great Labor Upheaval* (Chicago: The University of Chicago Press, 1942).

17. Ginger, *Debs*, 136–166, 184; Gashman, *America*, 168–171; HDL letter to editor,

New York Journal, 18 October 1896; Eugene V. Debs to HDL, 24 July, 15 August 1894; HDL to Debs, 23 November 1894; and Florence Kelley to HDL, 18 July, 1 August 1894, all in HDL, Wisc.

18. HDL to Samuel Gompers, 30 July and 14 August 1894 in HDL, Wisc. and "Enemy of the Trusts: Henry D. Lloyd, Chicago Populists' Nominee for Congress," *Chicago Evening Post*, 5 September 1894, clipping in HDL, mf.

19. "Address of HDL to a People's Party meeting, October 6, 1894," HDL, mf. "People's Party Speech at Tattersal's, November 3, 1894," in HDL, mf.; HDL to Willis J. Abbott, 8 October 1894, in HDL, Wisc; CLS, *Lloyd* I, 251–252; *C.T.*, 21, 26, 28 October 1894; and JBL diary, 27 September 1894, CHS.

Lloyd was pictured as a People's Party Candidate in *The Chicago Spotlight*, 17 October 1894. He was nominated as the Populists' candidate for lieutenant governor as well but declined the position. See unidentified clipping, 15 September 1896, HDL, Wisc.

20. CLS, ibid.; *C.T.*, 4, 8 November 1894; Destler, *American Radicalism*, 204–209; Nelson, *Martyrs*, 227–228; and Goodwyn, *Populist*, 103–104.

21. Ethelbert Stewart to HDL, 12 October 1894 in HDL, Wisc. Benjamin O. Flower to HDL, 21 October 1894; Clarence S. Darrow to HDL, 12 October 1894; Darrow, et. al. to HDL, 22 October 1894; C. A. Starr to HDL, 3 March 1895; J. M. Bale to HDL, 5 April, 7 May 1895; all in HDL, Wisc. and Darrow to CLS, 17 May 1906, in HDL, mf.

Also see "Boycott Still in Force," *Chicago Chronicle*, 14 June 1896 in HDL, mf.; and E. P. Hassinger to HDL, March 1895 and 4 May 1895, both in HDL, Wisc.

22. William H. Harvey, *Coin's Financial School*, ed. Richard Hofstadter (Cambridge, MA: Belknap Press, 1963), 175; Oren Stephens, "'Coin' Harvey: The Free Silver Movement's Frustrated Promoter," *American West*, 8 (September 1971): 4–9; and I. T. Alvord to HDL, 2 September 1896, in HDL, Wisc.

23. HDL to Judge Miller, 17 August 1894; HDL to William T. Stead, 21 August 1894; Harvey, *Coin*, 145–147; HDL to J. C. Manning, 7 February 1895; Ignatius Donnelly to HDL, 26 May 1895; and HDL to Donnelly, 28 May 1895, all in HDL, Wisc. and Thorelli, *Anti-Trust*, 358–363.

24. Frances E. Willard to HDL, 17 January 1895, in HDL, Wisc. R. H. Howe to HDL, 13 November 1894; Clarence Darrow to HDL, 22 November; HDL to Darrow, 23 November 1894; HDL, "Platform of the People's Party, Chicago, February 1895"; HDL to E. Benjamin Andrews, 19 February 1895; Green to HDL, 3 February 1895; all in HDL, Wisc.; *Labour Leader*, 4 May 1895, clipping in HDL, mf.; HDL, "Municipal Ownership Speech," HDL, mf.; "What the People's Party Platform Means," broadside dated 8 March 1895, State Historical Society of Wisconsin; and Destler, *American Radicalism*, 250–251.

25. HDL to Richard T. Ely, 14 March, 2 April 1896 in Ely Papers, Wisc. and HDL to H. I. Grimes, 10 July 1896, in HDL, Wisc.

26. Florence Kelley to HDL, 18 June; HDL to Thomas J. Morgan, 11 July; Bayard Holmes to HDL, 11 July; HDL to R. I. Holmes, 10, 13 July 1896; all in HDL, Wisc. and HDL, "The People's Party," typed manuscript for *C.T.*, 26 July 1896, in HDL, mf.

27. HDL, "The Populists at St. Louis," *Review of Reviews*, 14(September 1896): 298–303; HDL, *Progressive Review*, 1 (October–November 1896): 75–77; CLS, *Lloyd* I, 257–265; undated clipping from N. O. Nelson, HDL, mf.; CLS Journal, HDL,

Wisc.,; Richard T. Ely comments on HDL to Ely, April 2, 1896, Ely Papers; and Sorge, *Labor Movement*, 157.

28. HDL to Richard T. Ely, 3 August 1896; HDL to William Hogan, 6 August; HDL to A. B. Adair, 10 October; HDL to Edward H. Rogers, 26 October; Henry Lloyd to HDL, 1 November 1896; all in HDL, Wisc.; and "Cow-Bird Politics," *Boston Times and Advertiser*, 17 November 1896, in HDL, mf.

29. HDL, "Populists," 302.

30. Goodwyn, *Populist*, 262 and Hofstadter, *Reform*, 107–108.

31. *Seattle Times*, 26 December 1896, in HDL, mf.

32. HDL to JBL, 25 February 1903; Anne Withington to CLS, n.d., circa 1906; Jessie Dale Pearce to CLS, 24 October 1907; and CLS Journal, all in HDL, Wisc.; William Bross Lloyd to Richard T. Ely, 12 July 1909; Richard T. Ely to CLS, 27 June 1916; and CLS to Ely, 13 July 1916; all in Ely Papers, Wisc.; Nicholas Kelley Oral History, Columbia University; William Bross Lloyd to Nicholas Kelley, 22 February 1905, 9 November 1915, 22 April 1916, and 19 December 1941; Henry Demarest Lloyd, Jr. to Kelley, 14 April 1942; all in Nicholas Kelley Papers, New York Public Library; "Interview with Mrs. Zelda Stewart Charters," 28 December 1939, Destler papers, Wisc.; Demarest Lloyd file, Nicholas Murray Butler Papers, Columbia University; "A Decision for the 'Octopus'," *Saturday Evening Post*, 7 July 1900, clipping in HDL, mf; *Chicago Daily Journal*, 8 June 1916, clipping in Lloyd-Schwimmer Papers, New York Public Library; John Hohenberg, *Foreign Correspondence: The Great Reporters and Their Times* (New York: Columbia University Press, 1964), 280; Robert W. Desmond, *Crisis and Conflict: World News Reporting Between Two Wars, 1920–1940* (Iowa City: University of Iowa Press, 1982), 339; and Jessie Lloyd O'Connor, "Discovering the World," *Harvey and Jessie: A Couple of Radicals* (Philadelphia: Temple University Press, 1988), 77–78.

33. JBL to HDL, n.d.; HDL to JBL, 27 September 1891; and JBL to Mrs. Edward Bemis, 13 January 1900; all in HDL, Wisc.; Bross MS diary, 10, 17, 28 November, 10, 20 December 1880; JBL MS diary, 12 April 1895, 14, 27 January, 3 February 1897, 11 February, 13 March 1898, 16, 17, 18, 19 January, and 26 February 1899; JBL, "Relative Values," undated speech, delivered to the Chicago Women's Club, circa 1890s; and various JBL obituaries; all in JBL, CHS.

Also see Noble M. Eberhart, *A Working Manual of High Frequency Currents* (Chicago: New Medicine Publishing Co., 1911), 208–212.

34. HDL to John Bigelow, 10 October 1896; HDL to Gladden, 5 October 1899; and HDL to Elderess Anna White, 12 December 1899; all in HDL, Wisc.; CLS, *Lloyd* I, 172; and Strauss and Howe, *Generations*, 222–223.

35. HDL to William Salter, 14 July 1895; *C.T.* as quoted in "Only Sneers," *The Better Way*, 7 January 1897; Frances E. Willard to HDL, 21 July 1897; Jessie Dale Pearce to CLS, 24 October 1907; "Watch House" poem, 11 September 1899; and HDL to Anna White, 12 December 1899, in HDL, Wisc.; all in HDL, Wisc.; *Boston Globe*, 24 October 1895 and *Chicago Times-Herald*, 24 July 1896, both in HDL, mf; JBL to Anita McCormick Blaine, 21 June 1896, McCormick Papers, State Historical Society of Wisconsin; and Mann, *Yankee*, 22–23; 159–163.

36. HDL notebook 9, p.89, circa late 1890s, HDL mf.; Aaron Lloyd to HDL, 2 January, 17 August 1894, 15 January 1895, 4 July 1898, 9 October 1899; Galloway, Lyman and Patton to HDL, 5 December 1894; CLS to HDL, 30 April 1896; and R. D.

Hill to JBL, 10 April 1905; all in HDL, Wisc.; William Bross Lloyd bill to JBL, 11 February 1904, in JBL, CHS; CLS, *Lloyd* II, 173; Hoyt, *One Hundred Years*, 178-181; Chamberlain, *Reform*, 17-21; and Wendt, *Tribune*, 316-321.

37. Among the numerous exaggerated accounts of Lloyd's wealth in the media were the *Dover* (New Hampshire) *Democrat*, 18 June 1890; *Boston Herald*, 18 November 1894; unidentified clipping, T.S.C. Lee to HDL, 12 August 1899; *Boston Globe*, 29 September 1903; and *Boston Herald*, 29 September 1903, all in HDL, Wisc.; and *Richmond Star*, 17 January 1895.

Regarding Lloyd's financial situation, see HDL to Edward W. Bemis, 3 February 1900; Bemis to CLS, 30 August 1906; and JBL to Richard T. Ely, 8 January 1904; "Not up to expectations," *Albany* (New York) *Express*, 14 February 1898; HDL to Eugene Higgins, 19 November 1898; James B. Pond to HDL, 14 February 1891; *Philadelphia Ledger*, 15 January 1902; all in HDL, Wisc.; HDL to Ely, 21 December 1895 and 18 October 1901, both in Ely Papers, Wisc. The Bross fortune was worth an estimated three million dollars in 1908 plus the family's one-fourth ownership in the *Tribune*. See *Chicago Journal*, 20 July 1908, in HDL, Wisc.

38. HDL, "Is Personal Development the Best Social Policy," reprinted in *Mazzini and Other Essays* (New York: G. P. Putnam's Sons, 1910), 190-200; "National Ownership of Coal Mines," and "The Failure of Railroad Regulation," both reprinted in *Lords of Industry*, 224-346.

39. CLS to HDL, 5 March 1898; HDL to Catherine Allen, 1 May 1900; and HDL to William T. Stead, 2 November 1901; all in HDL, Wisc.; Strauss, *Generations*, 225-226; William Allen White, *In the Heart of a Fool* (New York: The Macmillan Co., 1918), 524 as quoted in Jernigan, *Lloyd*, 147; and Thomas, *Alternative*, 344.

8

Muckraking and Other Reforms

The defeat of William Jennings Bryan in the 1896 presidential election disgraced many of the reform leaders in the United States but not Lloyd. *Wealth*, Lloyd's anti-fusion position, and his success on the podium furthered his reputation as an advocate for social justice. At times, the admiration merged on idolatry. One supporter told him, "I trust to always find in you a '*chevalier sans feur et sans reproche*' [a knight without fear and above reproach] whose motto is 'noblesse oblige.'" Unlike most of his Populist counterparts, however, Lloyd also remembered that he needed support for his reforms from the many, not the few. He made a list of the top six historical "Enemies of Mankind" in his notebook, ranging from the original Christians, to the Protestants, English Puritans, American Colonists, Abolitionists, and ending with "the workingman." "All of which shows the value of what is called Public Opinion and gives to those who seek immortality a hint as to the side they should enlist on," he noted.[1]

In spite of his success, Lloyd was despondent over the demise of Populism. Many of his reform efforts dating back to Haymarket had been negated by the same kind of clandestine political manipulations that had derailed the Liberal Republican party in 1872. Lloyd's only release from his frustration was his writing, and the period between 1896 and 1903 was the most prolific of his career. He produced three books and numerous magazine and newspaper articles, all advocating reforms such as cooperatives, binding labor arbitration, old-age pensions, and minimum wage laws. He became involved in the early stages of muckraking and was helpful to several writers, most notably Ida M.

Tarbell. Ultimately overwork, stress, and his precarious health all contributed to his death at the age of fifty-six.

Out of the ashes of Populism, Lloyd's next cause was cooperativism. He was attracted to the concept of shared work for mutual benefit out of his instinctive sense of altruism and his conviction that the cooperative movement was still anonymous enough in the 1890s to furnish him with another book. Cooperatives were neither new to Gilded Age America nor entirely foreign to Lloyd. They had been introduced to this country in the 1790s and as a result of Populism had experienced a temporary rise in popularity in parts of the country during the 1880s. Lloyd's first encounter with a cooperative came during his 1885 European tour, and the last chapter of *Wealth* contained a brief discussion of the cooperative ideal. He wrote in his notebook at about the same time:

What Party do you belong to?
  The Cooperative Commonwealth.
What school of economy?
  The C.C.
What God do you worship?
  The C.C.

He told an audience during the 1894 People's Party campaign, "I will not veil, or soften, or ambiguify my belief that there is no way out of the present situation, but the Co-operative Commonwealth, and that is the only live issue before us today."[2]

He was introduced to the cooperative ideal by three different sources. Lloyd considered the first, an eccentric Danish immigrant, "one of the greatest thinkers of our time." Laurence Gronlund's 1884 *The Cooperative Commonwealth* was the first American book to discuss Marxism, and it was instrumental in introducing a number of Gilded Age liberals, including William Dean Howells and Edward Bellamy, to the German social philosopher. Gronlund argued that "socialism is not so much the cause of the poor and weak as of the capable, gifted and cultured," a statement that appealed to upper-class reformers like Howells. Lloyd learned of the book from a Boston friend in 1888 and was so impressed with its contents that he invited Gronlund to be a part of his Labor Congress at the World's Columbian Exposition in 1893. It was only after Lloyd came to know Gronlund personally that he discovered the eccentricities of the man. When not threatening suicide, Gronlund literally survived through the generosity of his friends. Lloyd learned with time to keep his distance from Gronlund but found much to admire in his plea for mutual cooperation.[3]

Lloyd met another cooperationist during his Populist campaigns, Julius A. Wayland, the publisher of a popular Indiana reform newspaper, *The Coming Nation*. Wayland supported a variety of cooperative projects with his paper's profits. The most involved was Ruskin, a three thousand acre cooperative colony set in the rolling farmlands of Tennessee, named after the English critic and modeled after Edward Bellamy's altruria in *Looking Backward*. Wayland wanted Lloyd to contribute to the project, but the financially strapped Lloyd refused, instead agreeing to lay the cornerstone of the Ruskin College of the New Economy, billed as the first socialist college in the world, in 1897. Both the college and the colony eventually failed, but Wayland moved to Kansas and started another reform newspaper, *Appeal to Reason*, which became the first mass circulation Socialist newspaper in America. Lloyd found Wayland's enthusiasm for cooperatives infectious and carried it into his own work.[4]

The most influential cooperationist in Lloyd's life was a St. Louis plumbing manufacturer named Nelson O. Nelson. Lloyd stayed with Nelson's family during the 1896 Populist convention, and he attended a national cooperative congress with him at about the same time. In the wake of the demise of Populism, Nelson talked Lloyd into joining the American Cooperative Union, one of many organizations spreading the cooperative gospel. When that group dissolved over the issue of monopolies, another group, the Brotherhood of the Cooperative Commonwealth, asked Lloyd to become its president, an offer Lloyd appreciated but ultimately refused. Not long thereafter, Nelson invited Lloyd to join him at the 1897 International Co-operative Conference in Holland, and Lloyd went, telling friends, "I had been warming myself by the picture of a fire. It would be better to go to the fire itself." He was so impressed by what he learned that he decided to write a book publicizing European cooperative methods for Americans. Nelson introduced him to two English cooperationists—Henry Vivian, secretary of the English Labour Copartnership Association, and Thomas Blandford, a colleague—and the two showed Lloyd various English cooperatives. Lloyd spent several weeks in England, filling an entire notebook with his impressions, and then hurried home to distill his thoughts into book form.[5]

The result a year later was *Labor Copartnership*, Lloyd's third book. He struck a deal with Harper Brothers again to pay for the printing plates and illustrations and guarantee a sale of fifteen hundred copies, in return for complete editorial control. Lloyd restricted his text to agricultural cooperatives, believing that American farmers would be more receptive to the cooperative ideal than industrialists. Evoking the Agrarian Myth of his own childhood and his experience with Populism, Lloyd explained, "I think our reformers, including our cooperators, are too municipal, too citified. I think they have largely lost the 'sense of the soil'." To appease his labor friends, who considered cooperatives a form of anti-unionism, Lloyd tempered his praise, hinting that there was room for compromise, not confrontation, between the two reforms. To make his prose interesting, he adopted a more pleasing, travelogue writing style, in contrast to the prosecutorial tone of *Wealth*, but it was still advocacy writing. It suffered from a couple of flaws. As in *Wealth*, Lloyd used too many unnecessary official statements and statistics to make his points, once again forgetting that he was not arguing before a jury. One reader complained, "When you were bringing your charges against the Standard Oil it was better to have court decisions than clear and vivid statements from your own pen; but in describing English cooperation where your attitude was that of an observer, one page of your say so was worth a dozen from the officials of these societies." The book was also overly emotional in places. One of Lloyd's favorite pitches was patriotism:

The achievement of America in uniting in one common life and one cooperative citizenship the African and European and even Asiatic types which elsewhere glare at each other with hatred across frontiers of bayonets is the greatest triumph of cooperation which the history of civilization has yet shown. . . . Cooperation can go on in America as in Great Britain and on the Continent. . . . What cooperation needs here, as elsewhere, is not philanthropy, but leadership; not endowment, but initiative.[6]

In spite of such short comings, *Labor Copartnership* attracted a respectable reading public and even made Lloyd a small profit, selling seventeen hundred copies. University of Chicago political economist Charles Zeublin rated it one of the most important economic books of 1898. It received favorable reviews in the *New York Journal*, *New York Herald*, *Brooklyn Eagle*, and the *Chicago Times-Herald* as well as in reform publications such as *The Kingdom*, *The Outlook*, and *Social Gospel*. Labor supporters were the biggest detractors. The Chicago Post called it a "blow to state socialism and a practical argument for individualism and private enterprise in the labor world." A.F.L. President Samuel Gompers, a native of England, had warned Lloyd to learn the anti-union activities of cooperationists during his English visit, advice Lloyd ignored. Gompers reprimanded him in 1899, "I think that there can be no question but that some of the very ablest men among the wage workers have been weaned from the trade union movement by reason of their connection with, and devotion to, cooperative associations. . . . In fact, the cooperative societies of Great Britain have adopted trade union rules in their establishments only as many other employers have, through the force and demand of trade union action." As much as he disagreed with Gompers, Lloyd could not abandon organized labor, which he equated to the working class and considered the core of his constituency. He wrote in 1898, "I never deny that the workingmen make great mistakes, but I insist that it is the duty of all of us to be on their side, never more so than when they are wrong." Sales of *Labor Copartnership* declined after 1898, even though Lloyd continued to preach cooperatives in his speeches. He told an audience in 1901, "All the clothes I have on my back were made by cooperatives and I consider myself the best dressed man in New York tonight." It was Gompers's opposition, rather than any change in Lloyd's thinking, that convinced him to downplay cooperatives in his subsequent writings and speeches.[7]

Lloyd's 1897 trip to Holland and England reawakened his enthusiasm for travel, and even though his wife could no longer join him, he decided to research the social question in Australia and New Zealand. The two countries had been an object of American intellectual curiosity since the early 1890s, largely for their innovative methods of mitigating the negative side effects of the industrial revolution. Lloyd believed that Americans were "still economic barbarians," incapable "of naturalizing all the reforms that have been successfully instituted in different parts of the world." "What is especially wanted at this point of our development," he wrote, "is a focusing into one view of all the different things that are being done of, by and for the people in different parts of the world in different provinces of effort." Although he was not optimistic of success, he told a correspondent, "Whether we can get this economic readjustment by means of the reforms in progressive taxation, government ownership, land restoration, cooperation, etc. which are now being pushed with such success in New Zealand and England, I do not know. I think we are bound to make the effort."[8]

He embarked for Australia and New Zealand in late 1898 with his oldest son Will as a traveling companion. His sister Caro warned the pair, "Don't give the cannibals their 'first taste' of sociology." They traveled by train and boat, arriving in the New Zealand capital of Wellington on February 12, 1899, amid a "regular Noah's ark of rain." Lloyd quickly confirmed that the country was all that he had hoped it would be. He later described New Zealand as an island of small, English-style garden cities surrounded by stretches of untamed wilderness, full of a "flooding tide of a new prosperity." Wellington had the world's first social security system, and Lloyd watched in amazement as pensioners, the "flotsam and jetsam of the work-a-day life of New Zealand" as he called them, picked up their monthly checks, secure in the knowledge that they did not have to live on the generosity of a relative for the rest of their life. Old-age pensions immediately became one of Lloyd's pet reforms. The highlight of Lloyd's New Zealand trip was his discovery of compulsory or binding labor arbitration. In an era when American labor-management relations were marked by open hostility and death, as was the case during the 1894 Pullman Strike, most of New Zealand's unions and companies resolved their differences through peaceful negotiation. Lloyd was so impressed by the humanity of compulsory arbitration that he told one New Zealander that he would have stayed in the country for the rest of his life had it not been for his invalid wife. He gathered data on the process in the hope that he could convince workers and employers to implement the process in the United States, forever ending the need for labor-management confrontations.[9]

Lloyd conducted a whirlwind tour of Australia in May 1899 but found too much there that reminded him of the United States. The one major exception was a minimum wage law in the state of Victoria that guaranteed laborers a living wage for their work. He was staggered by the implications of that concept, especially how businessmen used Social Darwinism to justify starvation wages, and took detailed notes to help promote the concept in the United States.[10]

His time ran out in late May, for he had promised to attend the Harvard University graduation of his second son, Henry Demarest Lloyd, Jr., on June 23. He managed to talk the captain of his steamer, the *R.M.S. Warrimoo*, into attempting a new trans-Pacific crossing record, and the ship docked in Vancouver, Canada, in mid-June, with only hours to spare. The Lloyds' Phineas Fogg effort attracted the attention of a *New York World* reporter who described their progress in a series of newspaper stories as the two traveled by train across Canada. True to his word, Lloyd arrived at Cambridge less than two hours before graduation, traveling some ten thousand miles in twenty-nine days. Jessie was happy to have him back home safely. "It is a blessed moment," she wrote in her diary, "when my arms are around my truest love once again."[11]

The trip yielded a cornucopia of information but presenting it posed a challenge for Lloyd. He wanted to promote Antipodean reforms without "getting a reputation of being a [Baron] Munchausen," a reference to an eighteenth-century German aristocrat whose travel accounts were synonymous with self-aggrandizement. Lloyd was also worried that Samuel Gompers would oppose compulsory labor arbitration before Lloyd had a proper opportunity to introduce the idea. Lloyd resolved both concerns by deciding to "simply tell the truth" in the writing style that he had first learned at the *Chicago Tribune*. The result was his two best books, both avoiding the heavy-handedness and overkill of *Wealth* and his other, earlier works.[12]

The first, *A Country Without Strikes*, was completed in less than four months writing time. Lloyd concentrated on what he considered to be the most important New Zealand reform, compulsory labor arbitration, describing the law which made strikes legal only as a last resort in a labor dispute. He described the inner workings of the country's arbitration court as it mediated disputes, arguing that governmental supervision was the only way to guarantee the fairness of a similar system in the United States. He noted that it took "a majority to maintain its welfare against the attacks of an anti-social minority." Lloyd held that arbitration had to be mandatory, writing that "the greatest economic question involved in compulsory arbitration is whether property and business shall be distributed by the methods of reason and brotherliness or by the methods of force and greed."[13]

Next, he produced a more thorough chronicle of his journey in *Newest England: Notes of a Democratic Traveller in New England, with Some Australian Comparisons*. The title did not refer to the American New England, which Lloyd considered as corrupt as Great Britain. Rather, he meant the newest New England, New Zealand, which Lloyd believed was the only industrialized country in the world providing a secure, comfortable, and equitable life for its citizens. Lloyd described his travels in a clear, engaging prose, peppering his observations with interesting photographs and anecdotes. He discussed compulsory arbitration, social security, and other reforms, or "political novelties" as he called them, in a low-key manner that relaxed rather than irritated people. The result was a nonfiction book "so much like a romance that I shall reread it immediately so as to get some of the facts to stick," as one reader resolved. Lloyd's new publisher, Doubleday, Page and Company (the Harpers had gone bankrupt following *Labor Copartnership*), was equally enthusiastic and promised to make the book "the most dignified and attractive volume that we have ever put forth."[14]

In spite of the obvious writing improvements in both *A Country Without Strikes* and *Newest England*, neither approached the success or impact of *Wealth*. Publisher Walter H. Page apologized to Lloyd in 1901, telling him that "they ought to have sold more . . . I wish we had known how to make them sell more." Still, some twenty-five hundred copies of each were purchased, making them respectable sellers. Reaction to *A Country Without Strikes* was the most favorable, with a variety of newspapers calling for an American compulsory labor arbitration law in its wake. Reviews of *Newest England* were divided, with newspapers such as William Randolph Hearst's *New York Journal* hailing New Zealand as the world's "experimental station for advanced legislation" at the same time that other papers called it "paternalism in government." E. L. Godkin complained, "Mr. Lloyd is so enthusiastic a democrat as to despise the ordinary ideals of human welfare." In the end it was Lloyd, not his critics, who was most responsible for mitigating the impact of his last two books. The only thing common to all of Lloyd's five books was his writing style. His eclectic assortment of topics, ranging from starvation strikes to the flora and fauna of New Zealand, confused all but the most strident of late nineteenth-and early twentieth-century readers who were used to predictable themes and patterns in their literature. Still, both *A Country Without Strikes* and *Newest England* did succeed in furthering antipodal reforms in the United States, one newspaper reporter observing that it was Lloyd who was responsible for "New Zealandising the rest of the world." Beyond the books, Lloyd spread word of his New Zealand and Australian reforms in *Atlantic Monthly*, *Good Housekeeping*, *National Geographic*, *Outlook*, and several other general interest magazines. He was interviewed by several newspapers and conducted a compulsory arbitration lecture tour in 1901. Of his impact, historian Peter J. Coleman has noted in his *Progressivism and Reform: New Zealand and the Origins of the American Welfare State*, "For a time, [Lloyd's] forums shaped the tone of the American debate on important issues as well as some aspects of the reform agenda itself."[15]

Wealth, *Country Without Strikes*, *Newest England* and Lloyd's other two books also proved something else about his nonfictional writing style, its lack of profitability. Lloyd confessed to a friend in 1902, "The difficulty is that there is no demand, no market demand that is, for reform literature. I have not got back from my books a tenth of what they cost me." In spite of such a finding, Lloyd always thought of himself as a nonfictional writer, explaining, "As to what I am, I only know that I am doing the best I can to expose the evils under which we suffer and to make known all the facts that seem to come within my province that indicate the lines of evolution towards the remedy." To another friend he observed, "Fancies are the million eggs of the mother codfish; facts are the one or two that reach maturity." His sister Caro observed that he tried to make his books readable, not dry, didactic, and scientific, and that he had an artistic nature that wove extra words into his writings as armaments to deal with the "sorry state" of his society. "Facts . . . were his weapons," she wrote, "Ideas, superstitions were to be slain. . . . He feared revolution by bullets and worked all the harder for new facts and inspirations."[16]

Beyond his own, Lloyd was involved in the research, preparation, or promotion of several other reform writings. The first was a book published at about the same time as *Wealth*. William T. Stead's *If Christ Came to Chicago*, which eventually outsold *Wealth*, was a morality play on the corruption and mammonism of Gilded Age America, especially its second-largest city. The front cover, which showed a lithograph of an angry Christ driving a horde of corpulent Chicago politicians and bankers from their temple-like buildings, accurately described the contents. The English-born Stead painted a sordid picture of Lloyd's hometown, naming some of its most distinguished residents as his chief culprits. His argument, as he explained to Lloyd, was "that the really disreputable in Chicago are not those who are supposed to be disreputable but those who are clothed in purple and fine linen and occupy the high places in the synagogue and the Board of Trade, etc." Stead wrote toward the beginning of the book:

The first impression which a stranger receives on arriving in Chicago is that of the dirt, the danger, and the inconvenience of the streets. . . . If a stranger's first impression of Chicago is that of the barbarous gridironed streets, his second is that of the multitude of mutilated people whom he meets. . . . I have never seen so many mutilated fragments of humanity as one finds in Chicago.[17]

Stead was the leading reform publicist in Great Britain even before he wrote *If Christ Came to Chicago*. His principal claim to fame was a series of newspaper articles on child prostitution in the mid-1880s that named some of England's leading political and business figures. For his exposure, Stead was briefly jailed under England's antiquated criminal libel statutes, which were finally revised in 1888. A few years later, Stead resolved to carry his crusade against immorality across the Atlantic, originally intending to study New York City when he made a side trip to Chicago. There he learned about Lloyd and the two met at least twice in early 1894 to discuss mutual concerns. Their meetings must have been memorable, at least for Stead, for the latter complained to Lloyd, "Nearly three whole months, a quarter of a year [have] elapsed since we parted, and there has not been one mail in these three months in which I have not anxiously looked for a letter from you." Lloyd applauded Stead's finished work, especially his criticisms of the same business and social leaders who had shunned Lloyd after Haymarket, but he disliked Stead's moralizing, a practice which reminded him of his father. Stead returned to Great Britain following the publication of *If Christ Came to Chicago*, but the two remained correspondents. Stead used Lloyd as a model for a character he wrote in a Christmas story in 1895, and asked Lloyd to put his reminiscences of the failed St. Louis Populist Convention to paper the following year.[18]

Lloyd aided in the preparation of another reform book during the 1890s, but with more disastrous results. The president of Iowa College, George A. Gates, invited Lloyd to address his graduating class in 1895. Out of an assumed friendship, he sent Lloyd a manuscript for review the following year. Lloyd was not particularly fond of Gates, and probably glanced at the writing, pronounced it satisfactory, and returned it to him without further thought. In 1897, Gates published "A Foe to American Schools" in the liberal theological magazine *The Kingdom*. The article exposed the grade and high school textbook publishing monopoly known as the American Book Company, revealing a systematic corruption of teachers, principals, and school boards to get the firm's often inferior textbooks used in schools. Gates was not as careful a researcher as Lloyd and did not have all of the evidence he needed to substantiate his charges. In turn, the American Book Company sued Gates and his publisher for defamation. Lloyd was both concerned and outraged by the suit, and felt partially responsible because had given a cursory approval to the manuscript. He was also afraid that the lawsuit would encourage other monopolists to harass critics, including himself. He set up a legal defense fund for Gates and provided him with moral encouragement and legal advice but his efforts were in vain. The book company won a $100,000 verdict against Gates, one of the largest libel judgments in the late nineteenth century. Lloyd was especially disappointed by the ruling because the overwhelming majority of Gate's charges were true and deserved to be publicized, but Lloyd understood the importance of accuracy and proof beyond a doubt.[19]

Beyond books, Lloyd was supportive of advocacy journalism in newspapers. He was fond of Joseph Pulitzer's *New York World* and to a lesser extent, William Randolph Hearst's competing *New York Journal*, the two circulation giants most associated with the yellow journalism of the late nineteenth century. He wrote in 1895, "The *World* and *Journal* are the two best friends the American people have in journalism, almost the only ones." Given a choice, Lloyd preferred the *World* because he believed that Hearst was an investor in New York City's streetcar monopoly and therefore a monopolist himself. He was also critical of Hearst for starting the *Chicago Examiner* in 1900, a morning newspaper which competed with and hurt the *Chicago Tribune*.

Lloyd frequently corresponded with Pulitzer and the *World*'s staff, offering a variety of story ideas and tips. He had so many suggestions that one of the editors told him, "If you continue making suggestions, I will have to put you on the *World*'s payroll!" Both newspapers were the object of clandestine censorship attempts by detractors who thought them crass and low class, so Lloyd championed them whenever he could, going out of his way to check public libraries to make sure they were available to patrons. He believed turn-of-the-century newspapers, even those which sensationalized, were necessary to publicize the evils of monopolies and promote the welfare of the working class.[20]

At about the same time, Lloyd tried, without success, to get the *Chicago Tribune* involved in advocacy. His entreaties were ignored by Joseph Medill, but Medill's son-in-law Joseph Patterson allowed Lloyd to write an editorial announcing a price reduction to one cent per copy of the newspaper in 1895. Lloyd optimistically wrote, "The *Tribune* in doing this is the first of the great newspapers of the world to place all the resources of a first-class modern journal within the reach of all the people." As it turned out, the price cut had more to do with competition than altruism, a motive that was never revealed to Lloyd even though he may have been suspicious, but it was a small victory in Lloyd's personal battle to make the *Tribune* more of a working-class paper. Lloyd offered other, intriguing story ideas to the *Tribune*. One came at the height of the Spanish-American War in 1898:

A lady who was recently at my house repeated to me the statement made to her sister, who is a trained nurse, by a soldier who had recently returned from the West Indies that the canned beef furnished to his regiment was absolutely unfit to eat. He said it was a mere mass of strings completely destitute of any nutritious quality excepting a little grease—if that could be called nutriment.

Lloyd was particularly concerned that the "meat" had been packed in Chicago, a charge probably true. No one at the *Tribune* followed up on the idea even though rumors about Chicago's meat-packers persisted for years. Ultimately it was an outraged public, inspired by Upton Sinclair's 1906 *The Jungle*, that demanded government inspection of meat-packers.[21]

The last reform book that Lloyd aided in his life was also the most important. Ida M. Tarbell's study of the Standard Oil Company, which began as a series of articles in *McClure's* in 1902 and was published in book form in 1904, finally fueled the public outcry against monopolies that Lloyd had dreamed of for *Wealth* a decade earlier. Tarbell was well aware of Lloyd, having been given a copy of *Wealth* by a friend shortly after it was published in 1894. She eagerly read the book, in part because she had been born and raised in the Western Pennsylvania oil region and partly because her father was one of the many independent refiners who felt he had been cheated by the Standard. She liked Lloyd's advocacy presentation but was confused by his altruistic solution. "I was more simple-minded about it," she admitted in her autobiography forty years later. "As I saw it, it was not capitalism but an open disregard of decent ethical business practices by capitalists which lay at the bottom of the story Mr. Lloyd told so dramatically."[22]

Lloyd did not know who Tarbell was when she began researching her series in late 1901, and he was concerned that she was being paid by the Standard to write a rebuttal against *Wealth*. He wrote to Roger Sherman, the Pennsylvania oil region lawyer, for information on Tarbell but discovered that Sherman had died in 1897. Sherman's widow Alma knew Tarbell personally, however, and she told Lloyd that Tarbell was "sincere in her intentions to write an impartial history but I think, as you, that she can not understand the situation in its fullest integrity." Other Lloyd contacts were leery as well, one offering the hope that Tarbell would take the Standard on but promising "of course I will not commit myself in advance as to her work and will watch the matter closely as you suggest."[23]

Such confidences made Lloyd more of a hindrance than a help to Tarbell in the initial stages of her work, and she later admitted that his warnings complicated her efforts. In fairness to Lloyd, Tarbell did little to ease his suspicions at first. She arranged to meet with Standard Oil Vice President Henry H. Rogers and continued her interviews with him until her first article appeared in 1902, an event she later characterized as the first instance of corporate public relations in American history. It was Rogers who had been instrumental in the controversy between Lloyd and the Reverend B. Fay Mills and other theologians and academics in 1897, and Lloyd feared that he was applying a similar pressure to Tarbell. As it turned out, the Rogers interviews proved to be one of the strengths of Tarbell's book, providing the Standard's side of the story that Lloyd had been unable to obtain, but Lloyd had no way of knowing that at the time. He interpreted their meetings as a sign that Tarbell had either willfully or unwittingly sold out to the company and warned his sources accordingly.[24]

Such differences between the two were mitigated in 1902 when Tarbell finally realized what Lloyd was doing and tried to arrange a meeting with him. Lloyd was in Europe at the time, touring Swiss cooperatives and the Germany of Kaiser Wilhelm II, but he sent her a cautious response, offering limited cooperation and a promise to meet with her upon his return. In September 1902, he invited her to his Rhode Island summer house, and she was immediately taken in by his gentlemanly charm and commitment to reform. In turn, Lloyd's fears were alleviated by Tarbell's determination and Victorian gentility. They walked about his property, talked of her research, and in the end he promised to give her copies of documents she had been unable to find and to send her Standard news clippings from his various services. She thanked him and asked if he had any interest in writing for *McClure's*.[25]

Although their meeting removed most of the doubts that Lloyd had about

Tarbell, it did nothing to alleviate his concern over her employer, Samuel S. McClure. Lloyd told an acquaintance, "Miss Tarbell, herself, seems to be doing her work with great fidelity and ability." Yet, McClure's promotion of the Tarbell series in his magazine was too evenhanded for Lloyd and he worried that the Standard had bribed or somehow influenced the magazine publisher. Lloyd reminded his sources of the havoc a well-written "white-wash of the Standard" would create, and one responded, "I had a very plain talk with [Tarbell], in fact, quite of number of them and she understands my suspicions and . . . she will carefully look out for the breakers ahead." Still, Lloyd remained skeptical, for as Tarbell recalled, at least two sources continued to refuse her entreaties until her first article appeared in the magazine in November 1902.[26]

Lloyd never lived to read the conclusion of Tarbell's series, but was pleased by what he saw. He wrote an encouraging letter to her following the first installment, citing a few minor errors, and she responded, "I shall be very glad if you will call my attention at all times to anything which seems to you like an incorrect or unfair inference on either side." Lloyd was more enthusiastic with the second part, writing, "When you get through with Johnnie I don't think there will be very much left of him except something resembling one of his own grease spots." His final comment came a month later when he wrote, "Your story grows more interesting every month."[27]

Beyond their direct contacts, Lloyd encouraged Tarbell in a less obvious way. The Harpers had asked Lloyd to revise *Wealth* during the summer of 1898, but Lloyd was preoccupied with his Australia and New Zealand study at the time and asked several of his oil region contacts if they would be interested in the project. The only positive response came from a sixty-nine-year-old former Pennsylvania newspaper editor and oil refiner named Marinus N. Allen. Lloyd gave Allen serious consideration until Alma Sherman warned him that he was an "excitable and irritable . . . man of ungovernable temper." Certain he was not the man to revise *Wealth*, Lloyd nevertheless encouraged Allen to preserve his memories of the Standard battle in some written form and Allen completed a manuscript of sorts in early 1900. He sent it for consideration to the Doubleday and McClure publishing company on the advice of fellow Standard opponent and friend, William W. Tarbell, Ida's brother. At the request of Samuel S. McClure, Ida Tarbell read the manuscript and ultimately rejected it because of its bad writing and unsubstantiated charges. She also told Allen that she believed McClure would not be interested in publishing a book on such a parochial subject as the Western Pennsylvania oil war. Less than two months later, Tarbell started researching her own study of the Standard, with the knowledge and financial support of McClure. Allen complained to Lloyd about plagiarism at the time his manuscript was rejected, but he eventually applauded Tarbell's efforts. Tarbell mentions nothing about Allen in her autobiography, suggesting only that McClure encouraged her to write about the Standard during a European trip.[28]

Even as he encouraged Tarbell, Lloyd harbored some resentment toward her. This was due in part to the vehicle for her series, *McClure's*. Lloyd did not have a favorable impression of the new generation of mass circulation magazines like *McClure's*, believing that unlike newspapers they were flippant and ill-suited to matters of serious intellectual discussion. He and the rest of his generation preferred the lesser read but more genteel *North American Review*, *Harper's Monthly*, or *Atlantic Monthly* magazines. This was true even though McClure had asked Lloyd to write for him as early as 1894, offers Lloyd refused. Lloyd died never knowing the impact that *McClure's* and other muckrake mass circulation magazines would have on early twentieth-century American public opinion. Beyond the magazine, Lloyd was piqued over the attention that Tarbell's articles received since she was essentially retelling the story that he had written nine years earlier. He confided to Henry George, Jr., "[the articles] were good as far as they had gone" but "presented nothing important beyond what had already been offered in *Wealth*."[29]

In return, Tarbell harbored serious misgivings about Lloyd, especially his political ideology, that she never revealed to him. Following his death in 1903, she told his wife Jessie, "He has left too large a mass of valuable work behind him to be forgotten." A few years later, Tarbell told Caro Lloyd that Lloyd had been a great help to her in her own book and "Rarely have I met a man who on immediate acquaintance I found so companionable, so animated and so full of fresh and healthy interests." However, Tarbell told Allan Nevins, John D. Rockefeller's biographer, in a 1939 letter that Lloyd was "a suspicious-minded man" and "I could never follow Lloyd. His book was of course an argument for socialism." Nevins used her misgivings to justify his attacks against Lloyd in his Rockefeller biography. Tarbell also neglected to make any mention of Lloyd in her autobiography beyond her first reading of his book in 1894, disregarding the advice and documents he provided to her, the Marinus N. Allen manuscript, and the change in public opinion that he had helped engineer.[30]

Despite the damage to his ego, the *History of the Standard Oil Company* was more beneficial than harmful to Lloyd. It was the most influential piece of reform literature he had ever been involved in, eventually eclipsing *Wealth* and his other works, and his contributions made Tarbell's work more devastating. The combined criticisms of Lloyd and Tarbell hurt John D. Rockefeller, more than either imagined. Rockefeller's reaction, as obtained by the *New York World* reporter who interviewed him, was kept from the public until the 1970s but his family was well aware of how he felt. Grandson David Rockefeller, Jr. told a British television interviewer in 1986, "In the case of Mr. Tarbell . . . he accepted cash and apparently didn't invest it very successfully and so he was in trouble and so was his daughter Ida and she became a very bitter person who devoted her life to trying to write unkind things about my grandfather and that and other articles that were written certainly were very derogatory."[31]

More importantly, Tarbell's work was the vindication of *Wealth* that Lloyd needed but could not provide himself. As long as he was the only voice in the wilderness, Rockefeller and the Standard Oil Company could ignore him as an eccentric, millionaire mugwump who knew nothing about modern business. When Tarbell began repeating Lloyd's assertions, even the most skeptical reader could no longer doubt Lloyd. The *Chicago Journal* was sarcastic but truthful when it observed in 1903 that "Henry D. Lloyd . . . has not lived in vain. He will be remembered as the man who enabled Ida M. Tarbell to become famous." At the height of the trust-busting movement in 1907, *Collier's* stated, "Tracing origins is unsafe, but if one were bent upon it, probably Henry D. Lloyd would be selected as the first influential explorer [of trust-busting]. After him, Thomas W. Lawson, Ida Tarbell, Lincoln Steffens, and other writers have aided the movement in the press."[32]

Was *History of the Standard Oil Company* better than *Wealth*? It is difficult to compare the two because they were written at different times and for different purposes. Lloyd's was the pathbreaking effort, a book designed to counteract the nearly universal late nineteenth-century attitude that monopolies were beneficial to society. With limited resources and nothing to use as a model, Lloyd exposed the Standard octopus as best he could. Thanks largely to Lloyd, the public perception of monopolies had changed significantly by the time Tarbell wrote her series of articles, and she had the opportunity to present a more specific, detailed account of the company's misdeeds than Lloyd had been able to do. In particular, her interviews with Henry H. Rogers, which probably would not have been possible without the negative publicity generated by *Wealth*, gave her the Standard's side so conspicuously absent in Lloyd's book. Tarbell used documents that were unavailable to Lloyd, although at least one was stolen from the Standard and therefore would have been unusable to the more ethically minded Lloyd. Tarbell's book is better remembered, and it was Tarbell who contributed directly to the dissolution of the Standard, but Lloyd was the pioneer who helped make her's and other's subsequent antitrust studies possible.[33]

In spite of such successes, Lloyd's personal and health problems were the biggest challenges in his later years. His overwork habit, combined with his chronic insomnia and high-strung emotions, aged him beyond his physical years. One of his sons' friends remembered him as a loner in his final years, a man often mentally and physically apart from his friends and family. In 1901, Lloyd complained to his sister Caro, "I have not been and am not fit to write. I don't get through with the things I must do to live." At about the same time he predicted to another friend, "I shall not live more than two years longer." Associates noted a steady deterioration in Lloyd's health in 1902 and 1903, a condition Lloyd blamed on a lack of sleep and "bad air." He wrote to Jessie in early 1903, "Why can't we fade out as the roses do—always fragrant and beautiful even in our decay?"[34]

Lloyd was preoccupied with Socialism in his final years. He had no interest in the immigrant-led, Marxist-type socialist parties of his day, denigrating them in his writings as "German," "amateur," and "sectarian socialists." Instead, he organized a local Fabian club, based on the more mild English form of socialism, wrote articles for William Dwight Porter Bliss's *American Fabian* magazine, and voted Socialist in several elections. But his reputation as a Socialist is exaggerated, due more to his sister's efforts than to himself. Caro Lloyd Strobell was a member of the Socialist Labor Party until her death in the 1940s. She maintained in the biography of her brother, written in 1912, that Lloyd would have become a Socialist if he had lived long enough. Lloyd did consider joining Eugene V. Debs's Socialist Party of America, writing in 1903, "My mind is moving towards the Socialistic party" and "Socialism comes with the grandest message of enfranchisement ever heard on earth." However, he never became a member of the S.P.A., and to this day, a Socialist Party of America application remains uncompleted in his papers. Most of his friends advised him not to join. Liberal journalist Samuel Bowles warned him, "I do not believe . . . that the Socialists as a party will attain extensive political power in this country." John Mitchell confided, "I believe it would impair your usefulness if you were to associate yourself with the Socialist Party." Economist John R. Commons called the idea a mistake, noting, "Your influence is certainly far greater unattached to a political organization." The Socialists didn't want him either. Debs rejected Lloyd, telling him, "I do not believe that Single Taxers, Socialists, and anti-Socialist trade unionists can successfully harmonize upon any proposition whatsoever." A. M. Simons, Socialist writer and the editor of the Chicago-based *International Socialist Review*, admonished Lloyd, "Those who take your position are not themselves workers but rather almost exclusively professional men." Lloyd was an independent thinker, an "opportunist" when it came to political ideas as William Dean Howells observed, and never doctrinaire enough to join any individual party. His friend Richard T. Ely tried to tell Caro Lloyd Strobell after Lloyd's death:

Certainly he was never willing, in any correspondence with him, or in any conversation, to commit himself definitely to Socialism. He seemed at times inclined to do so but always held back at the last feeling that he wanted to be free. The only thing to which he did commit himself without reservation was the fearless pursuit of truth.

Unfortunately, historians of American reform and radicalism have been misinformed about Lloyd's rejection of the Socialist Party of America, and the party's rejection of him, and continue to maintain incorrectly that Lloyd was a party member.[35]

As a Chicago property owner, Lloyd followed at least one local reform issue with interest in his final years—the city traction or streetcar monopoly. During the Populist Chicago mayoral campaign of 1895, Lloyd demanded "that stop shall be put to the whole maggot-breeding" streetcar system, which licensed streetcar monopolies to rich businessmen through corrupt city contracts. In

1903, Lloyd wrote to the *Chicago Tribune*:

The people of Chicago are being amused with a pretty play on words of municipal ownership. . . . And while the people are thus being entertained, the issue immediately vital, whether our system be municipal or private, is being cleverly and assiduously kept out of discussion, and even out of sight.

Lloyd turned his full-time attention to the streetcar situation at about the same time as he wrote his letter, joining with Jane Addams and other urban reformers to support of a publicly-owned and operated transportation system. To headquarter their cause, Addams volunteered the use of her settlement home, and Lloyd made his first visit to Hull House. He was captivated by what he saw, remarking, "It's a club that can accomplish the impossible for other clubs—the free association of men and women under the same roof."[36]

As the summer drive to municipalize the streetcars mellowed into the fall of 1903, Lloyd claimed not to be "up to par." He blamed his condition on "the weather—with its Chicago trimmings of dust, smoke and noise." In mid-September, he contracted a chest cold, but continued to work on the streetcar issue, speaking to groups nights and resting during the day. In his last letter, he wrote Jessie on September 20:

I have slept almost continuously for 36 hours, except that I had to get up last night to go to a meeting—just had to, no matter what the headache or the cold might say. This morning I am all right. The headache has reached the dwindling point, and the cold has "set" in my bronchial region, and nothing new now remains but to wear it out.

That night he spoke briefly to a gathering of the Chicago Federation of Labor, calling on the group to endorse a "Traction Emergency Call" he had written. The group gave its approval and named Lloyd to head a delegation that would speak at a city council meeting a week away. Lloyd never attended the meeting. He was coughing uncontrollably by the end of the night, but refused a carriage ride home, preferring one of the same open streetcars that he was protesting against. He arrived home chilled and exhausted. A friend called upon him two days later and found him so sick that he could not get up. A doctor sent for Jessie and their sons when he was diagnosed with pneumonia. A friend brought news of a streetcar franchise victory in Toledo, Ohio, on Saturday, September 26. "Good," Lloyd responded. He lapsed in and out of consciousness the following day and died on Monday, September 28, 1903, at the age of 56.[37]

Caro Lloyd blamed her brother's death on the germs and squalor of Chicago's streets, writing, "In the gutters of the principal business streets, I saw oats growing in the accumulated dust and filth." True or not, Lloyd's obsessive preoccupation with work and his emotional personality weakened him as well. His remains were cremated and buried beneath a rock next to an Episcopalian church in Winnetka that he rarely attended, and Jessie's ashes were buried in the same spot a year later. Lloyd was the object of many tributes in the wake of his death. *Out West* called him a "martyr to the cause of the common people." The *Saturday Night Dispatch* observed, "Died at his post on the firing line may be said of Henry Demarest Lloyd." A memorial service was held at the Chicago Auditorium in late November 1903. Speakers included Mayor Samuel M. "Golden Rule" Jones, United Mine Workers President John Mitchell, Jane Addams, and Clarence Darrow, with unions paying the entire $650 fee for the service. Mitchell told the audience, "[Lloyd] did not belong to Chicago alone, but to America and the world." Darrow noted that Lloyd was "one of those few rare souls who have the courage to condemn the errors of the present." Lloyd left no epitaph for himself, but he observed in a 1900 speech, "We dream of a Utopia and we are getting an Altruria right now. Beneath all the evils that we see about us there is the well-developed beginning of an ideal life." In the end, it was for that ideal that he became a writer and gave his life.[38]

NOTES

1. Samuel Leavitt to HDL, 20 January 1896, HDL, Wisc. and undated small notebook entry G-9, circa 1887, HDL, mf.
2. John Hossack to HDL, 30 March 1897; G. E. Pelton to HDL, 22 May 1895; HDL to Aaron Lloyd, 31 December 1896; undated HDL quote, circa 1894; all in HDL, Wisc.; Stanley B. Parsons, "The Role of Cooperatives in the Development of the Movement Culture of Populism," *Journal of American History*, 69(March 1983): 866–865; Edward K. Spahn, *Brotherly Tomorrows: Movements for a Cooperative Society in America, 1829–1929* (New York: Columbia University Press, 1989); HDL notebook 26, p. 9, circa 1894, HDL, mf.; Derek C. Jones, "American Producer Cooperatives and Employee-Owned Firms: A Historical Perspective," in Robert Jackall and Henry M. Levin, *Worker Cooperatives in America* (Berkeley: University of California Press, 1984), 37–56; Foner, *Labor*, 76–77; Gashman, *Gilded Age*, 148; and Gronlund, *The Cooperative Commonwealth* (Cambridge, MA: Belknap Press of Harvard University, 1965, 1884).
3. Laurence Gronlund to HDL, 12, 20, 27 May, 24 July 1893, 10 December 1894, 18 June 1897, 20, 22 October 1898; HDL to James L. Cowles, 20 October 1898; HDL to E. L. Shuman, 1 November 1899; all in HDL, Wisc.; Spahn, *Brotherly*, 176–180; Bell, "Marxian Socialism," in Egbert and Persons, *Socialism* I, 270–273; R. Laurence Moore, ed., *The Emergence of an American Left: Civil War to World War One* (New York: John Wiley and Sons, 1973), 81–100; and Mann, *Yankee*, 232–233.
4. J. A. Wayland to HDL, various dates, 1894-1895; A. S. Edwards to HDL, 14 April 1896, 24 May 1897; Ray G. Edwards to HDL, 30 January 1899; all in HDL, Wisc.; "Wealth Against Commonwealth Notice," *Appeal to Reason*, 2 May 1896; "For a Socialist College; Corner Stone of First Institution of kind laid at Ruskin," *New York Herald*, 20 June 1897 and *Richmond* (Virginia) *State*, 7 August 1897, both clippings in HDL, mf.; HDL Ruskin Address Pamphlet, Destler Papers, WI; Elliott Shore, *Talkin' Socialism: J. A. Wayland and the Role of the Press in American Radicalism, 1890–1912* (Lawrence: University Press of Kansas, 1988); Spahn, *Brotherly*, 231–235; CLS, *Lloyd*

II, 61–67; Chamberlain, *Reform*, 54–55; and Destler, "Radicalism," 356–358.

5. HDL to Thomas Blandford, 12 September 1898; HDL to Elderess Anna White, 15 April 1897; N. O. Nelson to CLS, 28 January 1905; Imogene C. Fales to HDL, 4 August 1896; in HDL, Wisc.; Spahn, *Brotherhood*, 214–216; CLS, *Lloyd* II, 59–61; Destler, *Western Radicalism*, 357–358; Selig Perlman and Philip Taft, *History of Labor in the United States, 1896-1932* IV, (New York: The Macmillan Company, 1935): 226–227; Gashman, *Gilded Age*, 168–171; HDL,"Labor Copartnership" notes, HDL, mf.; and Thomas, *Alternative*, 344–346.

6. HDL, *Labor Copartnership: Notes on a Visit to Cooperative Workshops, Factories and Farms in Great Britain and Ireland, in which Employer, Employee and Consumer Share in Ownership, Management and Results* (New York: Harper and Brothers, 1898): 334–336.

7. HDL to Henry Vivian, 4 January 1900, JBL, CHS; HDL to William Clarke, 8 August 1901; HDL to James H. Ferris, 13 June 1897; Ferris to HDL, 16 June 1897; Frances E. Willard to HDL, 7 September 1897; Samuel Gompers to HDL, 2 October, 13 November, 17 November 1897, 1 April 1898, 21 July 1899; HDL to Henry Vivian, 17 November 1897; HDL to Dr. Henry B. Fay, 10 March 1898; HDL to Eltweed Pomeroy, 6 April 1898; Ignatius Donnelly to HDL, 11 August 1898; HDL to the Reverend B. Fay Mills, 10 November 1898; HDL to M. L. Lockwood, 23 November 1898; HDL to Robert Patterson, 13 December 1898; Harper and Brothers to HDL, 4 January 1899; Charles B. Spahr to HDL, 14 September 1898; Bert Stewart to HDL, 14 September, 16 November 1898; Charles Zeublin to HDL, 22 September 1898; James D. Corrothers to HDL, 26 September 1898; Henry Keenan to HDL, 14 November 1898; all in HDL, Wisc.; *New York Journal*, 27 August 1898; *New York Herald*, 11 September 1898; *Brooklyn Eagle*, 28 August 1898; *Chicago Times-Herald*, 27 August 1898; *The Kingdom*, 10(December 8, 1898): 159–160; the Reverend Washington Gladden, "Social Progress of the English People," *The Outlook*, 60(24 December 1898): 1002–1004; *Social Gospel*, 1 (October 1898); and various notebook quotations; *New York Journal*, 21 December 1901; and *Boston Budget*, 9 February 1902; all in HDL, mf.; CLS, *Lloyd* II, 90–93; John H. M. Laslett, "Socialism and American Trade Unionism," in Laslett and Lipset, *Failure of a Dream*, 118–169; and Destler, *Empire of Reform*, 391–398.

8. Richard J. Seddon to HDL, 22 March 1893, in JBL, CHS; Fred W. Boys to HDL, 1 September 1893; HDL to Ely, 30 September, 1, 18 October 1893; Robert Stout to HDL, 22 March 1894; Edward Tregear to HDL, 28 April 1894; Henry Latchford to HDL, 25 June 1894; HDL to Anna White, 17 October 1898; HDL to E. B. Watson, 19 October 1898; HDL to James L. Cowles, 20 October 1898; HDL to M. L. Lockwood, 23 November 1898; all in HDL, Wisc.; A. G. Fradenburgh, "Social Experiments in New Zealand," *Outlook*, 49(7 April 1894): 620–621; Peter J. Coleman, *Progressivism and the World of Reform: New Zealand and the Origins of the American Welfare State* (Lawrence: University Press of Kansas, 1987), 45–75; CLS, *Lloyd* II, 94–124; and Mann, *Yankee*, 126–144.

9. JBL MS diary, 30 January, 26 February 1899, JBL, CHS; HDL to Richard T. Ely, 26 October 1898; HDL to Carroll D. Wright, 10 November 1898; HDL to Eugene Higgins, 19 November 1898; HDL to Lee Meriwether, 26 November 1898; Willis J. Abbot to HDL, 7 December 1898; HDL to James D. Corrothers, 8 December 1898; HDL to Abbot, 13 December 1898; CLS to HDL, 23 December 1898; HDL to Carroll D. Wright, 27 December 1898; Wright to HDL, 31 December 1898; "H. D. Lloyd in

Honolulu; Well-Known Chicago Sociologist on His Way to Australia," undated *Chicago Record* clipping after 18 January 1898; all in HDL, Wisc.; *New York Times*, 19 March 1899 in HDL, mf.; CLS, *Lloyd* II, 98–111; and Thomas, *Alternative*, 346–347.

10. CLS interview with William P. Reeves, 13 October 1904, in CLS Journal, HDL, Wisc.

11. JBL MS diary, 23, 24 May 1899, JBL, CHS; HDL to George J. Holyoake, n.d., circa June 1899, in HDL, Wisc.; *Montreal Gazette*, 23 June 1899 and *Boston Herald*, 24 June 1899, both clippings in HDL, mf.; and CLS, *Lloyd* II, 111.

12. HDL to Richard T. Ely, 17 July 1899; HDL to James Rhodes, 11 August 1899; HDL to George Jones, 14 September 1899; William P. Reeves to HDL, 3 July 1899; all in HDL, Wisc. and *Boston Herald*, 27 June 1899, in HDL. mf.

13. HDL, *Country Without Strikes: A Visit to the Compulsory Arbitration Court of New Zealand* (New York: Doubleday, Page and Company, 1900), 175; HDL to Wright, 18 October 1898; Willis J. Abbot to HDL, 4 November 1899; Horace C. White to HDL, 26 May 1900; all in HDL, Wisc.; Gompers, *Seventy Years* II, 131–143; and CLS, *Lloyd* II, 112–117; Destler, *Empire of Reform*, 413.

14. HDL, *Newest England: Notes of a Democratic Traveller in New England, with Some Australian Comparisons* (New York: Doubleday, Page and Company, 1900); Walter H. Page to HDL, 9 February, 17 August 1900; Aaron Lloyd to HDL, 3, 10 December 1900; HDL to Aaron Lloyd, 7 December 1900; John Swinton to HDL, 2 November 1901; and William G. Eggleston to HDL, 19 May 1902; all in HDL, Wisc.; and HDL, "Ethical Progress of the Nineteenth Century," paper delivered to the New York State Conference of Religion, 20 November 1900, HDL, mf.

15. Aaron Lloyd to HDL, 3, 10 December 1900; HDL to Aaron Lloyd, 7 December 1900; Walter H. Page to HDL, 9 August 1901; Frank Doubleday to HDL, 27 September 1901, 3 October 1902; and J. H. Steffee to HDL, n.d., circa 1902; all in HDL, Wisc.; sales records of *A Country Without Strikes* and *Newest England*, 1 August 1904 and various reviews, all in HDL, mf.

Also see HDL, "A Visit to the Compulsory Arbitration Court of New Zealand," *Outlook*, 63(9 December 1899): 877–879; "New Zealand Newest England," *Atlantic Monthly*, 84(December 1899): 789–794; "Some New Zealand Scenes," *Ainslee's Magazine*, 4 (January 1900): 752–759; "A Living Wage by Law," *Independent*, 52(27 September 1900): 2330–2332; "Problems of the Pacific: New Zealand," *National Geographic Magazine*, 8 (September 1902): 342–351; "Australasian Cures for Coal Wars," *Atlantic Monthly*, 90(November 1902): 667–674; "Fact and Fancy About New Zealand," *Boyce's Weekly*, 4 February 1903; "New 'Song of the Shirt'," *Sunday School Times*, 21 March 1903; and "The Abolition of Poverty," *Good Housekeeping*, 37(September 1903): 216–220.

16. CLS, *Lloyd* I, 306–307; HDL to Mr. Skillman, 7 October 1895; HDL to Samuel Bowles, 25 July 1898; HDL to William Sand, 18 January 1900; HDL to John C. Reed, 21 June 1903; and CLS Journal; all in HDL, Wisc.; and HDL, notebook 11, p. 62, circa 1902, in HDL, mf.

17. William T. Stead, *If Christ Came to Chicago* (New York: Living Books, 1964, 1894) as quoted in Cook, *City Life*, 62–63.

18. HDL to Dr. Albert Shaw, 19 May 1891; Stead to HDL, 11 November, 1, 18 December 1893, 12 January, 23 May, 6, 23 June, 7 September 1894; 5 November 1895; and HDL to Stead, 21 August 1894; all in HDL, Wisc.; Joseph O. Baylen's, "A

Victorian's 'Crusade' in Chicago, 1893–1894," *Journal of American History*, 51(December 1964), 418–434; Stone, *Fifty Years*, 200–204; Grenier, "Muckraking," 258–261; McDannell, *Christian*, 100–101; Hofstadter, *Reform*, 186–198; Harold S. Wilson, *McClure's Magazine and the Muckrakers* (Princeton, NJ: Princeton University Press, 1970), 86; Peter Lyon, *Success Story: The Life and Times of S. S. McClure* (New York: Charles Scribner's Sons, 1963), 151; and Frederic Whyte, *Life of W. T. Stead* (New York: Houghton Mifflin, 1925).

19. George A. Gates to HDL, 3 June 1896, 2, 14, 21 December 1897; the Reverend Herbert W. Gleason to Victor Lawson, 24 May 1897; Gleason to HDL, 2 December 1897, 6, 13 January 1898; H. H. Hilton to HDL, 7 December 1897; Gleason to Gates, 12 January, 3 February 1898; Melville E. Stone to HDL, 18 January 1898; Gleason to Stone, 26 January, 3 February 1898; Stone to Gleason, 28 January 1898; D. C. Heath to HDL, 8 April 1898; Kingdom Publishing Company to HDL, 8 April 1898; T. W. Wilson to HDL, 14, 16 April 1898; D. C. Heath to HDL, 11, 28 December 1894; HDL to Heath, 19 December 1894; all in HDL, Wisc.

Also see George A. Gates, *A Foe to American Schools: A Vacation Study* (Minneapolis: The Kingdom Publishing Company, 1897); Mrs. Isabel Gates, *The Life of George Augustus Gates* (Boston: The Pilgrim Press, 1915), 18–24; Exman, *Harper*, 187–189; and Donald Sheehan, *This Was Publishing: A Chronicle of the Book Trade in the Gilded Age* (Bloomington: Indiana University Press, 1952).

20. HDL to Samuel Bowles, 5 December 1895; Bowles to HDL, 19 December 1895; HDL to Joseph Pulitzer, 14 January 1896; 1 January 1898; Charles B. Spahr to HDL, 23 March 1897; William T. Stead to HDL, 7 December 1897; HDL to Arthur Brisbane, 23 April, 25 May 1897; Willis J. Abbot to HDL, 25 January 1898; HDL to Mr. Keeler, 19 November 1898; W. Van Benthuysen to HDL, 15 September, 7 October, 27, 29 December 1899, 15 January, 27 November 1900; Florence Kelley to HDL, 14 October 1899; HDL to Edward Bemis, 27 February 1900; Willis J. Abbot to HDL, 14 June 1900, 20 August 1903; HDL to CLS, n.d., circa 1897; untitled HDL article, *New York Journal*, 25 August 1897; HDL writing as "Radical," *Springfield* (Massachusetts) *Republican*, 22 April 1898; all in HDL, Wisc.; *The Public*, 3 (30 June 1900): 177, in HDL, mf; and Casill, *New York Memories*, 228–231.

21. *C.T.*, 11 November 1895; HDL to Samuel Bowles, 5 December 1895; HDL to Robert W. Patterson, 8 December 1895; HDL to Mr. Keeler, 19 November 1898; and HDL to Edward Bemis, 27 February 1900; all in HDL, Wisc.; "The Chronicle's Triumph," *Chicago Chronicle*, 12 November 1895; F. A. Russell, "The Newspaper and Periodical Publishing Industry in Illinois from 1880 to 1915," (Ph.D. diss., University of Illinois, 1915); HDL, "Radical," *Springfield* (Massachusetts) *Republican*, 22 April 1898, clipping in HDL, mf; HDL, "Food Adulteration in Congress," *C.T.*, 9 March 1880; and James Harvey Young, *Pure Food: Securing the Federal Food and Drug Act of 1906* (Princeton, NJ: Princeton University Press, 1989).

22. Brady, *Tarbell*, 123; Tarbell, *Day's Work*, 204–205; Lyon, *Success Story*, 189–193; H. Wickham Steed, *Through Thirty Years, 1892–1922* I (Garden City, NY: Doubleday Page, 1924), 47–48; and *Standard Oil Company of New Jersey, et al. v. United States*, 221 U.S. 83 (1911).

Of Ida Tarbell, Allan Nevins subsequently wrote, "It is true, I think, that Miss Tarbell followed [Lloyd] too much." See Nevins to Dr. Philip Benjamin, 14 December 1953, Tarbell Papers, Allegheny College.

23. Alma S. Sherman to HDL, 16 December 1901, 21 January, 12 March 1902; James W. Lee to HDL, 30 December 1901; all in HDL, Wisc.; Sherman to HDL, 21, 23 December 1901, 2 March 1902; HDL to Sherman, 19 December 1901; Ida Tarbell to Sherman, 9, 11 March, 23 June 1903; all in Sherman papers, Yale University.

24. Thomas W. Phillips to HDL, 30 December 1901; George Rice to HDL, 26 January 1902; James W. Newlin to HDL, 17, 24 March 1902; all in HDL, Wisc. and Tarbell, *Autobiography*, 214.

25. Ida M. Tarbell to HDL, 28 March, 29 September, and n.d. before 29 September 1902; Tarbell to l21, Caroline Stallbohm, 4 April, 31 October 1902; HDL to Tarbell, 6 May 1902; Tarbell to CLS, 16 May 1905; all in HDL, Wisc.; Brady, *Tarbell*, 132; and Tarbell, *Day's Work*, 231.

26. Lewis Emery, Jr. to HDL, 10 March, 25 March, 9 April 1903; HDL to Emery, 30 March 1903; Ida M. Tarbell to Emery, 23 March 1903; all in HDL, Wisc.; Emery to Alma S. Sherman, 10 March 1903, Sherman Papers; Brady, *Tarbell*, 138; and Tarbell, *Day's Work*, 231–233.

27. Ida Tarbell to HDL, 17 November 1902, 15 April 1903; HDL to Tarbell, 3 May 1903 and fragment, 11 April 1903; Tarbell to JBL, 9 November 1903; all in HDL, Wisc.; Tomkins, *Tarbell*, 60; Ida Tarbell, *History of the Standard Oil Company* (New York: McClure, Phillips, 1904).

28. M. L. Lockwood to HDL, 15 July 1898; M. N. Allen to HDL, 1, 13, 25 August, 23 October, 10, 23 November 1898, 20 August 1899; 27 May, 1, 7, 12, 17, 28 June, 21 July, 28 October 1900 and n.d., circa August 1898; Alma S. Sherman to HDL, 23 August 1898; HDL to Alma S. Sherman, 5 March 1902; Allen to HDL, 1, 7, 12, 17 June, 8 September, 14 October 1900, 6, 8 June, 9 November 1901, 5 March, 2 April, 19 November 1902; 8 December 1902; Allen to CLS, 27 August 1905; all in HDL, Wisc.; Roger Sherman to M. N. Allen, 21 October, 3, 9 December 1878, 1 January, 10 February 1879, 6 February 1880; Roger Sherman to Mrs. M. N. Allen, 28 November 1893; all in Sherman Papers, Yale University; *The Petroleum Gazette*, 19 February 1916; McLaurin, *Sketches in Crude*, 344, 363–364; Brady, *Tarbell*, 120–132; Samuel S. McClure, *My Autobiography* (New York: Frederick A. Stokes Co., 1914), 238–240; Tarbell, *Day's Work*, 202–211; Lyon, *Success Story*, 202; and Wilson, *McClure's Magazine*, 134–138.

On the timing of Tarbell's project, see John M. Siddall to Ida M. Tarbell, 9 September 1901 and Tarbell to Siddall, 11 September 1901, both cited in Brady, *Tarbell*, 263. Tarbell never mentioned the Allen manuscript to anyone apparently, instead, crediting Samuel McClure with the idea. See Tarbell, *Day's Work*, 202; Brady, *Tarbell*, 121; and McClure, *Autobiography*, 238–239.

29. Samuel S. McClure to HDL, 27 February 1894; John Mershau to CLS, 2 July 1906; Albert Kimsey Owen to CLS, 11 September 1907; and Henry George, Jr. to CLS, 21 September 1907; all in HDL, Wisc.

30. Ida Tarbell to JBL, 9 November 1903 and Tarbell to CLS, 16 May 1905, both in HDL Wisc.; CLS, "Ida Tarbell whom I saw November 5, 1909," MS note dated 7 April 1936, HDL mf.; Allan Nevins to Tarbell, 21 April 1939; Tarbell to Nevins, 24 May 1939, 22 April 1940; Chester M. Destler to Ida Tarbell, 21 April 1943; Destler to Allegheny College Librarian, 29 May 1944; and CLS to Tarbell, 14 November 1939; all in Tarbell Papers, Allegheny College; CLS to Tarbell, 21 January 1935, Tarbell Papers, Drake Well Museum.

31. Mrs. Frank S. Tarbell to Ida M. Tarbell, 6 August 1893, as quoted in Wilson, *McClure*, 138; David Rockefeller, Jr. as interviewed by Ted Brocklebank for the Grampian Television series "Oil," transcript provided by Grampian Television PLC; Earl Lathan, *John D. Rockefeller: Robber Baron or Industrial Statesman* (Boston: D. C. Heath, 1949), v–vii; Carr, *John D. Rockefeller*, 133; Hawke, *John D.*, 213–217; Filler, *The Crusaders*, 102–109; and Zahler, *Paradox*, 159–160.

32. *Chicago Journal*, 17 February 1903; *C.T.*, 29 September 1903; *Rochester Herald*, 30 September 1903; *Springfield* (Massachusetts) *Republican*, 30 September 1903; *Boston Herald*, 30, 31 September 1903; *Denver News*, 1 October 1903; *Oil City* (Pennsylvania) *Derrick*, October 1903; *Boston Post*, 29 November 1903; "The Origin," *Collier's*, (9 November 1907): 9; all clippings in HDL, mf.; and CLS, *Lloyd* I, 236.

33. Tarbell, *Standard Oil*; Robbins, *Tarbell*, 12–16, 20–22, 211–212, 255–259, 330–336; Hawke, *John D.*, 215–218; Miller, "Ida Tarbell's Second Look," 223–241; and Allan Nevins, "Letter to the Editor," *American Historical Review*, 50(April 1945): 677–688.

On Tarbell's admitted use of stolen documents, see Tarbell, *Autobiography*, 213–228; Tarbell, "Standard Oil-Rachel Crothers Group" speech, n.d., circa after 1911, Tarbell Papers, Drake Well Museum; and Clifford G. Christians, "The Pentagon Papers as Stolen Documents," *Media Ethics*, Clifford G. Christians ed. (New York: Longman, 1991), 96-100.

34. HDL to Major Huntington, 7 July 1900; HDL to Catherine Allen, 1 May 1900; HDL to CLS, n.d., circa 1901; HDL to JBL, 11 January, 9, 20 March 1903; HDL to Aaron Lloyd, 3 May 1903; HDL to Moritz Pinner, 23 May 1903; Nicholas Kelley to CLS, n.d., circa 1906; all in HDL, Wisc.; CLS, MS conversation with Miss Moxley and CLS, *Lloyd* biography edited fragment, both in HDL, mf.; HDL, "The Judicial Destruction of Law," *National Progress*, 1 (August 1903): 80–82; and Thomas, *Alternative*, 344.

35. HDL to E. B. Gaston, 7 August 1899, reprinted in *Fairhope* (Alabama) *Courier*, 15 September 1899; Thomas J. Morgan to HDL, 20 October 1900; Willis J. Abbot to HDL, 16 May 1901; Samuel Bowles to HDL, 26 November 1901; *The Standard*, 21 February 1902; William E. Smythe to HDL, 21 September 1902; Hiram Vrooman to HDL, 9 May 1902; HDL to Vrooman, 22 May 1902; John Spargo to HDL, 12 July 1902; William E. Smythe to HDL, 21 September 1902; George Williams to HDL, 18 February 1903; HDL to JBL, 21 February 1903; HDL to Williams, 1 March 1903; Clarence Darrow to HDL, 19 March 1903; HDL to William Mailly, 2, 20 April 1903; Mailly to HDL, 4 April, 4 May 1903; HDL to Samuel Bowles, 6 April 1903; Bowles to HDL, 8 April 1903; HDL to John Mitchell, 17 April 1903; A. M. Simons to HDL, 14 May, 13, 19, 24 June 1903; HDL to Jugo Poetzsch, 21 May 1903; John Mitchell to HDL, 27 May 1903; HDL to Richard T. Ely, 2 June 1903; Ely to HDL, 5 June 1903; John R. Commons to HDL, 5 June 1903; HDL to Thomas J. Morgan, 8 June, 28 June 1903; HDL to Eugene Debs, 8 June 1903; HDL to Commons, 12 June 1903; N. O. Nelson to HDL, 22 June 1903; Eltweed Pomeroy to HDL, 22 June 1903; Eugene V. Debs to HDL, 22 June 1903; Morgan to HDL, 25 June 1903; HDL to Morgan, 28 June 1903; *C.T.*, "HDL Memoriam," 30 November 1903; Simons to CLS, 2 February 1905; notes on CLS interview with William Dean Howells, n.d., circa 1905, CLS Journal; Richard T. Ely to CLS, 4 August 1916 in Ely Papers, Wisc.; H.L. Koopman to CLS, 22 February 1907; all in HDL, Wisc.; "A Large Straw in a Strong Wind," *Boyce's*

Weekly, 29 April 1903; "Why I Join the Socialists," HDL notebook 7; CLS, "A Talk With Fraulein," n.d., circa 1905; all in HDL, mf.; CLS to Ely, 17 August 1916, in Ely Papers; HDL to JBL, March 1903 as quoted in CLS, *Lloyd* II, 254–255; CLS, *Lloyd* II, 253–279; Destler, *American Radicalism*, 250–251; Thomas, *Alternative*, 344–346, 352–353; Lens, *Radicalism*, 171–193, 208–215; Robert N. Stow, "Conflict in the American Socialist Movement, 1897–1901: A Letter from Thomas J. Morgan to Henry Demarest Lloyd, July 18, 1901," *Journal of the Illinois State Historical Society*, 71(May 1978): 133–142; and Ginger, *Debs*, 316–332.

Also see Nelson, *Martyr*, 102–126; Aileen S. Kraditor, *The Radical Persuasion, 1890–1917*(Baton Rouge: Louisiana State University Press, 1981): 205–247; Egbert and Persons, *Socialism*, 3–20; and R. N. Berki, *Socialism* (New York: St. Martin's Press, 1975), 9–22.

36. HDL to JBL, 20 July 1903; HDL to Thomas J. Morgan, 8, 29 June 1903; Daniel L. Cruice to HDL, 29 June 1903; Ethelbert Stewart to HDL, 27 July 1903; HDL to JBL, 21 February 1903; HDL to Ethelbert Stewart, 27 July 1903; HDL to Edward Bemis, 2 August 1903; and George Schilling to HDL, 6 August 1903; Ethelbert Stewart to HDL, 4 August 1903; HDL to JBL, 9 September 1903; HDL to Anne Withington, 13 September 1903; all in HDL, Wisc.; JBL MS diary, 14 February 1904, JBL, CHS; HDL, "Municipalities Should Own and Control Street Railways," *Chicago Inter-Ocean*, 4 March 1895 and "Profit from Low Fares," *C.T.*, 1 June 1903, both clippings in HDL, mf.; CLS, *Lloyd* I, 270–273 and *Lloyd* II, 284–290, 297–301; and Jane Addams, *The Excellent Becomes the Permanent* (New York: The Macmillan Co., 1932), 43–46.

37. HDL to CLS, 12 September 1903 and HDL to JBL, 20 September 1903, both in HDL, Wisc.; CLS, *Lloyd* II, 301–305; JBL MS diary, 26 September 1903, in JBL, CHS; William Bross Lloyd to CLS, 22 January 1935; CLS MS on HDL's death, n.d., circa 1903 and 1905, HDL, mf.; Caroline Stallbohm to Nicholas Kelley, 21 January 1907, in Kelley Papers, New York Public Library; and Destler, *Empire of Reform*, 521.

38. HDL, "The Ethical Progress of the Nineteenth–Century," *Unity*, 29 November 1900; CLS on Lloyd's death, CLS Journal, HDL, Wisc.; Nina Gray Lunt, "Character Sketch of Jessie Bross Lloyd," n.d., circa December 1904, JBL, CHS; *In Memoriam," Henry Demarest Lloyd, 1847–1903* (Chicago: Thomas P. Halpin Co., 1903); *Saturday Night Dispatch*, 3 October 1903 and *Chicago Sunday American*, 8 November 1903, both clippings in HDL, mf.; *Chicago Record*, 8 November 1903, in Lloyd Family Scrapbook, New Jersey Historical Society; CLS Journal; Amy Aldrich to JBL, 11 October 1903; *Out West*, November 1903; Thomas J. Morgan to JBL, 24 March 1904; "The Arrival of a Thinker," *Denver News*, 21 October 1901; all in HDL, Wisc.; *Unity*, 8 October 1903 and Lilian Whiting, "The Useful Life of Henry Demarest Lloyd," *Chicago Inter-Ocean*, 9 October 1903, both in Lloyd Family Scrapbook, New Jersey Historical Society; JBL to Mrs. Simon Sterne, 19 December 1903, Sterne Papers, New York Public Library; *Columbian Quarterly*, March 1904, Columbiana Collection, Columbia University; Willis J. Abbot, "Men and Matters of Moment," *The Pilgrim*, November 1903, Drake Well Museum; and B. O. Flower, "Henry D. Lloyd—An Apostle of Progressive Democracy," *Arena* (December 1903): 651–656.

Conclusion: What Is Done By the People Lasts Forever

Henry Demarest Lloyd's beloved Wayside still stands in late twentieth-century Winnetka, a small brick structure surrounded by the urban sprawl of Chicago, but there are few other tangible remnants of Lloyd's life or work. The Amoco Oil Company, formerly the Standard Oil Company of Indiana, operates a twenty-four hour self-service gasoline station and food market in the heart of Winnetka, just blocks from Lloyd's home. The stranglehold of the oil octopus is even tighter in the late twentieth century than it was when *Wealth Against Commonwealth* was written, and Americans have now fought a foreign war to preserve the precious flow of petroleum. The forty-hour work week went into effect in 1940 under the Fair Labor Standards Act, but the new international economic order, now preoccupied with European and Asian competition, has doomed the generation of late twentieth-century Americans to work past 40 hours. Organized labor is in decline in the United States, some would say in disarray, and companies no longer have to shoot or beat striking employees, just replace them. International monopolies, known as cartels, operate outside of any national or international laws, exploiting and polluting with little fear of retribution. Social Security, the national retirement system that Lloyd once envisioned, is jeopardized and may fail, just as hundreds of other private and public old-age pensions. The world's religions continue to shun modern social, political, economic, and medical changes, as Lloyd once decried in "The New Conscience." The Rule of Gold, as Lloyd called capitalism, reigns supreme with the defeat of communism in the Soviet Union and Eastern Europe.

As much as Lloyd has been recognized as a leading late nineteenth-century reformer, it is his writings that have become his true legacy. Lloyd was a man of words, a journalist and nonfiction writer who used alternative media forms to plead for an improvement in social conditions. The injustices of the Industrial Revolution as magnified by the Haymarket Square bombing encouraged Lloyd to crusade for the rights of the poor—consumers, workers, farmers, and aged. In doing so, Lloyd produced an enviable body of writings, including the 1881 "Story of a Great Monopoly," his seminal 1894 book *Wealth Against Commonwealth*, and a body of speeches.

Lloyd also set a standard for journalists and writers who followed him. Charles Edward Russell observed, "[The Story of a Great Monopoly] was a turning-point in our social history; with it dawned upon Americans the first conviction that this industrial development of which we had been so proud was a source, not of strength, but of fatal weakness." Of Lloyd, Russell said, "He planted the seed; his fortune, very unusual in such men, was to see the tilth in a thousand places and in ways of which he had never dreamed." Progressivism advocate Walter Weyl joined Lloyd's bid for binding arbitration during the anthracite coal strike of 1902. The strike "was a turning point in Weyl's life. Drift and uncertainty gave way to the challenge of a cause," wrote Weyl biographer Charles Forcey. Lincoln Steffens was inspired by the rising interest in late nineteenth-century journalistic realism fueled by Lloyd, noting that "The prophets of the Old Testament were ahead of me, and—to make a big jump in time—so were the writers, editors, and reporters (including myself) of the 1890's who were finding fault with 'things as they are.'" A young Walter Lippmann, working for Lincoln Steffens and *Everybody's* magazine in 1910, recalled that "We were looking not for the evils of Big Business, but for its anatomy. We found that the anatomy of Big Business was strikingly like that of Tammany Hall: the same pyramiding influence, the same tendency of power to center on individuals who did not necessarily sit in the official seats, the same effort of human organization to grow independently of legal arrangements."[1]

Lloyd's style of writing declined in the wake of World War I, but did not die. Lippmann began his path breaking "Today and Tomorrow" column for the *New York Herald Tribune* in 1931, joined by Drew Pearson and Robert S. Allen's syndicated "Washington Merry-Go-Round" the same year and Joseph Alsop's "Capital Parade" in 1937. Dorothy Day's *The Catholic Worker* began a record of advocating "personal activism" to achieve nonviolent social justice in 1933. Commentators such as Upton Close, Dorothy Thompson, Walter Winchell, Gabriel Heatter, and H. V. Kaltenborn brought advocacy journalism to radio. Edward R. Murrow's dramatic broadcasts from the rooftops of London in 1939 were proof of something that Lloyd knew well, the power of the spoken word. Murrow's famed 1954 "See It Now" broadcast on Joseph McCarthy was Lloyd's kind of writing, as was his 1960 "Harvest of Shame" documentary on the substandard living conditions of migrant farm workers. Murrow concluded the later broadcast in words reminiscent of Lloyd: "The people you have seen have the strength to harvest your fruit and vegetables. They do not have the strength to influence legislation. Maybe we do." I. F. Stone published his advocacy newspaper between 1953 and 1971. Many erroneously assume that advocacy journalism was born in the New Journalism era of the 1960s and 1970s, in the works of Tom Wolfe, Joan Didion, Gay Talese, Truman Capote, Garry Wills, John Gregory Dunne, Joe McGinniss, Norman Mailer, and Hunter S. Thompson and the so-called underground and alternative press, but it was only revived. *San Francisco Bay Guardian* publisher Bruce Brugmann explained in 1976, "I aim my derringer at every reporter and tell him, by God, that I don't want to see an objective piece of reporting. . . . This is not dishonest journalism. It is 'point of view' journalism."[2]

One hundred years after the appearance of *Wealth Against Commonwealth*, the kind of writing Lloyd championed is proliferating, especially in the broadcast media. "You're more show biz than you are journalist," *L. A. Times* Washington Bureau Chief Jack Nelson told former talk show host Phil Donahue at a newspaper editor's conference in 1989. "Explain the difference," retorted Donahue. MTV's "The Week in Rock" newscaster Tabitha Soren called it "advocacy journalism" when the cable channel successfully challenged thousands of young people to "Rock the vote" in 1992, and presidential candidate Bill Clinton was only too happy to join the effort. Former Vice-President Dan Quayle decried the "networks' advocacy journalism in support of Clinton concepts" in 1994. *The New York Times* media critic Walter Goodman proclaimed, "Serious advocacy is welcome on the [television] screen as long as it is done without mirrors." CNN war reporter Christiane Amanpour openly flaunted U.S. Bosnia policy in a global forum with the president of the United States even as she was the cable news service's highest paid correspondent. Black journalist Jill Nelson wrote in a book that all African-American journalists function as advocates, "Ambassadors from the colored catch-all, black America, explaining and justifying not only ourselves but also the mythical, monolithic black community," a sentiment echoed by Pulitzer Prize-winning *Chicago Tribune* columnist Clarence Page. Small-town newspaper editor Alexander B. Brook argued that all small-town newspaper editors are advocates for the same reason. Society of Professional Journalists' award winner Virginia Lautzenheiser said she was an advocate journalist, and "I'm proud of it." Nonfiction authors such as Joe McGinniss and Dan Kurzman make up dialogue for their historical books, and a 1967 Supreme Court decision has virtually licensed the fictionalization of real life events for made-for-TV movies, in an ironic coming of circle in the controversy that Lloyd faced over the writing of fiction or nonfiction.[3]

Henry Demarest Lloyd's reputation lives on as well. *Washington Post* media reporter Howard Kurtz considered Lloyd and Lincoln Steffens as role models for late twentieth-century journalists. "These news hounds," Kurtz wrote in his 1993 book, *Media Circus: The Trouble With America's Newspapers*, "would have instinctively sniffed out major scandals of the 1980s such as the wholesale looting of the Department of Housing and Urban Development by politically-connected fat cats and the great savings-and-loan swindle." Lloyd wrote shortly before his death, "We had rather fail seventy times seven with the people and succeed at the last, than succeed without the people at the first attempt. What is done by the people lasts forever." If nothing else, Lloyd's words still serve as a credo for those who aspire to write or speak for those without a voice in our society.

NOTES

1. Charles Edward Russell, "Introduction," in CLS, *Lloyd*, I, v–ix; Charles Forcey, *The Crossroads of Liberalism: Croly, Weyl, Lippmann, and the Progressive Era, 1900–1925* (New York: Oxford University Press, 1961), 66–67; Lincoln Steffens, *The Autobiography of Lincoln Steffens* (New York: Harcourt Brace and Co., 1931), 357; and Ronald Steel, *Walter Lippmann and the American Century* (Boston: Little, Brown and Co., 1980), 36–40.

2. Janice Scott Anderson, "The Rhetorical Theory and Practice of Walter Lippmann: Advocacy Journalism as Rhetorical Discourse," (Ph.D. diss., University of Wisconsin, 1981), 98–260; Leann Grabovy, "Joseph Alsop and American Foreign Policy: The Journalist as Advocate," (Ph.D. diss., University of Georgia, 1988); Nancy L. Roberts, "Dorothy Day and *The Catholic Worker*, 1933–1982," (Ph.D. diss., University of Minnesota, 1982); David Streitfeld, "It's not easy being weird; Hunter Thompson's an insider these days," *Washington Post*, 23 August 1994; Dave Wadsworth, "Few lessons learned from Watergate scandal," *Denver Post*, 12 June 1994; Leonard Downie, Jr., *The New Muckrakers* (Washington, D.C.: The New Republic Book Co., 1976), 175–201; and David L. Protess, et al., *The Journalism of Outrage* (New York: Guilford Press, 1991), 42–47.

3. Stephen Kinzer, "Where there's war there's Amanpour," *New York Times*, 9 October 1994; Thomas B. Rosenstiel, "To journalists, technology is a blessing—and a curse," *Los Angeles Times*, 24 September 1994; Hillel Italie, "True stories; Writers often walk a fine line between non-fiction and fiction," *C.T.*, 20 September 1994; Larry Fiquette, "Why is the press so negative?," *St. Louis Post-Dispatch*, 21 August 1994; Dan Quayle, "GOP airs its views on health care reform," *Arizona Republic*, 2 August 1994; Doug Cress, "United '94 ethnicity shapes his perspective, Rivera says," *Atlanta Constitution*, 28 July 1994; Marcia D. Davis, "Race matters: Conflict in the newsroom," *St. Louis Post-Dispatch*, 17 July 1994; Dan Hulbert, "Rocking TV journalism," *Atlanta Journal and Constitution*, 26 May 1993; Chris Willman, "MTV's 'Gangsta Rap' an objective debate," *Los Angeles Times*, 25 May 1994; Julie Kosterlitz, "Journalist, heal thyself," *The National Journal*, 26 March 1994; Walter Goodman, "Advocacy Journalism: A Medium's Strength," *New York Times*, 17 March 1994; Rob Ehrgott and Virginia Lautzenheiser, "Profiles in excellence: The stories behind the Sigma Delta Chi awards," *Quill*, 81(June 1993), 100–101; Alan Miller, "Press no longer on a roll," *San Diego Union-Tribune*, 2 May 1993; Carin Pratt, "Small-town newspaperman makes

good," *Christian Science Monitor*, 22 July 1993; Martin Zimmerman, "'Liberating Schools' makes case for choice," *Los Angeles Times*, 23 April 1993; Liz Viall, "Crossing that line," *The Quill*, 79(November-December 1991): 17–18; and *Time, Inc. v. Hill*, 385 U.S. 374, 87 S.Ct. 534 (1967).

Bibliographical Essay

No study of Henry Demarest Lloyd can be undertaken without reference to his remarkable collected papers, which are preserved at the State Historical Society of Wisconsin. A microfilmed edition of the papers was produced by the Society, as described in *The Papers of Henry Demarest Lloyd: Guide to a Microfilm Edition*, edited by F. Gerald Ham (Madison, 1971), and is available in many research libraries and archives. The Society continued to collect Lloyd-related items after completion of the microfilm. These documents, including a journal kept by Lloyd's sister, Caroline Lloyd Withington Strobell, as she researched and wrote her Lloyd biography, have not been microfilmed. They remain in the society's archives in addition to Chester M. Destler's unorganized notes and materials, which were donated to the Society by his family in 1993.

In the wake of Lloyd's unexpected death, the Lloyd family gave the task of organizing his papers to Richard T. Ely, who taught at the University of Wisconsin at the time. Ely removed documents that he felt were too personal or private and returned them to the family. Some were donated to the State Historical Society of Wisconsin in the intervening years but the most personal were kept from researchers until they were donated to the Chicago Historical Society in 1987 by Georgia Lloyd Beshears, Lloyd's granddaughter. Included in the Jessie Bross Lloyd papers at the CHS are Jessie's diaries, which chronicled many of her husband's activities, personal letters, and some of Jessie's writings. Perhaps someday someone will do a study of her. The CHS also has diaries and other documents written by William Bross, Lloyd's father-in-law. A collection of Lloyd family documents kept by New Jersey members of his family is available at the New Jersey Historical Society.

Other manuscript collections yielding significant Lloyd-related documents include the Richard T. Ely and McCormick Family papers, State Historical Society of Wisconsin; Roger Sherman papers, Yale University Library; Nicholas Murray Butler and Edmund C. Stedman papers, Columbia University Library Special Manuscript Collection; Jane Addams, David A. Wells, Lyman Trumbull, and Carl Schurz papers, Library of Congress; Nicholas Kelley, Simon Sterne, and Lloyd-Schwimmer papers, New York Public Library; William M. Salter Papers, Knox College Archives; Ethelbert Stewart papers, Southern History Collection, University of North Carolina at Chapel Hill; Ida M. Tarbell papers, Allegheny College; Ida M. Tarbell papers, Drake Well Museum; the Columbiana Collection at Columbia University of New York City; and various Aaron Lloyd documents at the New York State Historical Society. Chester M. Destler prepared a detailed bibliography for his Lloyd biography that was too long to publish but is available in manuscript form at the Library of Congress. Quotations from the William O. Inglis interview of John D. Rockefeller have never before been incorporated into a Lloyd biography. The entire conversation is available on microfilm with a helping guide, *John D. Rockefeller Interview, 1917–1920, conducted by William O. Inglis*, compiled and introduced by David Freeman Hawke (Westport, CT, 1984).

Most of Lloyd's writings up to his death in 1903 were incorporated into this study. The more important ones include his *Chicago Tribune* editorials, 1874–1883; "The Story of a Great Monopoly," *Atlantic Monthly* (1881); "The Political Economy of Seventy-Three Million Dollars," *Atlantic Monthly* (1882); "Our Land: The Story of the Dissipation of Our Great National Inheritance," *Chicago Tribune* (1883); "Making Bread Dear," *North American Review* (1883); "Public Land Frauds," *Chicago Tribune* (1884); "Lords of Industry," *North American Review* (1884); "The New Conscience," *North American Review* (1888); *A Strike of Millionaires Against Miners of the Story of Spring Valley* (Chicago, 1890); *Wealth Against Commonwealth* (New York, 1894); *Labor Copartnership: Notes on a Visit to Cooperative Workshops, Factories and Farms in Great Britain and Ireland, in which Employer, Employee and Consumer Share in Ownership, Management and Results* (New York, 1898); *Country Without Strikes: A Visit to the Compulsory Arbitration Court of New Zealand* (New York, 1900); and *Newest England: Notes of a Democratic Traveller in New England, with Some Australian Comparisons* (New York, 1900).

Lloyd's will directed that his secretary, Anne Withington, and his sister, Caro Lloyd Strobell, publish his uncompleted writings. *Man, the Social Creator* (Chicago, 1906) was edited and rewritten by Jane Addams and Anne Withington, and *A Sovereign People: A Study of Swiss Democracy* (New York, 1907) was essentially written by John A. Hobson from Lloyd's fragmentary notes. These works were not consulted for this study because of length considerations and their uncertain origins. Lloyd's final three books are compilations of speeches and writings delivered or completed before his death and are cited within. They are *Men, the Workers* (New York, 1909), *Mazzini and Other Essays* (New York, 1910), and *Lords of Industry* (New York, 1910).

Nineteenth- and early twentieth-century newspapers and magazines used include issues of the *Chicago Tribune*, *Chicago Daily News*, *Chicago Times*, *Chicago Chronicle*, *Chicago Herald*, *Chicago Inter-Ocean*, *New York Tribune*, *New York Sun*, *The New York Times*, *Boston Herald*, *Detroit Free Press*, *The Free-Trader*, *People's Pictorial Tax-Payer*, *Atlantic Monthly*, *Boyce's Weekly*, *Harper's*, *North American Review*, *Forum*, and *Nation*.

Existing Lloyd biographies are discussed in the introduction. They include Caro Lloyd Strobell's *Henry Demarest Lloyd, 1847–1903: A Biography*, 2 vols. (New York, 1912); Chester M. Destler, *Henry Demarest Lloyd and the Empire of Reform* (Philadelphia, 1963); E. Jay Jernigan, *Henry Demarest Lloyd* (Boston, 1976); Harvey O'Connor, "Henry Demarest Lloyd: The Prophetic Tradition," in Harvey Goldberg, ed., *American Radicals: Some Problems and Personalities* (New York, 1957), 79–90; Daniel Aaron, *Men of Good Hope: A Story of American Progressives* (New York, 1951), 133–171; and John L. Thomas, *Alternative America: Henry George, Edward Bellamy, Henry Demarest Lloyd and the Adversary Tradition* (Cambridge, MA, 1983).

A variety of secondary sources were used in the preparation of this biography. Particularly useful titles on nineteenth- and early twentieth-century journalism include Dan Schiller, *Objectivity and the News: The Public and the Rise of Commercial Journalism* (Philadelphia, 1981); Robert Miraldi, *Muckraking and Objectivity: Journalism's Colliding Traditions* (New York, 1990); Michael Schudson, *Discovering the News: A Social History of American Newspapers* (New York, 1978); Edwin and Michael Emery, *The Press and America*, 6th ed. (Englewood Cliffs, NJ, 1988); Sidney Kobre, *The Yellow Press and Gilded Age Journalism* (Tallahassee, FL, 1964); Hazel Dicken-Garcia, *Journalistic Standards in Nineteenth-Century America* (Madison, WI, 1989); Gerald J. Baldasty, *The Commercialization of News in the Nineteenth Century* (Madison, WI, 1992); Carl Hausman, *The Decision-Making Process in Journalism* (Chicago, 1990); and Gunther Barth, *City People: The Rise of Modern City Culture in Nineteenth-Century America* (New York, 1980), 58–109.

Nineteenth-century reformers and the culture of reform are discussed in John G. Sproat, *"The Best Men:" Liberal Reformers in the Gilded Age* (New York, 1968); Peter J. Frederick, *Knights of the Golden Rule: The Intellectual as Christian Social Reformer in the 1890s* (Lexington, KY, 1976); Robert H. Walker, *Reform in America: The Continuing Frontier* (Lexington, KY, 1985); Thomas Bender, *Community and Social Change in America* (Baltimore, 1976); Roberta Garner, *Social Movements in America* (Chicago, 1977); Kathleen McCarthy, *Noblesse Oblige: Charity and Cultural Philanthropy in Chicago, 1849–1929* (Chicago, 1982); and Warren Susman, "The Persistence of Reform," in *Culture As History* (New York, 1984).

Post bellum business is discussed in Edward Chase Kirkland, *Dream and Thought in the Business Community, 1860-1900* (Ithaca, NY, 1956); Saul Engelbourg, *Power and Morality: American Business Ethics, 1840-1914* (Westport, CT, 1980); Thomas K. McCraw, *Prophets of Regulation* (Cambridge, MA, 1984); Naomi R. Lamoreaux, *The Great Merger Movement in American Business, 1895-1904* (New York, 1985); and Steven L. Piott, *The Anti-Monopoly Persuasion: Popular Resistance to the Rise of Big Business in the Midwest* (Westport, CT, 1985). Information on the Standard Oil Company can be found in John B. Clark, *The Federal Trust Policy* (Baltimore, 1931); Hans B. Thorelli, *The Federal Anti-Trust Policy: Organization of an American Tradition* (London, 1954); Ralph W. and Mauriel E. Hidy, *History of the Standard Oil Company (New Jersey): Pioneering in Big Business, 1882-1911* (New York, 1955); Harold F. Williamson and Arnold R. Daum, *The American Petroleum Industry: The Age of Illumination 1859-1899* (Evanston, IL, 1959); Ernest C. Miller, *Pennsylvania's Oil Industry* (Gettysburg, PA, 1974); and Bruce Bringhurst, *Antitrust and the Oil Monopoly: The Standard Oil Cases, 1890-1911* (Westport, CT, 1979).

Index

About the Author

RICHARD DIGBY-JUNGER is an Assistant Professor of Journalism at Western Michigan University, Kalamazoo. Before embarking upon an academic career, he worked as a broadcast journalist in Minneapolis-St. Paul, Milwaukee, Duluth-Superior, and Madison, and was recognized for his investigative reporting.

Recent Titles in
Contributions in American History

The Moment of Decision: Biographical Essays on American Character
and Regional Identity
Randall Miller and John R. McKivigan

Christian Science in the Age of Mary Baker Eddy
Stuart E. Knee

Northern Labor and Antislavery: A Documentary History
Philip S. Foner and Herbert Shapiro, editors

Loyalists and Community in North America
Robert M. Calhoon, Timothy M. Barnes,
and George A. Rawlyk, editors

Abraham Lincoln: Sources and Style of Leadership
Frank J. Williams, William D. Pederson,
and Vincent J. Marsala, editors

Zebulon Butler: Hero of the Revolutionary Frontier
James R. Williamson and Linda A. Fossler

Clio Confused: Troubling Aspects of Historical Study from the
Perspective of U.S. History
David J. Russo

Federal Antitrust Policy During the Kennedy-Johnson Years
James R. Williamson

The Home-Front War: World War II and American Society
Kenneth Paul O'Brien and Lynn Hudson Parsons, editors

Portrait of an Abolitionist: A Biography of George Luther Stearns
Charles E. Heller

No King, No Popery: Anti-Catholicism in Revolutionary New England
Francis D. Cogliano

James Glen: From Scottish Provost to Royal Governor of South Carolina
W. Stitt Robinson

ISBN 0-313-29957-9

90000>

EAN

9 780313 299575

HARDCOVER BAR CODE